Romancing the Real

*Folklore and Ethnographic
Representation in North Africa*

Sabra J. Webber

uɲɲ

University of Pennsylvania Press

Philadelphia

Library of Congress Cataloging-in-Publication Data

Webber, Sabra Jean.
    Romancing the real : folklore and ethnographic representation in
North Africa / Sabra J. Webber.
        p. cm.—(Publications of the American Folklore Society. New series)
    Includes bibliographical references and index.
    ISBN 0-8122-8236-1
    1. Tales—Tunisia—Qulaytīyah. 2. Oral tradition—Tunisia-
Qulaytīyah. 3. Qulaytīyah (Tunisia)—History. 4. Qulaytīyah
(Tunisia)—Social life and customs. 5. Folklore—Africa, North.
6. Oral tradition—Africa, North. I. Title. II. Series:
Publications of the American Folklore Society. New Series
(Unnumbered).
GR353.52.Q53W43   1991
398'.09611—dc20   91-3348
                                                           CIP

Romancing the Real

University of Pennsylvania Press
Publications of the American Folklore Society
New Series

General Editor, Patrick Mullen

For
NESRIA BEN YOUSSEF
and
ELIZABETH WARNOCK FERNEA

من كل قلبي

And in Memory of
GACEM LENGLIZ
and
AMOR BEN SLIMÈNE

Contents

Illustrations

FIGURES

MAPS

Acknowledgments

My thanks first to the people of Kelibia—especially the family of Si Mohamed ben 'Ali Najar: Si Mohamed himself, Nesria ben Youssef, Malek,
Moncef, Leila, and Adel. I learned a lot about Kelibia and its ways and
even more about "living right" from them. I could not have done the research for this study without the enthusiastic support of Malek, the interest
and indulgence of Lella Nesria, and the stories of the following: Mohamed
Gharbi, Hmida el Bidwi, Fafani Khoudja (Zenaidi), Gacem Lengliz,
"Hamdan" ben Slimène, Si ben Youssef, and Khalti Jamila. I am pro-
foundly grateful. My thanks also to the scholars at the Institut des Belles
Lettres Arabes and to members of the archives in Tunis.

My deep appreciation to Richard Bauman for his sustaining, encourag-
ing, and down-to-earth letters during the initial fieldwork phase of this
project and to Elizabeth Warnock Fernea for more that I can say, but especially for her visit to Kelibia. "You must be very proud to have such a
friend," Lella Nesria said of her later, and I am. Particular thanks to Salem
Ghazali as well as to Malek Najar for uncompensated help in transcription
and translation that went far beyond attention to terms in a text to providing and continuing to provide cross-cultural translations of their own society—lovingly, but without blinders. Malek and Marie Thérèse Najar kept
lines of communication open over the years when Kelibia seemed awfully
far away.

Of those who read and commented on this work over the years, I have
first to thank Cornell Fleischer, who sent back from Turkey in 1986–87 over
forty pages of comments, questions, and criticism. His support and that of
Kay Fleischer during the conclusion of the writing process are incalculable.
Other readers whose contribution of time and energy was way beyond
anything hoped for or expected were Amy Shuman (who actually read two
versions), Mike McDougal (who read pieces of several versions and also
did much of the initial transliteration work in the Appendix), Gary Eber-
sole (who not only read my work but who also shared insights gleaned
from his own recent manuscript submission), Marilyn Waldman (who
made many helpful comments upon comments), and Salah Khoudja (who

read the manuscript as well). Others who generously helped with translit-eration details were Frederic J. Cadora, Keith Walters, and Salah Khoudja. Christine Khoudja kindly brought Salah's comments back to the States from Saudi Arabia for me. I also thank Marilyn Waldman as director of the Division of Comparative Studies and Frederic Cadora as chair of Judaic and Near Eastern Languages and Literatures for taking practical steps to be certain that the manuscript was completed in a "timely fashion," that is, before tenure review. I have been very fortunate in my academic "homes" from the point of both scholarly engagement and pragmatics. The Center for the Study of Islamic Societies and Civilizations awarded me a Rocke-feller Residency fellowship in 1988–89 that provided the time and scholarly atmosphere needed finally to finish the manuscript and enjoy my child's second year—something that most tenure-seeking moms and dads proba-bly miss. Besides Cornell, I especially thank scholars with me at Washing-ton University during 1988–89—Peter Heath, Ahmet Karamustafa, Mohamed-Salah Omri, Steve Caton, Dale Eickelman, and John Bowen—for inspiring conversations and encouragement. I thank Robert Fernea and Patricia Smith each for a telephone conversation offering just the right in-sights at exactly the right time. John M. McDougal and Diana Phillips helped with translations from the French. Joyce Bell, Marguerite Oleiki, and Diana Phillips typed and typed. Diana Phillips and Antonia Mortimer ably assisted with bibliography and proofing. Beverly Schillings helped with myriad "final" details. Brenda Hosey ably kept disaster at bay during the time I was both endlessly "finishing" the manuscript and serving as acting chair of the Division of Comparative Studies. Kirin Narayan, Mar-garet Mills, Patrick Mullen, and Paul Stoller sent me wonderfully detailed and constructive reviews. I have gratefully incorporated many of their sug-gestions and insights. Alison Anderson, as managing editor, showed much appreciated sensitivity to textual nuances. Michael Zwettler provided the epigraph.

I thank the Fulbright-Hays Dissertation Research Abroad program (1978–79) for funding my field research. The National Endowment for the Humanities Independent Research Fellowship program (1982–83) pro-vided the means to spend time in Paris, Aix-en-Provence, Morocco, and Tunisia doing archival research for, especially, Chapter 4. The Ohio State University College of Humanities personnel under the deanship of G. Mi-cheal Riley were generous in their provision of research and writing time, helped make financially possible my time in St. Louis, and provided funds for the drawing and reproducing of maps and photographs.

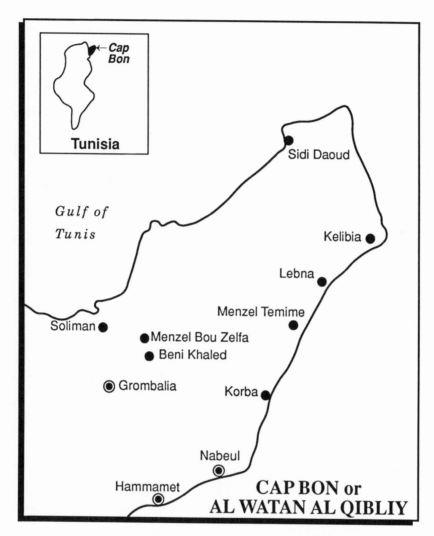

Map 1. Tunisia. Some locations referred to in the text are indicated.

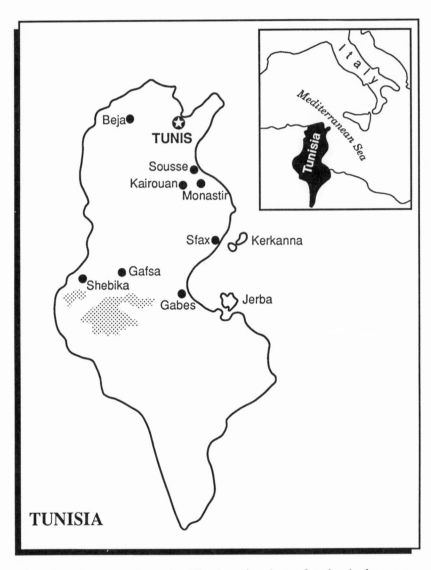

Map 2. Cap Bon or al Watan al Qibliy. Some locations referred to in the text are
indicated.

Preface:
The Presence of the Past or
Romancing the Real

We went down
To the beach of Kelibia
We swam and we ate
Tuna and sardines and
A plate of hot peppers

(children's song)

In northeastern Tunisia there is a peninsula that juts into the Mediterranean toward Italy. In Arabic the peninsula is called al Watan al-Qibliy, "the tribal homeland," or, from the town of Korba northwards, Dakhlet al Maouine (Ma-wīn), "the homeland of the descendants of Maouia," the region's most important holy person. The French call the peninsula the Cap Bon. On the eastern side of the "Good Cape," with the Mediterranean bathing the eastern and southern edges, lie the port and town of Kelibia.

Kelibia, an Arabic-speaking community of about thirty thousand, has existed for at least two thousand years. Like Tunisia itself, it is a Mediterranean crossroads, open to the sea but dependent upon its agricultural hinterland. The town's harbor, craggy lookout, and rich farmland have been mixed blessings. Like larger and better known Mediterranean coastal communities—Alexandria, Latakia, Tangiers, and, in antiquity, Carthage—Kelibia has long had to cope with its desirability as a destination for visitors, refugees, invaders, and colonizers.

My Romance: Entering the Field

Some two millennia after Kelibia made its debut in recorded history, in March, wearing snow boots and a mini-skirt and just short of my twenty-second birthday, I—visitor, invader, refugee, colonizer and, according to a fiery young university student in town, member of the CIA—and my fellow Peace Corps volunteer, Christine, were delivered by an assistant director of Peace Corps Tunisia who, we had been told by more seasoned volunteers, had once lived with BEDOUINS. In any case, she left us in the middle of the "road to the beach" with some surprised Kelibians, a farewell gift of a candy bar each, and a copy of an invitation from the Tunisian government to start a Kelibian nursery school and kindergarten.

Later that spring, busing the three-hour drive from Tunis to Kelibia, we were struck by the un-Peace Corps-like abundance and variety of agricultural products in evidence. Still today, as the bus skirts the Gulf of Tunis to the north and enters the Cap Bon area at Soliman, an old Andalusian town, great fields of various grains and groves of olive trees flash by. (Joseph Weyland reported that even in 1926 the Cap Bon had 34 oil mills with 45 crushing machines and 180 presses, most run by electricity, plus 37 mills operated by animals.) Nearing Menzel bou Zelfa, which has an orange festival every year, one finds orchards of oranges, lemons, and mandarins. Arriving at Korba, one first catches sight of the Mediterranean. This is a brushy area—mastic trees, jujube bushes, dwarf palm trees, rosemary, and so on.

Finally, continuing up from Korba, the real beginning of the Dakhla, one enters the most fertile area of the Cap Bon, starting about Lebna and extending up to the other side of Kelibia. Barring the produce of the oases, every crop that can be grown anywhere in Tunisia can be grown on the Cape, and almost any crop cultivated on the Cape can grow in the Dakhla, with cereals such as corn, barley, oats, beans, and maize growing best. This abundance explains why, as Augustin Bernard noted in 1924, *maraîchage* (market-gardening/truck farming) is a "spéculation ancienne" of Kelibia. One catches glimpses of the sheep, goats, and cattle raised in the area, as they are moved along the roads.

From the dwarf palms in this area along the sea baskets are fashioned, and straw mats are woven from the rushes gathered in the brackish water left standing along the seashore. Some of the brackish area was *habous* (religious) land, we learned, and often mats for mosques or lodges or the shrines of holy people were woven from rushes gathered there (story 7, for example).

As one drives up to Kelibia past cultivated fields and meadows of wild flowers, the first evidence that the town is near is the reappearance of the sea on the right, and then, in the distance, Kelibia's imposing Roman-Turkish fort overlooking both the land and the Mediterranean. Every once in a while, crossing the bridged wadis that lead down to the coast, one passes a small whitewashed stone house trimmed in blue. Later in the summer, one sees on such houses red peppers strung out to dry, or tomatoes drying on the rooftops so that they can be ground up and stored for winter. Any sunny day one sees sheepskins or colorful thin rugs (*kelims*) airing on windowsills or hanging from porch or balcony rails.

Nearer Kelibia, more and more houses appear—the sun sparkling on the blue water and green fields and reflecting off the collection of whitewashed houses stretching down to the sand in a typically Mediterranean scene.

In the town the street scene is somewhat different depending on the day of the week. There is more activity on Friday near the four mosques, which are located close to the town center. Every town in the area has its special market day and Kelibia's is Monday. And on Monday, souk day, the town is especially crowded. Women as well as men rise early to go to the large, otherwise empty area on the west side of town to try to get a bargain on old clothes or blankets woven farther south, or to acquire livestock or dried beans or nuts or ingredients for folk medicines or for beauty products such as henna or fabric for dresses or drapes. The new, large, covered market in the center of town, which houses several small poultry, fish, meat, and produce shops, also teems with activity on Monday. The entire front and side of the market are surrounded by colorful displays of vegetables and fruits brought in from the countryside.

Because of the fertility of the surrounding land, proximity to the sea, and pleasant climate, there is an abundance of basic foods for sale almost any day. Beef, lamb, chicken, and fish are usually available (although not always affordable) as are eggs, milk, and cheeses of various sorts if shopping is done early in the morning. Fresh hot bread can be obtained almost hourly during the day from a number of little neighborhood shops. Once we knew the names, we could easily purchase vegetables such as cauliflower, lettuce, turnips, artichokes, cucumbers, turnips, cabbage, radishes, eggplants, carrots, onions, potatoes, peas, squash, and more in season, as well as watermelon, figs, prickly pears, grapes, tomatoes, mulberries, apricots, quinces, pomegranates, lemons, mandarins, plums, and at least three varieties of oranges. Condiments include cumin, caraway, aniseed, and garlic.

The main streets belong to the men and children. On either side of these streets and in alleys men carry on their businesses in open-fronted or semi-open shops or, in all but the worst weather, sitting in the outdoor cafés found in the center of town and in the center of every neighborhood. In fact, in good weather the two cafés on opposite sides of the main square are often so crowded that the tables and chairs of each almost reach the center of the street, blocking passers-by. This phenomenon, we were to learn, seemed remarkable to the older men, who remember when people did not drink coffee at all and when there were no coffee houses in town.

Children often play in the narrower streets, as well as in the courtyards of their own homes. Thus, a pedestrian or a passing vehicle might interrupt a ball game or, in the appropriate season, a game of marbles, hopscotch, or tops. And, in the spring, there are often small boys and girls running along with homemade or store-bought hoops.

Romancing Kelibia

Despite the imposing presence of the old fort high on a hill overlooking both town and sea and our romantic knowledge of numerous Roman and Phoenician ruins in the Kelibia area, I did not imagine those chilly early spring days the intricate, multiple layers of the past through which Kelibians perceived each other and their community. As a child of a post-World War II San Francisco suburb, I had shared no communal history with my suburban neighbors and fellow townspeople. But in Kelibia, because simple introductions to the newcomers were often accompanied by lengthy accounts of past personal and familial ties between the introducer and the introduced, the importance of breadth and historical depth in defining relationships soon became very obvious. Without knowing particularly why these accounts were important, we were socialized to believe they were important and soon were telling haltingly our own relationship vignettes.

On my many visits to Kelibia between 1967 and 1983 I came to expect and enjoy these historical accounts. Tellers' reminiscenses were inspired not only by introductions but by landmarks in the town, or by visits among old friends. The sexes are segregated in Kelibia, so opportunities for lengthy chats or in-depth, serious conversation tend to be with members of one's own sex. At some point I began to wonder what men would have to say and to what extent men's and women's perceptions of the community differed. Women's social space was traditionally confined to homes, to shrines, to the baths, and to the graveyard at Friday dawn (a religiously good time to visit and pray over deceased parents, siblings, or children), while men socialized in the communal town space and more often ventured outside the community. Men frequently, but not always, were the ones to occupy the mediating position between the home and the community and between the town and the rest of the world.

When I returned to Kelibia in November 1978 for an extended visit, this time planning to do dissertation fieldwork, both older brothers of the family with which I had lived in the past were in town. The elder, Malek, in his late twenties, had married, and now lived with his French wife, Marie Thérèse, and their daughter down by the beach. He worked in town as a sports teacher. The other brother, Moncef, two years younger, was a government horticulturalist at a vineyard near Tunis. He returned to Kelibia every weekend since he was engaged to his father's brother's daughter. This situation was providential for me, for it broadened my possible field of inquiry to include (part of) the men's world in addition to the women's. Townspeople considered these two young men suitable chaperones for me. I had first been a member of their parents' household in 1967 when they were schoolboys, so that, in a sense, they were perceived to be my brothers. I thus had intermediaries for access into the men's world. The situation was especially important since my long association with the town and with its children, my youth when I first came to live in Kelibia, and my gender meant that most people never quite saw me as a researcher or a scholar, but as a person who was attached to the town and to some of its inhabitants and therefore had contrived a means to return for an extended visit. I was expected to comport myself as a proper, unmarried Kelibian woman. This meant, among other things, not visiting, unescorted, men unrelated to me.

So as not to tarnish the family's reputation or cause inconvenience, I consulted with family members (especially with Lella Nesria, the mother of Malek, Moncef, Leila, and Adel) about my fieldwork project. I had devised three alternative programs for my research, one of which was a study of townspeople's representations of Kelibia's past, and together this is the one we decided I should do. It was Malek, the eldest brother of the three, who offered to help me find men who could tell me about Kelibia's history. Malek was very attached to his community and proud to be a Kelibian. He also knew someone from almost every family in the town. He was willing to accompany me once or twice a week to record what men remembered about their town, about their heroes, and about their own lives. Moncef, one of the other brothers, also helped. Later, while I was suffering through the translation process—tape to page, Arabic to English—I would cause him to neglect his bride-to-be and their wedding plans in order to explain the difference between a scythe and a sickle, or to bring me another "Turk-ish" ("Arab," "Greek") coffee from the café across from his parents' home.

With the help of Malek and Moncef, I discovered that men, like women, did talk a lot about the past, and that their observations often took the form of stories. (In the women's world, they more rarely, but sometimes, did.) Like proverbs or lullabies, local history stories turned out to be a part of what might be called the "everyday folklore" of Kelibia, nuggets of lore embedded in everyday life rather than those presented as special, public events. They were told by a fairly wide range of people in the town—adults of both sexes and of various socio-economic groups. They occurred spon-taneously and unpredictably, often in the midst of conversation. So the research required a great deal of cultural immersion, but did not have to be conducted only during a particular season or at a particular rite of pas-sage, or on a special day of the week. These portable and low-key narratives turned out to be called *hikayat*.

Romancing the "Real"

My discovery of these stories added a new dimension for me to previously published collections of Maghribian oral literature. Since they dealt with highly local material, I found them to have an immediacy of time and place that dominated any fantastic, pedagogical, or epic element—what is typi-cally considered "folkloric." This is not to say that they did not contain those elements. But, in most cases, the fantasy and didacticism were clev-erly embedded because the narrator's primary task was to reinforce the be-lievability of his or her account by naming witnesses, participants, locations, and a thousand community details familiar to the audience at hand. The stories offered philosophical truths, as do Sufi tales or fables, but accepting that truth depended on accepting the historical "truth" of the account.

Hikayat submerge in local detail the markers of timelessness and of the transcultural that are the traditional allure of folklore studies—markers in folktales, epics, or fables, for example, that can be drawn upon to speak to the interests or concerns of folk other then those producing them. These local stories are emphatically placed in and are dependent on specifications of time, place, and actors. They are semiprivate: they are told by, directed toward, and most meaningful to the members of a community rather than outsiders. In fact, they were elicited by requests to hear about town history, not to be told stories. Nevertheless, most researchers surely would not take them seriously as history, for as story, and oral story told in Arabic dialect at that, their "truth" is suspect.

In earlier studies I had overlooked them myself because of my fascination with the many traditionally more foregrounded and studied verbal art genres of Tunisia, like lullabies, nursery rhymes, jokes, proverbs, folktales, and riddles, all of which have less "slippery" boundaries than these stories of the past. I discovered, however, that although, or perhaps because, the narratives were not so overtly marked by performative indicators as musical or theatrical events, nor so recognizable as an internationally shared, old, and venerable genre of lore, they were more pervasive in the town in terms of performers and occurrence and more integrated into the lives of group members than the more foregrounded folk genres (possibly excepting proverbs). As a genre the narratives were obviously flourishing in the community.

In form and content, hikayat are a genre that suited at the time of my study the needs of certain social groups. These stories provided me with a means by which to explore "local" identity and the past upon which that identity is built. Because these stories constitute a genre of folklore especially adaptable to life in a rapidly changing Tunisian town, they encouraged analysis of how folklore forms change in a changing world and of how they are involved in transforming that world. I discovered that the stories can be tailored to people's differing daily schedules. Some can be told in less than five minutes. Thus, city folk more in tune with the eight-hour day than with the cycle of the seasons can also make use of them. They are appropriate for fifteen-minute coffee breaks or business lunches as well as for evenings in cafés or afternoons spent drinking tea under shade trees. They can also be tailored to a variety of practical interests of the storytellers and audiences.

Kelibians effectively were using their traditional expressive forms to cope with the complexities of life in the late 1970s—the experiential distance between generations, increased movement of strangers into the town and of Kelibians abroad, and the encroachment of foreign, not to mention governmental and big city, interests and ways of life. Kelibians for centuries have been affected, and often adversely, by contact with the outside world at the same time that they have needed and profited from that contact. I found that they were using hikayat to accommodate selectively certain outside practices or to render changes imposed upon them as harmless as possible.

The stories were spun from threads of the past that were chosen by their *raconteurs* to comment on present society and to prescribe for the future. They were one medium through which change is confronted and new configurations held up for consideration. When a storyteller can gain the interest and respect of his or her audience, then the possibility for reconstructing some aspects of the social structure exists. This potential contribution of a storyteller to emergent culture should not be surprising: it is just what all art, including folk art, can do.

Folklore, like other aesthetic forms, is rhetorical, dynamic, and adaptive. It is potentially a force for both stability and change, repression and liberation. It is a phenomenon that is manipulated by its performer and subject to negotiation by its audience within communally determined bounds. But even those bounds may be knocked askew, especially when participants have frequent and intense contact with other cultural models. Folklore enables a particular performer in collaboration with his or her audience to appropriate selectively ideas or practices from other groups in a manner aesthetically and practically agreeable to his or her own community. (Of course this artistic appropriation could also involve severe critique of the "other" rather than incorporation, or could incorporate form or content but subvert the original "message.")

Each of the following chapters focuses on one aspect of the relationship between hikayah-telling events and historical, social, and political processes. Folkloric analysis of verbal art is drawn upon to illuminate other domains of Kelibian society and vice versa. Chapter 1 addresses the question of the derivation from town history of the underlying touchstones of Kelibian world view that then inform town perspectives on present "realities" and on the narratives and that provide a bond for narrators and audiences. I stress the fact that the actions and reactions of the raconteurs and audiences of the town, like the actions of the protagonists in the stories, are influenced by shared community understandings, in addition to each townsperson's individual experience. The chapter concludes with a description of the contemporary town of the stories (1978–79), emphasizing both its enduring and its changing features.

Since Chapter 1 is centrally directed at the problem of how history might become story, much of the subject matter in both sections of this chapter refers to or explains or elaborates on subjects that will be mentioned in the stories themselves. I describe three points, "givens"—the town's history as understood by longtime community families; certain facets of current Kelibian world view; and a collection of human, natural, and manufactured town icons and stories about them. With these points, I fill in a triangle, speculating on the role of tradition (history) in the stories, as well as on the means by which the stories act upon history (tradition) and upon the social and iconic aspects of the community—a demonstration of process, the continual rethinking and reinterpreting and negotiating of time past and time present.

Chapter 2 describes the common properties of a particular, pervasive set of male storytelling events, a narrower corpus related not only by subject matter such as past events and extra-ordinary town members but by the situational, structural, and social contexts in which the majority of the stories were told. By taking into account the structural relationships between narrator and audience as well as the respective structural positions of narrator and audience vis-à-vis the community past becoming present and looking toward the future, one is able to begin to understand the complex message of the stories. I consider just how the structure(s) of the storytelling events and the formal features of the stories help determine the significances of the texts. The chapter juxtaposes the past (as represented in the male hikayat) and the present (as represented by the narrator and his audience). It becomes clear that older townsmen negotiate with each other and with younger men as to what it means to be a man of the town by drawing upon relevant stories about special townsmen of an earlier era.

Chapter 3 centers on the dramatis personae of the hikayat and argues that these particular figures in order to be understood must be linked to their real life counterparts, to North African history, and to the past and present situation of the community itself vis-à-vis the outside world. To support this argument, Chapter 3 focuses more closely on the story content, integrating it with data incorporated from the previous two chapters. Central to the self-portrait that emerges from consideration of context (Chapters 1 and 2), and content (Chapter 3) of these hikayat is Kelibian management of Kelibia's status as a crossroads. It analyzes four of the dramatis personae who appear consistently in the stories—holy figures, secular heroes, "holy fools," and town characters—all people from the community. Each has a role to play in defining townspeople's views of their places and the place of Kelibia in a larger cultural history, over space and through time.

Chapter 4, partially as a response to the ongoing "crisis" in the doing and textual rendering of ethnography, situates my study vis-à-vis certain other ethnographic approaches to traditional expressive culture. It addresses the stigmatized status of folklore, particularly of North African folklore, and some reasons both historical and current for that stigma. Not only did this negative perspective on folklore arise for historical reasons—colonialism, imperialism, and theories of social evolution used to sustain them—but from a privileging, in western literary theory, of the written over the spoken and, in the Arab world, of the standard or classical Arabic over the colloquial. The chapter offers an alternative assessment of folklore, and especially verbal art, as a personal and group resource, and suggests that colloquial verbal art, like hikayat, is embued with a certain quiet power of its own. I indicate more specifically in what ways my work on folklore as central to the issue of process has been influenced by the theory and practice of certain past and current scholars. Just *because* it is an art form dismissed by most of the dominant, this "ephemeral" artistic medium was fit for cooptation by the adversary community, or an adversary group within the community, and could become a response to those who would devalue the hikayat or their cultural creators.

If the dominant hear this response at all it may be in a folk medium they have trouble taking seriously. Still, political jokes are taken very seriously in Cairo, and a folk national culture form in Algeria, the veil, was seen by the French as an impediment to the breakdown of Arab culture and combatted as such.

The discussion in this chapter illustrates how the intellectual history of a region can clarify or throw into sharper relief attitudes Kelibians have about their other, the westerners who colonized them. Kelibian hikayat are part of an ongoing dialogue that is addressed to outsiders as well as members of the town. The chapter takes account of the current scholarly dialogue concerning the political implications of conducting fieldwork in anthropology and folklore among the other, and explains my own stance.

In addressing a folk form as an artistically powerful resource for a Mediterranean town, I find myself responding to the challenge of recent social science scholarship in the United States that urges the dialogic study of less "exotic" social groups. First, I have rejected exoticism and "otherness" in favor of looking for what I could learn through study of creative expression in a more familiar kind of cultural setting. The pervasiveness of folk traditions in all social classes and in urban and rural settings has led many North American folklorists and anthropologists recently to seek out just such less studied and less "exotic" people as these middle class families in a northeastern Tunisian town. Many Kelibians are educated and cosmopolitan. They have hopes, anxieties, and goals quite familiar to me from the American context. They are not very definitively either exotic or other. Thus, rather than study the folklore of so called "uncontaminated," isolated, "traditional" groups and bemoan their passing, I could focus on local legends that addressed important community concerns that arose precisely because the community in which they were told was not isolated—either from the past, or from the outside world, or from thoughts about the future.

Malek (who used to whistle "Yellow Submarine" as he strolled in the family garden), Moncef (who has jokingly incorporated into his vocabulary several of the more impressive mistakes I have made in Tunisian Arabic), Leila (whom I have called *ukhti*, "sister," since she was nine years old and whom I nursed through her tonsillectomy), and Lella Nesria their mother (who tried her best to teach me proper Kelibian behavior while constantly forgiving, understanding, and hiding my peccadilloes from the rest of the town) are difficult to think of as the "other." Yet they and the other townspeople turned out to be sufficiently dissimilar (from me and from each other) to help me learn the differences between us and to allow me to "bring them home" or to find their "fit" within my own cultural context. Attention to my position as, at once, a community member and an outsider in a community very familiar and yet strange, in a culture both western and eastern, where I, a female in a male setting, heard stories lying on the margin between public and private, provided the tensions and contradictions that finally sparked the denouement set forth in Chapter 4 of this book.

The second way in which this study addresses current directions in social science research in the United States lies in its concern with the relationship between student and studied. Anthropologists are accused (often by other anthropologists) of robbing the studied of their right to speak for themselves in the international arena, of privileging interpretation over what is being interpreted. (Writers now accuse theoreticians of this as well, of course.) If the group studied was remote enough, its name for itself did not even have to appear in the ethnography about them: an ethnographic theory could be set out and proved *on* them. Yet ethnographers are in general agreement today that their writings carry political implications both for the group under study and for the researcher. They emphasize the importance of listening for the voices of culture members as they self-consciously respond to the intrusive presence of their other, the necessity of remembering Michel de Certeau's admonishment to listen for the "shared discourse." To this end, and because my encounter with the Kelibians was clearly dialogic, I have included most stories in their entirety and have placed them in the text rather than relegating them to the appendix. I have fitted my words around theirs and sometimes around those of fellow ethnographers and folklorists, in search of a shared discourse among us—me, my Kelibian readers, and my non-Kelibian readers—as the conversation continues.

Do studies of communal affect and of communal or folk aesthetics/poetics romanticize social groups and obfuscate social disjunction and difficulty or even encourage its continuation through refusal of the folklorist (and the folk) to face up to the fact that folklore is mystification—a way of keeping have-nots happy and oblivious of their exploitation? I found romancing the "real"—a "real" of which people are very much aware—to be a coping strategy and not at all the same thing as *romanticizing* the real. Romancing the real is a social means toward maintaining communal value and vitality through the rough times and despite relentless pressures from the world market, technological hegemony, an intrusive central government, or colonization. Folk poetics (folklore) is, by definition almost, anti-canonical discourse, the discourse of resistance of small groups, be they communal, occupational, ethnic, or regional, to larger forces, and hikayat are one kind of Kelibian communal dialogue addressing the community situation(s) vis-à-vis those more comprehensive forces.

My interest in Kelibia is in understanding the source of its strength. Romancing, or celebrating past moments in the unfolding lives of individual members of the community in all their power, tragedy, humor, and tenderness is part of this. Romancing is not to lose sight of the, at times, all *too* real but rather to play with it, to take time (out) to reperceive, reappreciate, celebrate the community, in this case, through the stories of its inhabitants.

I am romancing (but not, I maintain, romanticizing) the real because Kelibians have something to teach me and others. Learning that this was so and then learning just what I needed to learn had all the pain and pleasure of a good romance.

Figure 1. Najar family, summer 1990.
Adults: (left to right) Nadia (fiancée of 'Adel) and 'Adel, Malek and Marie Thé-
rèse, Nejoua and Moncef, Lella Nesria and Si Mohamed, Ouajdi and Leila.
Children: Inez (daughter of Moncef and Nejoua), Myriam (daughter of Malek and
Marie-Thérèse), Sirene (daughter of Leila and Ouajdi), Abir (daughter of Leila and
Ouajdi), Mehdi (son of Malek and Marie Thérèse), Selma (daughter of Leila and
Ouajdi) and Amin (son of Moncef and Nejoua).

Notes on Transliteration and Performative Aspects of Narration

Tunisian Arabic is rarely written and is difficult even for Tunisians to read or write because of its nonstandardization. There is a good deal of variation by region and even by town, at the levels of word choice and pronunciation. In Kelibian practice itself, there is a good deal of variation. Diverse renderings of the language into Western script add further complication. I have chosen to do the following: If I have taken a proper name from a French source, I use the French spelling. If a townsperson has written a name in western characters for me (most likely following a French transcription), I have used his or her spelling. When quoting from a western language text, I retain the spelling of proper names used therein. Thus, the same word in this book may be transliterated differently depending on its source.

In the body of the work, well-known words are transliterated in their traditional forms. For example, I use *wa'li* rather than the Tunisia-specific *uli'* (stress on the first and second syllables respectively), *dervish* for *derwish*, and even Kelibia for *Qalibiya*; "i" usually indicates a high front vowel, sounding like the "ee" in "feet." This is always true for those "i"s at the end of words and often but not always true when they fall at the beginning or middle of a word. In *hikayah*, though, the "i" sounds like the "i" in "pity." Other than in the transliterated texts in the Appendix at the end of the book, plurals for Tunisian words except *hikayat* and *khurafat* are formed by adding "s" rather than by using the Arabic plural.

Other names, and untranslatable words such as those for various coins, land dimensions, and so on, I have transliterated as simply as possible. I use only three vowels for both long and short variants, and environmentally caused allophonic variations of the vowels are not shown. Glottal stops occur irregularly when spoken Arabic is classicized, but they are not phonemic to Tunisian Arabic. Thus, I have used the apostrophe instead of the ﻉ to indicate the Arabic ع . In some Tunisian words, the ڨ replaces the Arabic ق , and in those cases, will be represented as "g" rather than "q." (The Arabic ج is never pronounced "g" as it is in Cairene Arabic.)

Throughout the text foreign words are italicized only the first time they are used. Transcriptions of four stories have been provided in the Appendix. There, a more detailed Tunisian-specific transliteration method has been used.

Performative aspects of narrative such as sound effects, pauses, and so on are indicated by typographical strategies. Ellipsis, for example, indicates a dramatic pause, voiced sound effects are in capital letters, various gestures are described in brackets, and more intense delivery (e.g., loud, rapid) by exclamation points. Any additions I make for clarity are also presented in brackets. As might be expected, asides by the narrator are in parentheses, and when he (or she) quotes someone, that person's words are put in quotation marks. In these hikayat as in some personal narratives in English, there is a great deal of rapid switching between past and present tense. This practice is at least partly dramatic strategy and will be the subject of a later study. In this work, if tense switches were confusing, I have standardized the tenses to make the text comprehensible.

Finally, in most cases, stories are not broken up for illustrative purposes. Since the hikayat are central to this study, I prefer to leave them intact even when their length might seem to exceed their relevance as examples. For the same reason, I integrate the stories into the text rather than placing them in an appendix. In rare noted instances, I have omitted asides, repetitions, or redundancies. For some sorts of studies or reinterpretations, these might be important, and I will try to supply anyone interested with the Arabic transcriptions of the paraphrased sections.

One may receive the misleading impression from some folklore collections that various traditional verbal art forms in a community or culture are equally viable at any particular point in time, and even that they describe a static, unchanging configuration; of course this is not the case. Verbal art forms like written ones have their time and place: in Kelibia right now, hikayat are told often, by most men and mostly by men. This trend toward personal experience and local narrative and away from folk, fairy, or fantasy tales, and even legend seems to parallel that which has occurred in the Western world. One suspects it may be because community- or small-group-specific subject matter is precisely that which one cannot ordinarily find on television, on the radio, or in books. In any case, the genre is taking a prominent place in the verbal art repertoires of many culture groups, and no doubt will be paid increasing attention by folklorists.

Introduction:
Hikayat and Social "Structures of Feeling"

> . . . for there is always something daunting—one might almost say sacrosanct—in the initiation of any act of language.
>
> (Roland Barthes)

> One story suggests another . . .
>
> (Kelibian saying)

Malek Najar's uncle, his father's older brother and a former sheikh of the town, told us to go talk to Si Mohamed Gharbi if we wanted to know about Kelibia's past. One afternoon in December he told us this story.

(1) Si Mohamed [war story]
And there are true dreams, and there are untrue dreams and from all of them here's one story I have:

In the year forty, the time of the war, France brought her soldiers [native troops from North Africa, I suppose] here to the town.

Sabra: In forty?

Yeah, the year nineteen forty, when she [France] was fighting the Germans. The army was brought here to the town. She put them in shops—in that shop of Khoudja's that's over there [gestures]. [It's] a garage now owned by the ben Ahmed sons. It's located at the corner of the impasse where the Amin house is. The soldiers slept there and she [France] wanted to convey them to France—to the front.

There was one soldier from Morocco, from Tef el-Leliq—a pious person. A young man who prayed and knew the words of God [the Koran] . . .

knew God's words. He was afraid to go to France—that there in France he'd die. He was afraid of death. So, in the afternoon around this time he went to that graveyard, and he recited the Koran and gave charity to the dead. And he said, "Oh God, I pray I don't go to the front over there where the soldiers are, where the war is, and I pray that virtuous people here among the dead will pray that I don't pass the draft examination" [so he would not go to the front]. And he went back to the store, where he spent the night with the other soldiers.

At night he was asleep and a woman came to him and nudged him on the leg with her foot.

Sabra: Is he dreaming now?

Yes! He's dreaming now. Oh, he's going to awake! A woman came to him and said, "Come on! Oh, sir, oh so-and-so wake up!" He woke up. Now . . . it was dark. The shop was closed up at night. He awoke and he heard the voice, the voice of a woman was talking to him.

Malek: He didn't see her?

He didn't see her. She said, "Bless you. You made us comfortable. Now, the tombs in the whole graveyard are full of light"—as if, for example, they all contained a lightbulb—"and you made us comfortable [but] get up and repeat such-and-such a *sura* [verse from the Koran]. That letter such-and-such, you see, you mispronounced. You mispronounced that specific letter in such-and-such a sura."

Malek: She said he was wrong.

Yeah. In place of a *nisba* ["ee"] for example [he pronounced "ah" or something else]. He got up. It was dark and the soldiers were sleeping— one snoring, and another . . . you understand. He looked this way and that and went back to sleep.

That woman returned, nudged him on his leg. He looked and found light. It was light in the store. He sat up. The woman was standing up in front of him. She had a lightbulb shining in the middle of her forehead.

Sabra: She wasn't wearing a veil or . . . ?

No. Nothing. He could look at her face. [She repeats her previous words, repeats that they are enjoying the light of the verses of the Koran chapter he donated, and again asks him to repeat the sura he erred in.] He studied her—what the woman was like. How her face was, her eyes, her nose, her eyebrows. How her chin was, her mouth, her hair. He studied her. After studying her he took the sura she told him about. He recited it until he got to the specific letter she had told him about. When he mispronounced it and the light disappeared from in front of him, he sat astonished. "I . . . am I awake or asleep? Am I sitting up or asleep? Wasn't there light shining in front of me? Wasn't there a woman talking to me?"

He got up from the middle of the soldiers. It was dawn—about four-thirty. He got up and went outside. At the time we had the shop across from the mosque. There used to be a barbershop there. We'd stay up there at night following . . . . making a map. I and a group of people. One was called Si Mohamed Trabulsi [Tripoli], Mohamed Ghanim [real name], who used to be an officer in the Turkish army. (Trabulsi had been captured by Italy and imprisoned. He escaped from Italy and came to Tunis here and from Tunis to Kelibia. We became friends.)

When war broke out between France and Germany we were following the war on a map—where exactly the fighting was every day. In other words, we didn't sleep. We were just listening to the news on the radio. The battle such and such is going on at such and such a place. Planes are bombing here. Tanks are here. Here one hundred head died, here one thousand died, for example, of the British or Americans or French or the Germans. [Continues talking about this for awhile.]

Well, when [the boy] came out of the shop he found a light on in our store as we followed the news. (A group of politicians, we were.)[1] "*As-salamu 'alaykum*," he said.

"And *'alaykum assalam*." He said, "Good day."

We said, "The same to you."

He came in and sat on the cement bench. He said, "You guys, I have a story I'd like to tell you."

We said, "Go ahead."

He said, "This area is the area of Sidi Maouia, an area of blessed people, a holy town!!"

That's right, it is Maouine and blessed."

He said, "And your cemetery on this side of town has saintly people in it."

We sat staring at him! "What do you mean?" [He tells them the story and Si Trabulsi asks him to repeat his description of the woman.]

The general [Si Trabulsi] said, "Bless you, that's my wife. That's my wife and she died in the year twenty-seven." (That means she had been dead thirteen or fourteen years when . . .) "That woman, my wife knew all of the sixty chapters of the Koran. She knew the Koran and she's Turkish, from Turkey." (Well, we said he was a Turkish general. He was in the Turkish army. He married a Turkish woman, an educated woman. She knew the Koran and when he escaped from Italy she heard he had come to Tunis. She came here to Kelibia. Yes, came here to Kelibia. She died in Kelibia and, if you want, I can show you her grave now.) Well, he said, "That's my wife." He asked him, "Do you know the tomb that you stopped at [when you recited the Koran]?"

He said, "I don't, but I remember the place where I stood. I know that."

He said, "Okay, let's get up."

We all got up and went out—the whole bunch together—everybody together—Trabulsi (the husband of the dead woman) and the servant of God [i.e., the narrator] and others. We started going, and he [the young soldier] was walking in front of us to show us where he had stood. Get along, get along, get along, until he was over the tomb of this woman, the wife of Trabulsi, who knew the Koran. He stopped right at her head. He said, "I stood here!!"

Trabulsi turned around and told him, "That's my wife's grave. That's the woman, the woman who stood before you last night . . . " [He reviews her actions.]

[And the boy wasn't sent to the front because France fell shortly thereafter . . .]

Si Mohamed illustrates in his story some effects of Kelibia's crossroads status as an Arab, Muslim, Mediterranean town. He calls attention to all that that status implies for community disruption and change, for unexpected influxes of new people with new ideas and technologies. He portrays to me and Malek a town of cosmopolitan inhabitants ready to handle these expected eventualities.

Such a town and such a story defeat any attempt by an ethnographer to study Kelibians in the anthropological manner prevalent through the 1950s; that is, to treat them as members of a homogeneous and isolated community far removed from the hustle and bustle of history by virtue of being located on a distant isle, or in an inhospitable desert, or in a treacherous mountain range.

Readers used to expect ethnographies to be like travelogues—to include the literary conceits of otherness: impossible geographies and exotic folk. But most ethnographers have realized that the old preoccupation with finding or portraying subject communities as isolated, homogeneous, and ahistorical derives more from traditional western models for thinking about and representing the "other" than from any inherent characteristics of their chosen subjects. If Kelibia is obviously not isolated, either from the past (in this case the war years) or from the rest of the world (France, Germany, Italy, Morocco, Turkey) or even from the hereafter (in the person of Trabulsi's wife and of Sidi Maouia) neither are those traditional subjects of ethnography—nomads, mountain people, islanders, or forest dwellers.[2] We now know that we can no longer think of, or write about communities as ahistorical, as timeless places awaiting the arrival of the West. We try to present them in a historical context intelligible to "them" and "us." We try to show how change is effected or discouraged in a particular community by community members themselves.

We also know that even those communities on islands, in deserts, or atop mountains are never homogeneous. Accurate description requires that we find the means to represent not simply communities but individuals and various subgroups within those communities.

Similarly, no community today is truly isolated. The "unspoiled" communities ethnographers wrote about in the past no longer exist, if they ever did. So we seek to place our chosen communities in their global context, to pinpoint the significance of the "micro" for the "macro," of the miniature for the big picture.[3] How then can a town such as Kelibia be evoked in contemporary ethnography? Although ethnography remains a "research process in which the anthropologist closely observes, records, and engages in the daily life of another culture . . . and then writes accounts emphasizing descriptive detail" (Marcus and Fischer 1986: 18), today ethnographers are challenged to describe communities not only within various historical and global contexts but from the inside out. The ethnographic task is to try to comprehend those elusive affective and analytic "structures of [community] feeling"+ that will convey to readers the process by which its uniqueness vis-à-vis other cultures endures.

Attention to reflexivity in field studies has led fieldworkers to realize (or at least to acknowledge), more than ever before, that we seek to engage and then write about cultures in other times and other places largely in order to reperceive our own times and our own places—in this sense, "bringing it all back home" (Berreman 1974).⁵ This juxtaposition of "home" from an ethnographer's perspective and "home" in *hikayat* (or local legends) like Si Mohamed's alerted me to what degree "periphery" and "home" in ethnographic writing are a matter of perspective. Kelibians—like any other group, no matter how remote historically, geographically, or culturally from "us"—also perceive themselves as central, even though they are fully aware that much of the rest of the world, erroneously, does not. In Si Mohamed's story he surely lets us know that all roads lead to Kelibia. In one night Turks, Moroccans, and an American (in 1978); Muslims and Christians; war (in story time) and peace (in 1978); the natural and the supernatural; oral and written; young (in story time) and older (in 1978); the living and the dead are all present. The search for the exotic is now tempered by the effort—impelled in large part by unresolved ethical problems with making human beings a subject of study—toward appreciating multiple perspectives, both within one community and globally, on such topics as centrality.

Meeting the challenge of contemporary ethnographic description and representation has resulted over the last thirty years in what George Marcus and Michael Fischer dub an "experimental moment" in ethnographic writing (1986), during which ethnographers have self-consciously examined and reworked fieldwork methodologies and goals, as well as the writing of ethnographies.⁶ Some ethnographers have experimented with portraying cultural affect through the lens of a dramatic incident or a cultural ritual. Others have worked with a significant "representative" life history, or have chosen to present a dialogue or series of dialogues between the ethnographer and one or more subjects. All of these modes of presentation have the effect of making room for the voice(s) of the community under study to be heard. To that same end, ethnographers today also tend to write open-ended works: to let certain social group phenomena remain unexplained or unincorporated into a "system" is not only acceptable but honest and inevitable. Tying up all loose ends is not clever: it is suspect and closes off dialogue. And scholars now study minutely how a community's political and economic interests influence and are influenced by the global networks in which they have been entwined over time. Finally, in most ethnographies today the ethnographer is self-consciously "present" in the texts.

None of these approaches guarantees representational success, of course. But in many cases, their authors consciously take steps to reconceptualize what it means to "know" a culture and move us, the readers, further in that direction.[7]

North African ethnographies now lie at the cutting edge of such experiments in representation. Fifteen years ago anthropologists working in the Arab world frequently expressed dissatisfaction with the paucity of contributions to anthropological theory from their ranks (for example, Fernea and Malarkey 1975). Out of that region had come disappointingly little of theoretical notice (partly because the area was not different, exotic, that is, "other," enough.)[8] However, for five years now, I have taught a course in experimental ethnography, using new-school ethnographies of the Arab world, and especially of North Africa. Pierre Bourdieu, Vincent Crapanzano, Jean Duvignaud, Kevin Dwyer, Lawrence Rosen, Dale Eickelman, Elizabeth Fernea, Clifford and Hildred Geertz, Roger and Terri Brint Joseph, Camille Lacoste-Dujardin, Henry Munson Jr., Abdellah Hammoudi, and Paul Rabinow, among others, have advanced the field's understanding of the workings of ethnographic representation and now are cited often in general theoretical discussion.

What is the position of folklore in all this? Ethnographers of the Maghrib, despite their common concern with affect and with the voice(s) of the other, tend to treat folklore—extra-establishment aesthetic culture—as "cognitive remnants" or as "increasingly anachronistic social mechanisms" (for a discussion of this phenomenon, see Marcus and Fischer 1986: 90), or they ignore it altogether. Yet in the effort to understand and describe the cultural experience of the other, careful attention to these traditional artistic forms is of central importance. In these forms we see or hear conveyed most clearly, and in their most compressed form, a people's negotiation and renegotiation of its "reality," in the context of both its historical and global settings. It is through the study of these art forms that we can come closest to an unmediated hearing of the individual and collective voice(s) of a social group. Thus do we understand from the inside out. Thus are we able to explicate "culture"-in-process—rather than culture represented merely as a reified product or as a cyclical (seasonal, yearly, generational) practice—in channels potentially accessible both to members of a society and to outsiders. Most important, it is in extra-establishment aesthetic culture (folklore) that we find displayed the structures of feeling of a social group that supply the centripetal force that gives relatively small groups the power to face oppression or the world system and remain culturally distinct and intact. In Si Mohamed's narrative we see what some of these components are for Kelibia. There is the desire and ability of Kelibians to understand and "master" the outside world as it is represented by the radio, the map, Trabulsi, the Moroccan, and me. There is the power of Islam— both in orthoprax form (the reciting of the Koran) and heteroprax (the evoking of a local holy person). There are educated people, both men (the group in the store and Malek and Si Mohamed) and women (Trabulsi's wife and me). There is knowledge of the past and stories about it.

As we try to place communities in global and historical settings, they begin to seem very much at the mercy of those larger forces—helpless and, finally, culturally nonviable. Folklore is a tool with which communities can reinforce and revitalize community identity when it seems the community should be falling apart under the onslaught of, say, western hegemony or the ups and downs of the global economy. To attend to community folklore is to attend to affect, to community "feeling tone" (Fernandez 1971), and thus its possibilities for cohesiveness and conflict. But it was when I learned to listen in the right register to a spectrum of Kelibian folk art forms, from gossip to greetings, that Malek, Si Mohamed, Lella Nesria, and others could help me understand Kelibian structures of feeling. Only then did various facets of community self perception about the nature and worth of their society begin to become clear. Folklore, like other aesthetic culture, is socially created fragments of "time out" within which alternatives to the norm, both aesthetic and social, can be experimented with, or within which the joyful essence of a community itself can be appreciated for a second, an hour, or an evening. Perhaps folklore and other art forms even have a charter to perform these tasks.

Folklore, in both form and content, is by definition communally centered and time tested. Thus it is an especially apt artistic medium through which to learn about community-shared concerns from the perspective of the culture members themselves. Given that reality is negotiated, where better to study the process of negotiation and renegotiation of a community world view than by searching for those artistic forms—be they musical, verbal, ritualistic, or iconic—that are centrally practiced by the members of a particular social group or subgroup? Folklore forms, like paintings, poems, or novels, take time to produce and savor. They demand heightened attention, and the audience expects them to be particularly significant.

I argue that the verbal art form I studied in Kelibia illustrates the powerful contribution that folklore and folklore theory can make to the evocation of any culture. Because Kelibia is so strikingly embroiled in historic and global exchange, certain very common types of occurrences that are less obvious, perhaps, in other cultures due to our geographical stereotypes of islands, deserts, and mountains are able to be studied *en clair*. Kelibian lore tests culturally agreed-upon boundaries and constructs alternatives to both the cultures Kelibians see around them and their own. Through informed study of a particular and pervasive Kelibian narrative form, the local legend or hikayah in social and historical context, I present not my analysis of Kelibians, but what I understand to be their representation of themselves. I try to hear and convey what I understand to be their side of things in the dialogue between "us" and "them."[9] At the same time, individual voices from within the town can be heard as each storyteller draws upon the rhetorical power of his or her art to persuade an audience of a particular point of view. Analyzing hikayat, in particular, provides a Kelibian representation of community life in process because, as will be shown, these stories are overtly about the past becoming present and about looking toward the future.

The definition of hikayah differs among the various dialects of colloquial Arabic. In Kelibia, the hikayah genre resembles the western folklore genres of local legend, memorate, local history narrative (Dorson 1952), or personal experience narrative (Labov 1972). Hikayat are "true" stories of the recent, two or three generations, past. The French colonial scholar Marcelin Beaussier defined them as *historiettes* in his French-Arabic dictionary.

Unlike other collections of narratives gathered in the Maghrib, hikayat cluster around local people rather than fictional characters or historical figures of national or international renown. Most of the one hundred hikayat

I recorded recounted ordinary townspeople's encounters with four types of memorable residents: the regional or town holy person (*wali*), the town holy fool (*dervish*), the town hero, and the town "clown" or "character." Even when a Kelibian hikayah features a religious figure, however, the focus of the story, unlike the focus of other collections of religious stories from the Maghrib, remains the town member who is the "eye" through which the marvelous doings of one of these holy people is witnessed. Narratives about a specific "man next door," told by the same or another "man next door" to a Kelibian audience that is free to comment and interject, give hikayat their special flavor. By their town-specific content and teller/audience context, hikayat represent and present Kelibia's particular dynamic.

The hikayah form lends itself easily to the analysis as a conversational genre, that is, to analysis as part of an ongoing social encounter rather than as a genre that is complete in itself. This approach emerges quite naturally from the Kelibian experience and has the effect of drawing the listeners' attention to correspondences between events in the story world and events in the contemporary world. Storytellers and audiences "naturally" achieve a conversational ambiance by the shared stories, thus demonstrating that conversational genres need not be limited to more ahistorical, short folk forms like riddles, jokes, and proverbs, or to stories of ongoing dramas like adolescent fight stories (Shuman 1986).

Within the spectrum of artistic communication, genres are defined relationally. In the Cap Bon region (although not everywhere in the Arab world), hikayat are juxtaposed to *khurafat*, fictional or fantasy tales. Hikayat are presented as true[10] by their tellers, but the truth, like that of legends, is open to negotiation or simple reevaluation between raconteur and audience and between one raconteur and another. However, as with many western local legends, their veracity does not necessarily preclude the presence of supernatural elements. Hence, stories of the marvelous doings of local holy figures and dervishes are included within the hikayah category.

Because of their historical and conversational components, hikayat constitute a particularly useful folklore genre to draw upon in an ethnographic study that aims at taking account of the town in both its historic and extra-town contexts. Hikayat are *about* ties between the community's past and present, just as they are *about* links among the narrators, the protagonists, and the audience—with three or more generations of community members present—and, especially in men's stories, *about* encounters with the outside world.

Community identity, then, is central in hikayah-telling. None of the people who told these hikayat was a professional storyteller or an "oral historian." Rather, each one's status as a community member worthy of special attention as a community spokesperson derived from three culturally determined factors. First, all narrators were older members of families with town roots, that is, their personal and familial histories were closely bound to the history of the town. Second, they had reputations for possessing some significant and accurate information about the past of the town or of town members; that is, the community judged them truthful raconteurs. And third, they were able (some more successfully than others) to present aesthetically pleasing narratives.

For the last reason, I study hikayat as artistically constructed texts. Rather than amassing them, as is often done, with the hope of uncovering historical or sociological detail, I present them separately. Recognizing that all culture, including cultural history, derives from social negotiation, my interest is in understanding something of a Kelibian artistic perspective on the past, present, and future. Narrators and audiences negotiate their shared, ever-changing community self-portrait by drawing upon past events in the lives of (mostly male) protagonists in Kelibia and their sometimes chaotic encounters with other Kelibians, Tunisians, or foreigners and by fashioning these encounters into stories. The significance of the stories is achieved by the teller's choice of information, the artistic arrangement of that information, the context in which it is presented, and the fit among these three aspects.

That the stories display social interaction, both in their content and in their situational context, is not surprising. Despite the advent of television, radio, a sophisticated educational system, and widespread literacy, Kelibia still privileges an intense interest in the doings of community members. Like members of other Mediterranean groups, most Kelibians place little value on being alone. Creative energy springs from day-to-day personal encounters and talk about them.

We can approach folk narratives in a number of ways. Often collections of texts are made to preserve the nostalgic detritus of an earlier age. Sometimes the goal is to offer a sample of some of the richer facets of a vital, living culture. Literary theorists carefully unpack selected culture texts in much the same way that literary or popular culture texts are studied. If history is brought into the analysis in, for example, a literary study of the famous Arab epics of the Bani Hilal tribe or of the hero Antar, it is the history of the art form and of its legendary events and figures rather than the history of the taletellers that is usually considered important. Sociolinguistic research into folk narrative is generally focused on speech situations or on performance events.[11] Text within situational context can be minutely studied. Finally, the sociopsychological circumstances of one particular storyteller or singer, or even audience member, might be the focus.

I draw upon all of these approaches in this work. Such a study requires a wide range of data and an integrative system of inquiry: text demands contexts; literary analysis must be integrated with social theory; the synchronic must draw upon the diachronic; individual situational studies must point to more basic cultural notions; and, finally, verbal art must mesh with other forms of expressive culture. With these multiple foci, textual and contextual, I intend to demonstrate the indicative *possibilities* of a "way of thinking" about traditional verbal art forms as they simultaneously constrain and encourage, and are constrained and encouraged by, the social, cultural, and personal matrices in which they appear. Specifically, Kelibian stories about the past become for me an entrée into understanding some levels of process by which one contemporary, postcolonial community manages its identity in the face of rapid social, political, and economic change.

Since this book is about a particular verbal art form, the hikayah, and the "fit" among folk legend, history, and anthropology, my analysis has benefited in particular from the insights of historians, literary theorists, folklorists, and anthropologists. Folklore theory and the closely related anthropological theory of those scholars who take a special interest in folk narrative, in historical process, and in the sociopolitical dimensions of fieldwork are central to all facets of my analysis.[12] Interwoven here are choices among approaches to verbal art (verbal art as performance), to anthropology (interpretation via culturally produced culture texts, dialogic fieldwork, and process- rather than product-centered ethnography), and to history (reflection by historians upon the fashioning of their own texts and the cultural codes that inform them).

My approach to the representation of Kelibian culture through hikayat is not exactly the "synecdochic rhetorical stance" described by James Clifford and others in which parts (in this case, hikayat) are "microcosms or analogies, of wholes" of Kelibian culture (Clifford 1983: 125). Rather, I maintain that hikayat, with the rhetorical potential of all art forms, are not a people's distilled "culture," but a resource, one source of "time out" for celebrating what is or what should be or for experimenting with or stumbling upon new visions of the possible past, present, or future.[13] Of course, other aspects of communal social or cultural life (including other folklore genres) also shape stories. As a folklorist, I center on hikayat as illuminators of community rather than vice versa, but I get around to both and, finally, the essential is the play between the two, since "both language and context are negotiable, interpenetrating, and fluid" (Beeman 1986: 3).[14] This ethnography of Kelibia, then, is "holistic" in the sense that hikayat are a key part of Kelibian everyday life and what is discovered about them has ramifications for all other parts of Kelibian society (Marcus and Fischer 1986: 60), just as Kelibian society must help explain hikayat.

Of course, the hikayah is not the only genre of the language arts to flourish in Kelibia. As everywhere in the Arab world, the language situation in Kelibia is complex. Artistic rhetoric there is both written and spoken, in both colloquial and modern standard Arabic, and it is axiomatic that all of these forms contribute in one way or another, separately and together, to the ongoing community discussion of "who we are." Spoken Arabic, whether colloquial or modern standard, is strikingly potent. "Everything from metaphysics to morphology, scripture to calligraphy, the patterns of public recitation to the style of informal conversation conspires to make of speech and speaking a matter charged with an import if not unique in human history, certainly extraordinary" (Geertz 1983/1976: 109). From this situation derives the allure of Arabic verbal art, its potential for ethnographic illumination, and its maddening complexity.

Besides an early and persistent exposure to a wide spectrum of verbal art forms—lullabies, nursery rhymes, rhyming games, proverbs, riddles, verbal duels, jokes, *Märchen*, joke tales, puns, nicknames, and so on—Kelibian men partake, at least peripherally, in a venerable literary tradition. Most do not spend much time reading. They peruse the daily paper and, perhaps, read from the Koran. But most Kelibian men are not illiterate, and every adult is committed in theory to literacy.

Until Tunisian independence, the educational system of the town, and thus that of the storytellers in this volume, was more or less uniform. Children, both boys and girls, attended the *kuttab* school at an early age. Age four was not considered unusual. Most girls were not encouraged to continue and often dropped out after learning to write their names or, perhaps, after memorizing a few of the most important Koranic verses.

The goal of kuttab study was the memorization of the entire Koran. Children sat cross-legged on mats on the floor for long hours. Their *'aarfi* (teacher) sat facing them. Each child would be assigned a verse of the Koran to learn—the particular verse chosen according to the ability level of the child. Each had a piece of wood and homemade ink and pen with which to write his or her verse. The 'aarfi selected groups of children to recite a verse together, beating time with a switch that was also used to nudge sleeping children or to punish mischief-makers.

Parents usually tried to ensure that their sons at least learned to read and write. If work kept boys from regularly attending the kuttab, they might be tutored by a relative or friend of the parents (see story 25). Few students managed to memorize the entire Koran, but those who did were ceremonially marched through the town to much public approbation. For the rare boy who mastered the Koran, the next step was to travel to Tunis and study at the Zeitouna Mosque. Going to study or work in Tunis was fraught with dangers, including tuberculosis. Accommodations for out-of-town students were cramped, and the Tunis of the late nineteenth and early twentieth centuries was full of the health hazards of premodern cities. Whereas Kelibia had the advantages of fresh food, fresh air, clean homes, and adequate sewerage, Tunis often damaged the students' health. Some died. And there were other hazards. Families in Kelibia tell of young men disappearing from the capital without a trace. Nevertheless, there were always a few Kelibians who made it through. Even fewer, during the French occupation, could read and write French.

The literary or classical Arabic learned at kuttab and the university, however, is a very different version of Arabic from the everyday colloquial Arabic in which hikayat are told. Classical Arabic, unlike colloquial Arabic, is not region-specific. It is the Arabic that is usually, though not always, written, and it is the Arabic that all literate Arabic-speakers write and speak. It is usually formal rather than informal, public rather than private or intimate, written rather than spoken, and sometimes acceptable as opposed to unacceptable. To complicate matters further, however, older women may often understand classical Arabic even if they do not speak it (except in prayer), and older men, I know, write poems in Tunisian Arabic, not thought of as a written medium.[15] Literary figures painstakingly employed in formal Arabic appear as well in folk forms ranging from riddles to cursing. Since the end of the colonial period, most boys and girls have attended western-style schools. Thus, the educational experience of many of the audience (the adult, younger generation) for the hikayat presented here is quite different from that of the raconteurs.

If an ethnography of speaking or an ethnography of communication for an Arabic-speaking community is ever to be accomplished, the social and cultural implications of this situation of diglossia (that is, two versions of the same language existing side by side over time and used for different purposes) must be addressed extensively by folklorists and anthropologists. Diglossia and the differences between verbal art in literate, restricted-literate, and nonliterate societies and all gradations in between have implications for Arabic verbal art that have yet to be fully explored, and are beyond the scope of this book.[16] For my purposes I would just observe that some scholars feel that among a literate population the existence of a formal Arabic allows that population to take liberties with the spoken informal Arabic otherwise not possible. Thus Arabic verbal art can tolerate permeable boundaries, can be much more flexible and creative than it otherwise might be (Gerhardt 1963: 416). Verbal art forms such as the hikayah contain words from a region-specific colloquial Arabic that, in Kelibia, include lexical items of Italian, French, Berber, Turkish, Spanish, and classical Arabic origin, a reflection of the Kelibian geographical "situation," lying as it does, on the edges of both the Mediterranean and Arab worlds. Thus the special creations of Kelibia become less comprehensible even to other Arabic speakers, even to other Tunisians, the farther one moves from the town. There is certainly a flavor of the private and in-group about Kelibian hikayat—in both their choice of subject matter and their choice of language. Only a close look *in situ* at historical, cultural, and cross-cultural dynamics of the town itself through Kelibian eyes can begin to make sense of its linguistic and cultural complexities.

The rich insights yielded by the current move toward collapsing together theory and praxis can be enhanced, quite evidently, by a concomitant understanding of social process, in the sense of changing theories and practices at both a global and a communal level, rather than attending only to cyclical movements or reifying practices already in place. Unless one concludes that social groups are unable to change *on their own*, a pervasive but dubious conclusion for two reasons to be discussed later, one is then led to ask what cultural resources a specific group possesses for appreciating and evaluating, and then maintaining *or* changing, practices. What cultural resources do communities possess for self-reflection and critique? Folklore, like other aesthetic domains within a culture, is one of these resources. In Kelibia, the hikayah is a powerful rhetorical tool for reflecting in certain ways on self or community.

In order to approach such a "way of thinking" about folklore, I have had to work through a number of conflicting attitudes or analyses of folklore and the folk held by scholars of the cross-cultural. As I will demonstrate in Chapter 4, some of these are products of colonialism and the association of the "folk," or the "folklore-ridden," with the non-European and the poor. Predictably enough the folk and the folklore for this and other reasons are associated with stasis rather than change, tradition rather than "modernity," and ignorant and provincial outlooks rather than sophisticated, cosmopolitan ones.

Hikayat studied in the contexts of the storytelling event, town history, and current situation reveal that at least some folklore forms are inherently neither at one end of any of the above spectrums nor the other, but a cultural resource for individuals and a community. They incorporate themes in Kelibian history that are of recurrent use to townsfolk in their fashioning and refashioning of world view and so have been distilled and presented by one storyteller after another to create and to argue for his or her complex vision of the ideal community. As James C. Scott argues, these visions are not simply escapism or fancy, but culture-in-embryo, an extra- or anti-establishment resource, ready, when the time is right, to be seized, expanded upon and adjusted, ornamented, and implemented by community members, or held in abeyance in times of oppression and danger, remaining "just a story, just talk" (Scott 1976: 240).

Local history "stories" often clustered around the four types of historical personages (walis, dervishes, heroes, and clowns or local characters)[17] mentioned above or around "exotic" phenomena (like Tayyes[18]) because these are community members, themes, or concepts that are pivotal in Kelibia and, thus, may serve as powerful cultural indicators. I will show that the four dramatis personae, while peripheral to everyday community life and anomalous in one way or another to expected community behavior, are at the same time absolutely central to community self-perception and evaluation.[19] The stories I recorded about them often dealt with a destabilizing outsider or stranger in the town, or with a crisis precipitated by outside events, or with a sort of picaresque situation where a protagonist leaves home to test his or her mettle outside the boundaries of Kelibia—just the sorts of crises that would precipitate both personal and community reflexivity. "Exotic" dramatis personae like walis, dervishes, heroes and clowns are linked again and again with the "everyday" Kelibian in these circumstances, I will argue, because these "exotics" are indicators to mainstream community members of both the periphery and the center of the community. As such, they are ideal resources for raconteurs and audiences interested in delimiting and evaluating the complexities of the relationships that Kelibia and Kelibians have with the outside world. Even when the community crises do not involve encounters with outsiders (some hikayat take place entirely within Kelibian boundaries, and with a cast of only Kelibian townspeople—living and dead), the hikayat that mark an appreciation of community potency that stands community members in good stead inside and outside community boundaries are also marked by the inclusion of these four dramatis personae, who *are*, in a sense, the community potency.

In order to understand just what a storyteller's story is conveying to her or his audience and community, however, and how the message is conveyed, one must draw together not only the performer's relation to her or his story world but also to her or his community and immediate audience. In the stories in Chapter 2 each male narrator is a link with the past (in story guise) and, in terms of his young audience, with the community at large and its fate. No raconteur is simply "passing the time" telling these stories. As with all performers each raconteur has an agenda embedded in his repertoire.

The performer's relationship to his or her own past is also an important factor. As illustrated by the contrast between what is acceptable behavior for storyteller as young protagonist and for storyteller as storyteller and older, established community member, we cannot conclude that differences in attitudes and approaches to life taken by younger and older community members are necessarily indicative of community change. Some differences simply represent two different stages in the life cycle. Younger Kelibian men will become more like older ones and judging from their stories, the older ones, were once like the younger in many ways.[20]

It is becoming clear that the stories in their capacity as evaluations of the past and creators of the future are addressed to an unseen as well as a present audience. If, in Jacques Lacan's terms, storytellers are addressing a third party, that is, embedded cultural structures (as much to challenge them as to reinforce them, in my opinion), they are addressing, consciously and unconsciously, not simply their own cultural codes but (through my presence as a western, Tunisian Arabic-speaking, non-Muslim woman) western hegemony past and present, past and neocolonialisms, and outsiders in general. The storytellers are providing the young men with cultural ballast to sustain them in (future) encounters and in competition with outsiders, be they Tunisois (people of the capital), or Europeans, or Americans who will automatically assume themselves to be culturally, and often financially, advantaged. Kelibians assume that *they* have a cultural, if rarely a financial, advantage. That advantage includes the Kelibians' willingness, nay their inclination, to compare and assess the people of other cultures in terms of their own. Both story context and content display an interest in encounters with members of the outside world, be they migrant workers, soldiers, tourists, or cattle rustlers. It is not only the story as art form that is focused on by raconteurs or audience, although it is evaluated in these terms. It is the communal credibility and personality of the teller, a person with a way with words, and the listeners' shared involvement as community with the story events, the past, and world events that is most necessary. Words thus become valuable coin of the realm.

Folklore can be a particularly important resource for community members of ethnic, religious, occupational, or regional groups lacking other effective means of defending community boundaries—whether geographic or social.[21] Symbolic resistance as expressed in folk forms is, of course, always the most important and practical form of resistance. As first expressions of "meaning," as a kind of societal fuel, this affect-charged resistance remains essential to the health and coherence of any liberating movement in, say, the arena of economics.[22] In studying these hikayat with their special regional flavor, I became aware that this sort of folk narrative, tied so specifically to a limited and delimited group and region, is a powerful resource for structuring a positive and adjustable image for the very kind of small, rural, Third World community, like historical Kelibia, that many scholars and intellectuals characterize as ignorant, stagnant, homogeneous, and powerless.[23] Because of the hikayat's region- or town-specific protagonists as well as other town-specific features of content, structure, and context, they are particularly suited to constructing a *community* identity.

Other topics, such as school experiences or a famous shipwreck, were usually presented in descriptive, rather than story, form. Never did the hikayat paint the "big picture" of history we would expect from political histories—the great uprisings, plagues, independence battles, land disputes. Emphasis is on personal control—over time and across space. The best of the hikayat are elegant, intimate miniatures that sketch in fine detail an hour or day in the life of a community member, significant for him or her, but also, as signaled by the presence of a shared community aesthetic, significant for the community-in-process, past, present, and future.

What emerges from the study of these hikayat is part of an ongoing dialogue among ethnographers about the place of history and folk narrative in ethnographic representation—an appropriate theme in the study of a Mediterranean culture group like the Kelibians since the Mediterranean region has such an abundance of history and folklore. Their town is another one of these Mediterranean places with "'more history than [it] can consume locally,'" (Davis 1977: 239) except that Kelibians, at least, are adept at consuming their history. Hikayat are one of the ways to cope creatively with both the destabilizing and the energizing facets of centuries of frequent, rarely controlled or asked-for cross-cultural contact. In Kelibia, at least, coping is part of the social process, but process is the equivalent not so much of social change as of continual reappreciation (reinforcement) or reassessment with an eye to *possible* judicious change.

Pursuing my thesis that even the most casual comparison of any town's situation with its local history narratives should show that raconteurs through their narratives *do* respond to, and act on, the specific historical circumstances of that town, I have found that indeed any single hikayah as well as the aggregate corpus reflects not just an individual but a collective insight and evaluation as well. Kelibia's world-view is derived from its historical circumstances, distilled and arranged to highlight community-shared knowledge about the town's past. Such common knowledge is one resource Kelibian community members draw upon in fashioning and re-fashioning community self-portraits: often through the medium of narrative. At the same time, however, narrative process and event become vehicles for the creation and maintenance of, as well as a challenge to, certain of these town-held interpretations of history, and thus are implicated in the revisions to world view that must take place from time to time in any viable society.

I do not find that this historical "reality" is created by hikayat, although they are one "force for both the conduct and perception of history" (Rosaldo 1980: 24). Rather, I find that a shared world-view is a synthesis, a changing product, of what both insiders and outsiders have chosen to remember, write, say, or do, about or in Kelibia. Certain events *really did* occur, at least, kind of, sort of, given artistic license and rhetorical strategy and several centuries. These are the traces on which reconstruction is based (cf. Paul Ricoeur). But only certain of these events and only certain players, structures, and geographical locations on the historical stage have been chosen to figure in hikayat. This complicated configuration has the effect of ensuring that no event is defined once and for all by a narrative and that neither Kelibia's culture nor its history can be pinned down. The creation is circular and involves not just written history, not just hikayat, their narrators, and audiences, but the stimuli of current events and of existing town "icons" whether natural, constructed, or human.

As I have pursued this study of Kelibian hikayat, I have become convinced that folklore is neither cultural cognitive remnant nor anachronistic social mechanism, but is in fact a resource that can contribute in a number of ways to the ethnographers' search today for theory and method (both field and literary) that will lead to "truer" representations of their subjects' experiences. First, multiple voices need to be presented within a text, not simply that of the ethnographer, or of one "representative native" within a supposedly homogeneous community. Attention to verbal art gives any individual subject of an ethnography at least a chance to speak around, if not through, the ethnographer. As both anthropologists and folklorists become increasingly sophisticated in the rendering of transcriptions and translations, we will hear the words of these subjects more clearly. And the significant cultural messages are those that are rendered artistically. They are not simply a reflection of the culture, but a multivocalic affective and practical pronouncement upon it. As Roger Renwick observes, "folklore of any sort . . . requires skill and effort to compose, learn, remember, and perform, and . . . consequently it would make little sense to expend such effort if the product were simply a verbal equivalent of the referent itself" (1980: 13).

Further, I would maintain that, in many cases, verbal art contains the key to the dialogue that ethnographers now see as essential to an ethically rendered ethnography. That is, in hikayah-telling events and other verbal art sessions studied by ethnographers, one can find a response not only to the fieldworker, but to what the fieldworker represents as foreign, western, non-Muslim (for example), male or female. Where else but in a culture's traditional expressive culture could we more naturally expect to find the "counterethnography of subjects" that is called for today (Marcus and Fischer 1986: 86)? After this study of Kelibian hikayat, I am convinced that it is not idealistic, but rather practical, to acknowledge that traditional subjects of ethnographies are "often equally, if not more aware of [the operation of the world system] . . . than the anthropologist himself" (Marcus and Fischer 1986: 86). They have had to be.

Folklore is an important resource for illustrating the necessity to draw upon history as a crucial theoretical tool through which to study the relationship between traditional expressive culture and social process. To illuminate this relationship I consider the interconnectedness of the hikayah-telling events with both the historical frame of reference of the community, fashioner of and fashioned by these narrative events, and the evaluative frames into which historically counter-hegemonic, especially Third World, folk discourse has tended to be placed. Both of these frames of reference in different ways guide my understanding of the social role of hikayat. Because Kelibia is very aware of the influence through time of diverse cultures, I argue that hikayah-telling speaks to both these frames of reference as well. Adult Kelibians are well aware of their own history, and they are quite aware of, though tolerant of, outsiders' perspectives of the town as a backwater. The social perspectives offered in these narratives are products of and responses to both of these histories. The latter is more overt, I am convinced, because of my presence.

A final note on diglossia and Arabic verbal art forms: If we concur that reality is socially constructed, that reality is negotiated, then the language through which it is negotiated most often is colloquial and not modern standard or classical Arabic. This situation holds true for even the most literate members of the Arab world. In the traditional privileging of classical Arabic by scholars both western and middle eastern, the richness, power, subtlety, intimacy and beauty of colloquial Arabic verbal art forms has been ignored or denied. Only in this century particularly in the last ten years, have Arab world scholars begun widely to attend to and take advantage of the social and rhetorical dimensions of colloquial Arabic verbal art genres. In a rigorous quest for cultural or cross-cultural enlightenment, these traditional aesthetic structures, with their concentrated communicative power and potential, must be attended to. This work is offered as a celebration of one of these speech forms and of the people who use it.

Notes

1. See Eickelman (1989: x–xi) for an account of similar news sessions in 1979 in an Omani oasis.

2. See Pratt (1986) for a discussion of the nonisolation of the !Kung, combined with the anthropological insistence on "timelessless."

3. These old ethnographic traditions did serve a purpose. They solved some research and representational problems, made a task that is seemingly undoable, at both the research and writing stages, a little more possible. Isolation of the subject community was a way to delimit research and to confine an account of a community under study tidily to one book. Paying attention to history, to an individual as an individual instead of as an abstracted representative, and to extra-community contact, including that with the anthropologist, makes both the research subject and the text harder to manage. Anthropologists new to the desert or the remote (from their perspective) countryside, with an imperfect grasp of the native language and operating under time constraints, are in a difficult position to observe process or to recognize differences, say, between one bedouin or one farmer and another. This is especially true since anthropologists tend not to be bedouin or farmers in their own cultures. Moreover, in their effort to grasp the norm, "*the* religion," "*the* kinship system," "*the* economy," they have little time to pay attention to the comings and goings of people on the peripheries of the community or to hear stories about what was or what should be. Traditionally, descriptions of the ongoing, stable system were what counted in mainstream ethnographic writing.

4. "We are talking about characteristic elements of impulse, restraint, and tone; specifically *affective* elements of consciousness and relationships: not feeling against thought, but thought as felt and feeling as thought: *practical* consciousness of a present kind, in a living and interrelating continuity" (Williams 1977: 132).

5. See Eickelman (1989: 372–395) for a discussion of the place of reflexivity in the doing and writing of ethnography today. Also see chapter 4 in this volume.

6. Again, see Eickelman (1989: 372–395) for a summary of these "moments" as they apply especially to middle eastern ethnography.

7. Non-North African examples of fairly recent ethnographies that combine engagingly more than one of these field and representational methodologies are Daniel (1984), Stoller and Olkes (1987), Ong (1987), Comaroff (1985), and Fox (1985). The liveliness of the "moment" is marked by the number of "philosophers of ethnography," notably George Marcus, Michael Fischer, Talal Asad, James Boon, James Clifford, Johannes Fabian, J. Ruby, Clifford Geertz, and Stephen Tyler, all of whom are themselves ethnographers and experimenters as well.

8. See Herzfeld (1987) for discussion of similar "problems" with anthropological studies in Greece, and Eickelman (1985) for a discussion of the situation in the Middle East.

9. At the conclusion of his article "Differential Identity and the Social Base of Folklore," Richard Bauman points out that in any artistic communication there must be a shared understanding between sender and receiver of the aesthetic conventions of the expressive system: "The auditor must be able to perceive the utterance as involving artistic elaboration in order to decode the artistic information built into it by the sender" (Bauman 1971a: 40). To understand the "artistic information" found not only in the stories I study here but in a very wide range of Kelibian communication both verbal and nonverbal is to begin to understand community affect, and thus the very essence of what makes a community cohere, what

ensures that a community will continue to endure meaningfully. Bauman observes that in asking what makes for such shared aesthetic understandings we are asking "a question of the fundamental nature of culture itself" (Bauman 1971a: 41). If my observations in Kelibia are valid cross-culturally, then attention to the folk aesthetic dimension of any community can lead us to understand components of affect in that community group. The more we understand about affect (both as an "instrument of conflict and aggression as well as solidarity" (Bauman), the closer we come to understanding the nature of (a) culture from the inside out. If it is at all meaningful to divide groups into "cultures," then there is also a need for translators between cultural aesthetics. (For cross-cultural explication as translation, see Anderson 1985.)

10. For a somewhat different usage in Turkish folklore see Boratav (1978) or Başgöz (1970). For yet another employment of the term among the Malays, see Errington (1979). See also Muhawi and Sharif (1988).

Among the hundreds of Berber and Arabic tales collected previously in the Maghrib, only the stories of the miracles of the walis, and sometimes those dealing with famous rulers or a famous city, mention specific names or places. Jeanne Scelles-Millie's classifications of stories are representative of types of stories found in most collections: animal stories, romances, factual stories of the "everyman" variety (mostly trickster tales), moral stories, marvelous stories, and religious stories (Scelles-Millie 1970).

My work differs from most Maghribian collections in its central concern with interpretation in light of ethnographic data and anthropological, folklore theory. Most text series are presented without any comment other than a brief introduction. In these introductions the texts are often represented as simply reflections of a culture (Benachenhou 1960), as escape from a grim reality (Reesink 1977), or as sugar-coated lessons from women to children (Scelles-Millie 1970). Often, the stories are felt to be a dying tradition. Study of the situational context of the tales, as well as their content and cultural context, would reveal that the reality is much more complex.

Two Maghribian works present a fuller analysis of a corpus of tales. Camille Lacoste-Dujardin's *Le Conte kabyle: étude ethnologique* (1970) and *Images and Self-Images: Male and Female in Morocco* (1978) by Daisy Hilse Dwyer. Lacoste-Dujardin's work is the more ambitious of the two. The stories upon which she draws are a series of eighty-five that were collected and published by Auguste Jean Mouliéras in 1890 and that Lacoste-Dujardin translated from Berber into French and published in 1965. Again, the stories do not concern specific, named individuals from *la vie quotidienne* either as protagonists or as storytellers. Rather, they concern character "types." Her approach is to study these stories as a mirror of Kabyle culture as it was just before colonization, on the brink of change. She establishes, by comparing summaries of various versions of the Kabyle texts with extra-Kabyle and extra-Berber versions of the same stories, that the Kabyle stories are of a definite type.

That established, she studies the Kabyle stories as revelatory of Kabylian conceptual, value, and culture systems. Most of the rest of the book is concerned with establishing the symbolic significance of types of places and types of characters in the stories. Places she groups together as symbolically significant for the Kabyles are, for example, cities, natural formations, railroads, villages, wells and so on. She also discusses the significance of various character types such as shepherds and hunters. Through the presentation of these types, a picture of the ideal Kabyle man or woman emerges as well as such examples of Kabyle world-view as the attitude that trouble is caused by leaving the group and resolved by returning to it (Lacoste-Dujardin 1970: 139).

The Dwyer book presents thirty-five tales from a corpus of ninety-five with an eye toward discovering "Moroccans' beliefs about maleness, femaleness, and sexuality" (1978: xi). Dwyer sees these tales as passing on an image of women and men that is "crucial in perpetuating women's subordination" (1978: 37). In such a study one would think it would be important to know whether specific stories were told by a man or a woman, but this information is not provided. In contrast, my approach to Kelibian stories depends on attention to just such ingredients of situational context.

11. Critics of sociolinguistic studies reproach scholars for failing to attend to the strictures that culture imposes on individual face-to-face exchanges (what Bourdieu 1977: 81 calls the "occasionalist illusion," that is, the idea that what is occurring in these exchanges can be explained without reference to unseen social pressures and presences). They maintain either that scholars give too much attention to individual strategies, thus failing to consider how actors' actions are informed by sociohistorical strictures, or that primary focus on the actor and on individual rhetorical strategies is a product of western (bourgeois) emphases that westerners then impose on other cultures. In this work, context includes situational, cultural, and historical components and considers how each informs the hikayat as well as vice versa. This approach is entirely consonant with the aims of anthropological folklore studies (cf. José Limón and Jane Young 1986 and references therein).

Critics of ethnographies, on the other hand, complain that these micro studies fail to address macro issues that are integral to the micro-culture under study. The perceived relationship between the larger world, the macro-system, and the Kelibian community I let emerge naturally from the hikayat. Gradually a picture of its "effect" on the town emerges. My particular focus is to show that Kelibians are not "helpless victims" of this larger system, though it is obvious that they have suffered and still suffer a good deal from their peripheral position (in the Wallersteinian sense).

12. For scholars whose works share an appreciation of the relationships among expressive culture, history, and social action, see E. E. Evans-Pritchard (1949), Jean Duvignaud (1970), Elizabeth Fernea (1965, 1970, 1975), Renato Rosaldo (1980), Clifford Geertz (1968, 1972), Richard Bauman (1971b, 1983b), Henry Glassie (1982), Dennis Tedlock (1983), James Boon (1977), and Pierre Bourdieu (1977). All of these scholars look at cultural process through the medium of one or more forms of traditional expressive culture—verbal art, material culture, religious rituals, secular

games, legendary folk figures—studied *in situ* and also take a special interest in the sociopolitical dimensions of fieldwork and in dialogical anthropology. Although their works are in many respects quite different from my own, the studies of Bauman (1971b and 1983b), Duvignaud (1970), Evans-Pritchard (1949), Geertz (1968), Glassie (1982) and Rosaldo (1980) also are informed by attention to the place of history in ethnography or vice versa, using one or another folk or popular culture form as a signpost.

13. It is in aesthetics, especially in extra-establishment or folk forms, that the possibilities for genuine social or cultural changes can be found. See Williams (1977: 132–135 and 125–126) for similar observations.

14. Speech act theory in its various manifestations is enticing, provocative, inspirational, and thus useful. However, there are barriers to its wholesale application to my data. I prefer not to let it "serve as an all purpose interpretive key" (Fish 1980: 244), at least for the interpretation of these verbal art forms. The kind of distinction that Austin makes between ordinary and performed speech—for example, that performed speech is parasitic upon speech's normal use—is not useful for me as a folklorist. Stanley Fish, among many others, suggests "that literary language may be the norm, and message-bearing language a device we carve out to perform the special, but certainly not normative, task of imparting information" (Fish 1980: 109). Also, the etic nature of the theory is difficult for a student of the cross-cultural. As an anthropologist, I must agree with Fish that "all aesthetics . . . are local and conventional rather than universal, reflecting a collective decision as to what will count as literature, a decision that will be in force only so long as a community of readers or believers (it is very much an act of faith) continues to abide by it" (Fish 1980: 109)—or, at least, we have to start from there as a working hypothesis.

None of my reservations about speech act theory prevents me from calling on the powerful insights into the workings of literary texts of such structuralists-formalists as Roland Barthes and Roman Jakobson, for examples, when I need them. For, "despite the uncertain status of speech acts in literature, the inclusion of this dimension of language . . . increases attention to interpersonal and discursive aspects of literature" (Fowler 1981: 18).

15. But see Belhalfaoui (1973) and references therein.

16. For further discussion on the relationship between classical and colloquial Arabic, see Geertz (1983/1976: 109–117), Sowayan (1985: 163–168), and Connelly (1986: 9–22). For a discussion of the effect of literacy, restricted literacy, or illiteracy on the oral literature of a folk, see Goody (1977: 124–128, 151–162), Connelly (1986: 266–269), Street (1984: throughout, including a critique of Goody), and Sowayan (1985: 168–182). See Zwettler (1976: 207–208) for discussion of the relationship between classical Arabic and the postulated early Arabic super-tribal poetic koine. Also see "Colloquial Arabic Poetry and the Egyptian Press," presented by Marilyn Booth to the American Research Center in Egypt, July 1987. To quote Margaret Mills (personal communication) "What literary *is* for various segments of the Muslim population [is] a particularly rich and challenging area in which to address the basic problems of literary theory and scholarship."

17. See Mullen (1988: 197–198, 115–116) for a summary of western folklorists' attempts to classify local character anecdotes.

18. تَيِّس —the Tunisian term for the legal procedure for reconciliation and re-marriage of a couple under classical Islamic law. Where a man has irrevocably divorced his wife, they can remarry only if she has in the meantime married another husband, that marriage has been consummated, and then the second husband has pronounced divorce (see Fyzee 1964: 149). Possibly I should not call this practice "exotic" since it in theory applies all over the Muslim world, but it is a very good way to ensure that men do not divorce their wives casually. It is clear from the story Si Mohamed told that a man who gets himself in the situation of having to go through Tayyes feels very foolish indeed. In this particular story the woman involved found the interim husband much more pleasing and the supposed stand-in refused to divorce her.

19. Patrick Mullen (personal communication) points out that these are what Erving Goffman labels "in-group" deviants (dervishes, clowns, or "characters") and "the eminent" (walis—also "morally mis-aligned"—and perhaps, heroes): "their special situation demonstrates they are anything but deviants—in the common understanding of that term" (Goffman 1963: 141). Goffman points out that the in-group deviant, and, I would say, the eminent character as well, is "often the focus of attention that welds others into a participating circle around him, even while it strips him of some of the status of a participant" (Goffman 1963: 141–142).

20. Failure to recognize these life-cycle differences is why one finds in folkways studies that "generation after generation contains the last basket weaver and the last ballad singer" (Glassie, 1982: 63). "As never before young men are wrenched out of the community, and drawn to jobs and films, but some still come to ceilis [Tunisian Arabic sahrah(s)]. They sit quietly after work, unable to tell tales, but they are listening, and some day they will" (Glassie 1982: 63).

21. See for example, Ong (1987), Comaroff (1985), and Taussig (1987) for uses of folk or vernacular religion (that is, personal, communal, or subgroup responses to establishment religion) as a source of communal as well as personal resistance to contemporary cultural domination. See as well Ahmet Karamustafa's important work in progress on the antinomian dervish (Washington University, work-in-progress).

22. Comaroff (1985: 262) points out that over-emphasizing "the division between the symbolic and instrumental, and between thought and action, can serve to blind us to the interdependence between domains which our ideology sets too definitively apart." (Again see Williams 1977: 132 and see also Abu-Lughod 1986.)

23. For example, in one of the better world history texts of 1986, the authors write of change-oriented cultures (meaning European and American) and tradition-oriented ones (meaning "the rest of the globe"). To illustrate the dichotomy, they juxtapose Berlin of 1914 with an Egyptian village of the same time. The authors state that "in important respects [the village] resembles villages all over the colonial world of the early twentieth century" (Findley and Rothney 1986: 42). Change is characterized as coming from the outside, meaning Europe. The village is described

as being much like those of ancient times since the sort of brick used to build houses is mentioned in the Bible, and since Roman-style lamps were used for light and clay or copper braziers used for heat! The extended kin group is described as all-important: "the individual counted for much less" (Findley and Rothney 1986: 47). Social roles "were highly standardized and little differentiated except in terms of sex and age" (Findley and Rothney 1986: 47). "Village society de-emphasized not only the individual but also larger social groupings" (Findley and Rothney 1986: 49). The section goes on to say that bright boys left home never to return and that villages had little sense of extra-village politics and were apathetic, because they were powerless. Finally, villages are characterized as full of spirits and nondifferentiated even to the point of fusing human, natural, and spiritual realms. Thus, for example, people drank muddy water because muddy water was what was best for irrigation and so must be best for them. Villages are also described as evasive, which, for good reason, they probably often were—hence their characterization by outsiders, as unable to carry on a meaningful exchange with them, as little differentiated, unchanging, isolated, and so on. In fact, as will become evident from the narratives contained herein, in at least in one colonial village (as Kelibia then was) even farm workers were very much differentiated, awareness of the global situation did exist, there were differences of opinion about spirits, and so on.

Chapter 1

Kelibia in Space and Time

A society is always placed in space and in time, therefore it is subject to what happens in other societies.

(Claude Lévi-Strauss)

A man came from the north
　You do not know who
On his feet yellow slippers
On his back a cloak of black.

(Kelibian riddle)

In speech is History made.

(Marshall Sahlins)

His eyes are like gold coins
And he is altogether wonderful
Many people are obsessed with him
　And he rides on the wind.

(Kelibian riddle)

In 1978, a man who had acquired a prime lot in Kelibia right in the shadow of the ancient fort, next to a well called the Bee Well, not far from the sea, was anxious to start building his home. Workers had scarcely begun digging the foundation, however, when they ran into a problem. Instead of mere rocks and sand, their shovels turned up ancient shards and mosaics. A Roman homeowner some two millennia earlier had preempted the homebuilder, who was forced in the name of preserving antiquity to build elsewhere.

The floor plan of the Roman villa the workers uncovered was typically Mediterranean—a large courtyard surrounded by what must have once been gracious rooms tiled with mosaic scenes of an ancient way of life. Before the mosaics were moved to the Bardo Museum in a suburb of

Tunis, Kelibians would come by to ask the guard for permission to brush away the protective sand. So did I. The floor of one room contained mosaics of the sea life still found offshore. Another floor depicted various flowers of the region. The largest room of the ancient home had three scenes: a horseman and his dogs chasing a rabbit, a man with a straw trap catching little birds to feed his hawk, and, last, the sportsman himself riding off with his bird ("from the north" with its "eyes like gold coins") to go hawking. Kelibians were amused and delighted to think that they still participate in a sport that was being practiced in their community nearly two thousand years ago.

How does history enter into a theory of change? How does it aid in the study of community process? Local history provides certain kinds of movements, diachronic movement-over-time in all its multiple dimensions ("long-term," "social," "short-term," to borrow from Fernand Braudel; or biological, geographical, physical; or narrative, poetic, mythic, among others) that work together with synchronic movements in and around (and in and out of) the town to produce changes particular to Kelibia. This dialectic of different notions of the synchronic and diachronic is roughly what must be addressed in any community study in order to begin to perceive process from the inside out. Of course, synchronic and diachronic are only artificially separated. At any point in town history diachronic movement incorporates synchronic movement and vice versa.

Together, the past and the outside world enter into the present lives of the Kelibians, and must be dealt with. That past is largely fashioned around accounts of the individuals and the waves of outsiders who have left their personal and cultural legacies to Kelibia. Evidence of these immigrants is abundant. A Roman-Turkish-French fort overlooks and dominates the townscape. The town's architecture bears traces of Turkish, Spanish, Italian, and French "cousinship." The music, foodways, and crafts of the inhabitants, their vocabulary, and their cosmopolitan perspective are lively tributes to multiple cultures. At the individual level, Kelibians, the progeny of immigrants most of whom arrived less than two hundred years ago, bear names that bespeak not tribal affiliations but distant places of origin or the occupation pursued by the first member of the family to arrive. So Kelibian appellations also evoke faraway lands or long-ago ancestors—distances of space or time. Furthermore, some older Kelibians in giving the geographical account of Kelibia will tell you that originally the town was a displaced piece of land that came from "as far away as Sicily." When the Mediterranean was formed by something "like an explosion," the piece of land turned completely upside down before settling in its present position.[1] That is why, they say, the town is called Kelibia. The Arabic root for the word Kelibia (actually Qalibiya) would be: QLB (the three consonants), which, as a verb, means "to turn over." From this perspective, not only have all the people been immigrants, but so is the very piece of land on which they live.

This chapter addresses the town's long-term historical movement and how that movement is understood and made use of by the community to form the interpretations of the more recent and personal past found in hikayah-telling events. Of course, received traditions and experiences can be used in the study of the communal relationships of any people. That Kelibia has so much commonly known history as a community, however, is both a resource and a burden. But in either case it provides a sense of (a small) place quite different from, and results in a community with a world-view quite different from, that found among nomadic or big city groups or among those whose community past is less intrusive, is centered on kin rather than place ties, or is simply unknown.

Kelibians today learn their history much as I learned it: from accounts by older members of the community, from books, from articles in Tunisian historical journals, from a radio series on Tunisian towns. This jumble of data is the vital resource from which Kelibian hikayat are fashioned. As Barbara Herrnstein Smith wrote, "our knowledge of *past* events is . . . most likely to be in the form of general and imprecise recollections, scattered and possibly inconsistent pieces of verbal information, and various visual, auditory, and kinesthetic images—some of which . . . will be more or less in or out of focus and all of which will be organized, integrated, and ap-prehended as a specific 'set' of events only in and through the very act by which we narrate them as such" (Smith 1980: 229). Such is the case for the Kelibians. From a jumble of facts the Kelibians weave personal accounts and communal narratives of the past.

But there is an intermediate step between jumble and narrative. Slightly distilled, the historical information in this chapter becomes the shared communal knowledge ("mentalité," to use Braudel's term) drawn upon in the stories that follow. It is fashioned into the touchstones that inform not only local history narratives but the world-view of Kelibians and Mediter-ranean people like them. I do not intend to treat either these historical accounts or the hikayat as hunks of rock out of which to mine nuggets of truth; I am not using statements people make about the past to reconstruct history. At times I have come across interesting contradictions between sources that I discuss and attempt to account for (see story 18). In general, however, I am concerned here with what members of a Mediterranean town, and Kelibians in particular, find interesting or useful about the past and, implicitly, how that contrasts with what western historians (or Ibn Khaldun[2] for that matter) attend to or neglect. For

to *historicize* any structure . . . is to mythologize it. . . . History . . . is never only history *of*; it is also history *for*. And it is not only history *for* in the sense of being written [spoken] with some ideological aim in view, but also history *for* in the sense of being written [spoken] for a specific social group or public. (White 1978: 103–104).

With White's admonishment in mind, I am relying for my data and analysis, "mainly on my informants' renderings, for what they lack in historical accuracy they more than make up for in cultural penetration" (Geertz 1968: 32). What they have told me in and outside the storytelling sessions has shaped what I have chosen to highlight about almost three thousand years of Kelibian history, the "story" of its history.

Still, the following is not a history that meets either folk or establishment canonical requirements. It is a grab bag of assorted historical bits and pieces from which I have pieced together some essential ingredients of the present Kelibian world view. First, Kelibia is a very old place that has seen the arrival and departure of many different (especially Mediterranean) culture groups. Second, the advent of so many groups has come about not simply because the town has permeable boundaries but because it possesses a centuries-old bounty and desirability—as a source of diverse and abundant food, as a military defensive position, as a fishing and trading port, as a place of beauty. We will see that ease of access and egress, beauty, and bounty have again and again over time been both the town's strength (in terms of cultural richness) and its weakness (in terms of its vulnerability to domination by outside forces). Third, to survive in such a situation has depended on knowing well one's physical surroundings and one's fellow community members and on paying close attention to the world-view of the "other," the intruder or outsider. These are the bases for the self-consciousness of Kelibia vis-à-vis its relationship to the outside world and to some extent explain its communal stance toward that world. History as process and product is present for practical as well as ideological reasons. In fact, they are the same.

From raw "historical" data historians everywhere derive such generalizations (always open to renegotiation) about the past from which to negotiate or assert the "givens" of the present and the future. Kelibians are no exception despite the fact that their medium is oral and their presentations in hikayat are more consciously artistic and sketched on a smaller canvas than that of establishment historians. In each hikayah, Kelibians personalize and particularize their rich historical resources and thus artistically construct purposive meanings and morals from the past, by which to help conduct the present and the future. Kelibians, I submit, understand these stories and the events from which they are fashioned "in the context of the longer trajectories of change" (Rosaldo 1980: 23). They, and I, use these resources in concert with the local history narratives to illuminate "as fully as possible the complex orchestration among events, institutions, and ideas as they unfold through time" (Rosaldo 1980: 23). None of us knows exactly the same historical details. Dates are misty. The veracity of some data may be disputed; but the generalities mentioned above emerge again and again.[3] The Kelibian "trends" that emerge, as one looks back over two thousand years of social history as it has been formed in part by its geographical and climatic structural continuities (*longue durée*), inform the "short-term" measures of the past that we find in individual hikayat and their contexts. Kelibian hikayah tellers, it became clear to me, draw upon their mutual, slower-to-change understanding of their wealth of past to measure and evaluate recent past events in hikayat-telling sessions. The events and qualities of the long-term past highlighted in this chapter turn out to be, quite naturally, those commandeered by Kelibians to serve as paradigms to be drawn upon to comment on the present and fashion the future.[4]

A Kelibian's oral history of the town often starts with the advent of his or her own ancestors to a particular district, even a certain house, in the town. From that point the history flows in fragments backward (immigration sagas), forward (recent history), and outward toward other town families, their histories, and beyond. I will begin my own account almost three millennia ago. It is a bare-bones narrative of Kelibia—a past reconstructed like a pot from shards using the bits and pieces of data I have acquired over the past twenty years.

*   *   *

Old Mother Tambu, my children
Asked God to give her flowers
Old Mother Tambu, my little ones
Washed her *jebba* [gown] in the river
Old Mother Tambu asked God to sustain her
    by bringing the rain.

Oh God, My Protector
If it is your will
Make the rain fall and
Give us some beans in the dewy morning
And, God, give us some peppers in the hot morning
And in the morning, corn for a full stomach.

(song for rain)

Europe and Africa draw very near at Kelibia. There are fewer than eighty miles between Kelibia and Sicily, and on a clear day one can catch a glimpse of the Italian island of Pantellaria from the fort overlooking the harbor. Although Phoenicians had occupied nearby Carthage (not more than a two day walk to the southwest) since the ninth century B.C.E. and most of present-day Tunisia since the sixth century B.C.E., the first recorded settlers of Kelibia itself were European immigrants from the Greek colony of Syracuse in Sicily.[5] Agathocles, the tyrant of Syracuse, had taken control of the town around 307 B.C.E., when the Phoenicians briefly lost most of that region of their Carthaginian empire to him and his allies. He had some sort of protective function in mind for his acquisition for he called it Aspis, or "shield." From the high ground in Aspis great expanses of both land and sea could be surveyed.

Agathocles's hopes for the city were never realized, however, for the area was soon reconquered by the Phoenicians. The little town of Kerkouane, which is only a half-day walk north of Aspis, was probably also reconquered at the time. Kerkouane, like Aspis, was an early part of a very ancient urban network with an impressive population in Mediterranean Tunisia.[6] Carthage, the capital, had, as Augustin Bernard (1924) points out, a population of 700,000 in its most populous days as a Phoenician city. In Kelibia Roman ruins and Phoenician ruins ("homey" ruins in this case that reveal little streets with their ingenious drainage system, intact bathtubs, and the outlines of various small houses with their room divisions and simple mosaic floors) provide the continuities to balance the historical discontinuities. Like the Roman ruins in Kelibia with their mosaic representations of flowers still found, fish still fished, and hawkers still hunting, nearby Phoenician ruins inspire among Kelibians a friendly feeling toward their ancient neighbors in their clever little houses and a pride at the fascination of outsiders with such Tunisian riches. Some would tell me of the crude little mosaic of the Phoenician goddess Tanit worked into the floor of one excavated house, and of how Tanit was the goddess of rain (among other things), and that the stick doll named Tambu, or Tangu, which children of Kelibia until recently constructed, dressed, and marched around town singing to make the rain come, is thought by some to be Tanit's descendant.[7] Here we witness the interweaving of items of material culture and folk literature, which together evoke and unite past and present in order to situate the Kelibian community meaningfully and affectively in its own space and time. Hawking stories like that of Uncle Hmida (see story 7), hunting riddles, memorializing poems written to hawks, the hawks themselves with their various paraphernalia, hunters, storytellers, hunting sites, and hunting mosaics are evoked by creative townspeople to tie past and present Kelibia and extra-Kelibia, insiders and outsiders, together—or to nudge or tear them apart.

In 256 B.C.E., the middle of the First Punic War, Kelibia, or Aspis as it was then known, had to be rebuilt after being ravaged by the Roman general Regulus on his march to Carthage. In 236 B.C.E. it was again pillaged by the Romans. It remained loyal to Carthage, however, and, as a result, it, like Carthage, was razed at the end of the Third Punic War in 146 B.C.E. Carthage later revived under the Romans to grow to a population of 100,000. The Romans, like the Greeks and Phoenicians, also recognized the strategic importance of Kelibia's location, and in 39 B.C.E. rebuilt near the old town, calling it "Clypea" (Kelibia, or Qalibiya, see page 31) which also means "shield."

It appears that then, as now, there was an established dichotomy between the people of the town and those of the countryside, the country people then being the fair-haired, Hamitic-speaking Berber tribes (some of whom gradually were absorbed into the towns and cities). Nevertheless, then, as now, certain connections were maintained with people of the countryside through kinship ties, religious ties (some of the earliest Christian converts were Berbers of the countryside), and trade, for instance. And as it is today, the town was surrounded by fertile countryside, and many of the townspeople farmed wheat and cultivated olive groves.

The area gradually and after a good deal of persecution became Christian under the Romans. The question of what sort of Christianty was to be practiced was never resolved. Donatists and Catholics were to compete, sometimes violently, off and on until the advent of the Arabs. When the Vandals, who were Arian Christians and who then competed with both Catholics and Donatists, gained control of Clypea and much of North Africa in the fifth century, the pastor of Clypea was exiled to Corsica. Despite the reputation of the Vandals as vandals, however, "commercial activities flourished in the towns, the crafts known in the Roman period continued, and agriculture provided the country with its needs of food" throughout their rule.[8] Long distance trade also continued.

It is thought that the fortress that dominates the Kelibian landscape today was first built by the Byzantines, one sign of the "insecurity and unsettlement of their post-Vandal period."[9] The Byzantines captured nearby Carthage in C.E. 534 and succeeded the Vandals as the dominant force in the area, but their internal struggles among various religious and ethnic groups and their external wars with the Persians and, later, the Arabs to the East made it effectively a less prosperous time than that of the Vandals.

The Arab invasion swept out of the east in the seventh and eighth centuries. Carthage fell to the Arabs for the second and last time in C.E. 705, and the new city, Tunis, was founded nearby. Today, Carthage is reduced to a suburb of Tunis. Many of the Christians from Clypea fled to the island of Pantellaria and others, perhaps, to Christian centers in the Morocco area, but what the Arabs called "Qalibiya" was at first a mixed Muslim and Christian town. Shortly after this conquest made in the last half century of the Umayyad dynasty ruling from Damascus, an Umayyad caliph sent ten religious scholars to the Maghrib to instruct Berbers. Doubtless this made for more committed converts in the Kelibia areas as in the other city centers. On the other hand, communities in the Tunisia region, including new Arab members, naturally avoided being governed by these far-off foreigners, and by the end of the first half century of 'Abbasid rule from Baghdad in C.E. 800, the Tunis region had managed to become fairly autonomous. Then as now Kelibia would have enjoyed the benefits of its membership in a cosmopolitan religious and commercial network with its inevitable links to Tunis and the great religious center of Kairouan and thence to Africa, Muslim Spain, and the East. But Jamil Abun-Nasr also reports that the Arab armies based in Tunis "were extortionist to the population and generally hostile to their rulers."[10] So the specter of outsider unfairness evident in a narrative like that of the oppressive Ottoman tax collector (see Appendix, story I) or the unfeeling cadi from Nabeul (story 6) were already old "stories." Some of the pressure was relieved when these hard-to-control troops were sent off by the Amir (ruler) to conquer Sicily. By the early tenth century all of the island was in their hands—thus determining that for more than two hundred years Kelibia would cease to mark the very northern periphery of Islamdom.[11]

* * *

The green paradise to which the [Hilali] tribe migrates is Tunis al-Khadra [Tunisia, the Verdant].

(Bridget Connelly)

The Cap Bon area of Tunisia was too far to the north to be hit by the second major Arab invasion into North Africa, when Arab tribes rode out of Upper Egypt in the mid-eleventh century. This fact is sometimes used by Kelibians and others to account for the persistence of Berber physical characteristics (fair hair and blue eyes) of a number of people in an area where Berber is no longer spoken. (At other times, townspeople explain these phenomena by saying they are the result of an intermarriage with European brigands or soldiers who could not bear to leave.) Although the advent into North Africa and the pillaging of Arab tribes like the Bani Hilal, itself the stuff of perhaps the most extensive and pervasive body of oral legendry in the Arab world, did evoke a crisis, especially in southern Tunisia and in the holy city of Kairouan, both the economy and the urban life of the region recovered. According to such scholars as John Ponet, Jean Pierre Bonnefant, Eric Wolf, Ezzidine Moudoud, and Fernand Braudel, until the late eighteenth century "urban development based on strong and complementary relationships between agriculture-industry-trade was . . . one of the most important characteristics of the spatial-economic organization [in the region of Tunisia]. This integrated spatial-economic organization was favored by a complex system of long-distance trade connecting Tunisia with the Middle East, Sub-Saharan Africa and the rest of North Africa."[12] Although Kelibia seems at this time to have been a less important factor in the external circulation system than during the Roman period, it still would have profited intellectually and economically from its proximity both to Sicily and to Tunis.

The Mediterranean area was long a scene of struggle between European Christians and North African and Middle Eastern Muslims, especially from the end of the fifteenth to the end of the sixteenth centuries. Although the town probably profited from the cultural contributions of Spanish Arabs forced from Spain in the fourteenth and sixteenth centuries, some of whom settled on the Cap Bon, it also suffered large scale destruction from the Christian-Muslim confrontation. Each side tried to gain footholds on the other's shores, and Kelibia's location on the sea and near Europe made it vulnerable in this tug of war. In the sixteenth century, when the Turks and Spaniards were fighting to dominate the area, Kelibia was attacked by the Spanish three times. Writing of his 1724 voyage along the North African coast, Jean André Peyssonnel notes that Kelibia appeared to have been a well-built and large city before its walls were breached, but that it was, by the time of his arrival, a very little village. By that time, the area had been under Ottoman rule for 150 years (since 1574). It was the Ottomans who rebuilt the old Byzantine fort.

Several Kelibian women and men have pointed out to me the remains of a tunnel built from the fort down to the sea so that *bint el-bey*, the daughter of the bey (ruler), could descend in privacy to bathe. There are the romantic or striking images of history that remain in one's mind—the dashing corsair, the princess—what become in the hikayat, albeit with a different cast of characters, history personalized.

*   *   *

A dolphin will appear from Monastir and before him nations will be helpless.

(Sidi Hmid Bou Bakkir's riddle)

When the Turks and Spaniards were fighting over Kelibia, Islam had been ensconced for seven hundred years. According to Abun-Nasr (1975/ 1971: 119) the subsystems of mystical religious brotherhoods and saints' shrines probably spread widely after the mid-thirteenth century, when Muslim political unity in this area broke down. Perhaps it was at that time that Muslims in and around Kelibia began to erect their share of these shrines that are so significant to the life of the town today and figure so prominently in the hikayat. Gradually, the town and countryside became dotted with the little domed, whitewashed shrines (*zawiyyas*) housing the graves of individuals who, by the time of their deaths, were perceived by their contemporaries to be walis, or "friends of God." These men or women were felt to possess an abundance of *barakah*, or God's grace, which in life and after allowed them to bestow blessings on those around them. Some were honored as well because they possessed more (religious) education than most of the country people, and others simply because they possessed a folk wisdom that was manifested in particularly keen observations on human dilemmas, in poetic predictions about the future, such as that above, or in a special ability to "read" or manage nature. These talents ensured local resources to answer vexing questions such as when rain would come or provided help in worrisome cases where, for example, the mother of a newborn could not nurse. Much later, just before independence, Sidi Bou Bakkir's mysterious predictions of a coming "dolphin" (p. 38) took on new meaning. Kelibians came to realize that the advent from the seaside town of Monastir of the liberator "dolphin," Habib Bourguiba, had been foreseen for decades, even, as Si Hamdan told me, "before Bourguiba's, 'the dolphin's' grandfather had been born." Si Hamdan remembers that the ubiquitous town watercarrier, another kind of mediator, would whisper the old dolphin riddle to men, women, and children on the doorsteps of their homes as encouragement that the end of French occupation was in sight.

Kelibians do not call these walis "Sufis." That term usually is reserved for more pan-Islamic, institutionalized holy figures around whom widespread congregations or brotherhoods have formed. *Sufism* denotes a special learned tradition with its *tariqah* ("path" to a mystical closeness with God), the legitimacy of which was acknowledged by such early orthoprax[13] Islamic scholars as al-Ghazali (d. C.E. 1111), who wrote in the eleventh and twelfth centuries. Three of these Sufi brotherhoods with their zawiyyas also existed in Kelibia, but according to Joseph Weyland, have not been active since the early twentieth century. They were Sidi 'Abdelqadir al Djilani from near Baghdad (d. A.H. 561), Sidi Mohamed bin 'Aissa from Meknes, Morocco, whose first lodge was founded in the sixteenth century (d. A.H. 933), and Sidi 'Abd as Salam al Asmar (Weyland's orthography). The local walis' descendants did not form brotherhoods of their own revolving around their ancestors, although conceivably they could have done so. Rather, they often affiliated themselves with one of the three pan-Islamic mystics. Sidi Maouia's representatives, for example, tended to affiliate with the brotherhood of Sidi 'Abdelqadir. Still, the Kelibian walis resemble Sufis in that both are thought to possess superior religious, moral, and ethical understanding and to be irreproachable (or less reproachable than most) in matters of personal piety. It is believed that walis, like Sufis, seek a personal, mystical path to closeness with God as a supplement to orthoprax Islam with its emphasis on the performance of the five religious pillars—the profession of faith, prayer, fasting, almsgiving, and pilgrimage to Mecca. In Kelibia, however, association with these walis is personal or familial rather than institutional or associational.[14] Most Kelibians do not see a contradiction in practicing "scripturalist" or "universalist" Islam and simultaneously in expressing their allegiances to and dependence on various communal and regional walis or *waliyyas*. (For a similar observation vis-à-vis a Moroccan community, see Eickelman 1976: 12.)

According to accounts by Si Hamdan and Si Mohamed, even non-Muslims recognized the power of walis. When the Ottomans finally became their rulers in the seventeenth century, Kelibians say that the Spanish, unwilling to abandon their wealth but unable to take it with them, built shrines to various Muslim "saints" and buried their gold under them, knowing it would rest undisturbed until they could find someone to fetch it. (It is said that the Germans and Italians did the same thing when they were ejected in World War II.) Rumors of wealth buried all around Kelibia abound. One story of the Bee Well (p. 29), I recall, was that the well was supposed at one time to be filled with diamonds. But when seekers tried to remove them, they turned to bees and flew away. Still another story by Si Mohamed says that a conjurer on pilgrimage in Arabia passed on to a fellow pilgrim traveling through Kelibia a charged piece of paper to throw in the Bee Well. In this version, bees emerged that then changed to *louis* or *lweez* in Kelibian Arabic (gold coins). Such fungible wealth as bees, diamonds, and gold coins still hidden around the town is one more indicator of the accumulated natural and manufactured adornments of Kelibia, where sunlight refracts diamonds and gold off the sea, the sand, the shining fruits of the orchards, and the whitewashed houses.

*   *   *

And Haneena is crying, her son's [a soldier] in Istanbul.

(excerpt from Kelibian lullaby)

The Ottomans who came to Kelibia in the latter half of the sixteenth century were soldiers and government officials charged with administering that outpost. They rebuilt the fort and took up residence there rather than in Kelibia proper, two and a half kilometers inland. The town in those days had only about ten family groups, all originating in Tripolitania or Algeria. By the advent of the Hussayni dynasty in 1705, however, when Tunis regained quasi-autonomy under a hereditary bey of Cretan origin, Husain bin 'Ali, Ottoman immigrants to Kelibia were intermarrying with other Kelibians, thinking of themselves as members of the town, and speaking Arabic.

Of the Turkish influence in Kelibia, André Louis writes: "Quant à l'épisode de l'occupation turque, il a fortement marqué la physionomie humaine de la petite ville de Kélibia, soit dans son architecture, soit dans ses traditions artisanales ou vestimentaires" (Louis 1964a: 6).[15]

To the Spanish, on the other hand, Louis attributes influences on "la culture condimentaire" and, perhaps, the refinement of artisanal products.

An important aspect of the institution of walis, which gained significance as the Ottoman Empire expanded into North Africa, was the practice of declaring a particular piece of land the property of a certain wali. Under Islamic law, land held in trust for the family of a particular holy man or woman or for a landowner's descendants (and, in theory, eventually designated for the religious community if the family died out) could not be divided or sold. Landowners actually become trustees, though continuing to enjoy the economic benefits of ownership. In North Africa this land was called *habous* or *waqf* land. As might be expected, this religious land was also free from the threat of confiscation by the state.[16] The landowners (habous trustees) were also frequently exempted from all taxes and from military service.

In the Kelibia area, as in other areas with fertile land, the habous tradition became economically significant because, as the Ottoman beys became strapped for funds, they relied on the *iqta'* system, whereby they compensated their military commanders with land grants—often someone else's land. In Kelibia, therefore, as elsewhere in the Middle East, the number of lands declared habous may have increased in the sixteenth century, as landowners attempted to avoid the iqta', and in the nineteenth century as heavy tax burdens were put on agriculturalists. Further, the land as waqf *ahli* or *dhurri* (family endowments) remained intact for their offspring, who continued to enjoy the revenues of the land either by farming it themselves or by renting it out to other farmers and then collecting a percentage of the crop. Around Kelibia much habous land was controlled until independence by one family, the Safis, as a means of keeping their wealth intact.

Of course, one should not speak of "Turkish" cultural influence in the singular because the Ottoman soldiers who came to Tunisia were recruited or drafted from a vast Mediterranean area, a fact of which Kelibians are well aware. In fact, not all the Ottoman soldiers who settled in Kelibia were of Turkish origin. The influence was eastern Mediterranean. For example, the Kordoghli and Gritli families are said to have originated in Cyprus and Crete, the Arnaout family in Albania, the ben Rejebs in Khurasan in Iran, and the ben 'Abdellatifs in Bulgaria. The metal-working Balajis are thought to have originated in Turkey. Their name means "[iron] door bar," or some say, "executioner's knife," after one of the products of their craft. Later on, the Balajis manufactured shovels and other iron tools in the town. The Zenaidis also were named for a skill, the making of rifle hammers. It appears that these and other Ottoman immigrants from Syria, Iraq, and several Mediterranean islands intermarried with the Arab ben Cheikhs, Bou 'Afifs, Samouds, and Zouaris from Tripolitania and with the Gharbis and Ridans from Algeria. Mediterranean piracy flourished well before the Ottoman colonization, and a legend holds that the Lengliz family derived its name from an English renegade. Names and family origins of the established members of the town are common knowledge and are reviewed frequently by adult members of those families that have long-term ties to the town. (Commitment to a particular school of Islamic law is not foregrounded in the town, perhaps because of the long-time Christian presence. Nevertheless, Ottoman families introduced the Hanafi school of Muslim law, while most Arab families were Maleki, though there was at least one Hanbali and one Ibadi family as well.)

Up until the beginning of the nineteenth century, Tunisia as a whole was doing very well under the Hussayni dynasty. According to Nancy E. Gallagher, the territory in 1800 was a prosperous one. Because of its centrality in the east-west and north-south trade routes and its own ability to supply both raw and manufactured goods, the territory had a brisk trade with southern Europe, the Levant, and sub-Saharan Africa. "Just under half of all ships landing at Marseilles from North Africa in the 1790s came from Tunis, then called the Shanghai of the Mediterranean" (Gallagher 1983: 33).

Other families well-known in the town arrived from inland Tunisia—

fleeing internal disorders (drought, famine, rebellion, and plagues) of the early- and mid-1800s.[17] Some of these families were the Najars, the Tanabanes, and the Khanissis. Surprisingly, no Andalusian or Jewish families settled in Kelibia, perhaps preferring towns closer to Tunis, such as Soliman and Nabeul. There may, at that time, have been some Italian slaves in town such as those, captured by Corsairs, in Tunis.

In Kelibia, as in other towns in the area, the names of old established families are not those of the tribes in the surrounding countryside. Neither are they for the most part names that would be found in neighboring towns. Long-time inhabitants of Kelibia and other towns in the Watan can often identify a person's Cap Bon town or city from his or her family name, and also name the region or country from which the family emigrated.

In the late nineteenth century, many Italians driven by hard times in their own country came voluntarily to Tunisia. One group was settled near Kelibia when a representative of the Italian consulate in Tunis bought a large parcel of land and then had his Pantellarian compatriots buy little lots of five to ten hectares. In the space of twenty years, almost a third of the population of Pantellaria, about three thousand people, came to the Cap Bon hoping to find fertile soil in which to grow peaches and muscatel grapes. Others came to fish. According to Père Louis, when a 1892 French law forbade the importation of wine stalks, the resourceful Pantellarians continued to bring in their muscatel vines by weaving them into the baskets in which they brought their possessions. Today, "Muscat Sec de Kélibia" is widely considered a superior dessert wine.

The French officially colonized Tunisia in 1881, beating out the Italians, who also wanted it and who actually had more settlers there at the time. In an early French government report on the Kelibia area, ("Zone Septentrionale," 1885, *Dossier des Affaires Indigènes*), Kelibia was described as a clean little town of 480 houses (the same size as its neighbors Korba and Menzel Temime), a town that was well-built and well-maintained. In addition to vegetables, the surrounding region was known for its abundance of fruits, beans, condiments and 16,000 feet of olive trees. Kelibia had four olive presses. Kelibia also shipped grains to the Sahel (the eastern coast of Tunisia) and charcoal to Tunis. Fishing was already important. In one summer, the report mentions, around 150 fishermen came from Malta, Sicily, and Tunisian ports to fish for sardines. Altogether the town had 120 artisans and tradespeople, including 42 wool weavers. An important population of Turkish descent was still to be found, and an important population of renegades as well.

As mentioned earlier, both the French and the Italians saw themselves as descendants of the Romans with the mission (and the right) to reclaim long-lost Roman lands—to "recivilize" them. Until the middle of the twentieth century, Kelibia had a very visible European population with a church, a Christian graveyard, and French doctors, administrators, and soldiers.

Several Europeans had farms in the area, but much of the land throughout the Cap Bon region was habous land—more than 2,000 hectares[18] in the Kelibia region. The 1885 *Dossier* on Kelibia reports that there were 800 hectares for one maraboutic family of the Majdoub in the center of the plain, 650 hectares for the Daoudine near Sidi Daoud in the West, and 620 hectares for "Henchir Arouret," which belonged to the zawiyya of Sidi 'Ali-Azouz. Joseph Weyland thought the primary reason for the slow colonization of the northeast region of the Cap Bon, the Dakhla, was this large expanse of habous land. He devotes a good deal of his essay to the discussion of ways the *colons* could legally gain access to this land. Though the French did take away many tax privileges from the habous families, they did not solve the problem of obtaining land ownership. Many foreigners and Kelibians alike were allowed, at best, only long-term leases of the land. This tug of war between the French and the indigenous Arabs and between the Kelibians and their rich landlords highlights the political and protective roles walis constantly assume. Despite the profligate ways of the holy people's caretakers (often absentee landlords like the Safis who lived in Tunis or Paris) certain obligations to the people had to be maintained in terms of religious tithes (land and animal bounty), sharecropper wages, education of children from the countryside, and so on. And these Muslim institutions were effective in discouraging the takeover of land by the Europeans. In both cases Muslim institutions carve out some breathing room for the underdog, a role the institutions themselves also assume, in a more personal way, in the hikayat.

In the early twentieth century, Weyland named several walis in and around Kelibia, besides Sidi Maouia, in whose name an individual or group could set up a habous foundation: Sidi Ahmed ben Hamouda, Sidi M'hammed Sahib el-Djebel, Sidi Maouia Cherif, Sidi Mohammed Daoud, Sidi M'hammed Zobeir, Sidi 'Abdel Moumen, Sidi Chaban, Sidi Ahmed el Mejdoub, Sidi Daoud Noubi, Sidi Ahmed ben Daoud, and Sidi Ahmed el Megaiz. In addition to those he mentions there were at least two wa-liyyas. One of them was Lella Khadhra (see page 129); the other was Lella Myriam (see page 129), who continues to be responsible solely for aiding new mothers who are unable to nurse their babies. Other walis were Sidi Amor ben Sahayek near Sidi Maouia, Sidi Mathkur to the northwest of the town, Sidi Bou Bakkir to the north, Sidi 'Ali Qsibi, just on the north edge of town, and Sidi Mqaddem, Sidi Kharfash and Sidi Bahri near the beach. Further, as indicated earlier, the town contained three Sufi brotherhoods or lodges dedicated to the teachings of famous Sufis from other parts of the Islamic world.

Thus, besides family endowments, there were more than twenty "friends of God" plus brotherhood lodges through whom it was theoretically pos-sible to secure one's land against confiscation or sale. The land and a share of its profits could be secured by and for the descendants of walis, but it could also be secured by a non-wali family group for a particular wali. These wali and non-wali family groups were also insulated from sale or confiscation of their land.

As mentioned earlier, the Safi family, said to be originally a bedouin group from Tripoli via Gabes, was the powerful landowning group around Kelibia. Other groups mentioned by Weyland as having lived in the Kelibia environs were the related tribes of M'daissa, Oulad-Naceur, Oulad-Diab, Oulad-Zerga, Oulad-Debabba, Oulad-el-Hadj, and Oulad-Dhemaida. He also mentions the Hajri tribe. These tribespeople were not of Kelibia proper, but inhabited the surrounding countryside and possibly had been in the area, at least seasonally, longer than the old families of the town itself. The 1885 *Dossier* mentions the grand bedouin families of ben Brahim, Bou Daffa, and Gouabés. Two-thirds of the land in the region, it continues, was in these bedouin families' hands.

Middle Eastern towns often seem to be made up of inhabitants not re-lated to the tribes of the surrounding countryside. E. E. Evans-Pritchard (1949: 43) makes the point in *The Sanusi of Cyrenaica* that townspeople, like religious leaders, tended to be outside the tribal system. He observes that between tribes and towns there is an economic and political interde-pendence and that townspeople usually dominate by a "monopoly of trade and influence in the administration" (1949: 44).

This dominance seems problematic in the Kelibia area. The Safis, at least, were absentee landlords, locked into a secure position by their ha-bous holdings. Kelibians, on the other hand, were largely in the position of having to rent most of their land and to work it for part of the profits or to work as laborers on Safi or other habous land. The habous system may have kept the French and Italians from acquiring as much land as they would have wished, but it left the Kelibians in a similar position, though with less money, less power, and less access to technical expertise. They were squeezed between the colonialists and the habous of the countryside. They also felt threatened by the nomadic or semi-nomadic tribes, who came to find work at harvest time. These migrants were stereotyped as "gypsies" often are. Kelibians tell stories of tribespeople stealing or attempting to steal half of what they harvested.

If the French had succeeded in breaking up the habous lands, they would have been bought by the French, not by townspeople. Thus, it was to the Kelibians' advantage to maintain the habous system, notwithstanding Zeis's petulant protest that since the habous had simply become a way of avoiding the exactions of the *pachas* (Ottoman rulers) and since "ce motif ayant cessé d'exister," it would be best to "abandonner cette dangereuse pratique"[19] (Weyland 1926: 63).

In Kelibia the Italians were much more intimately associated with the Muslims than were the French. As mentioned earlier, these Italians had come in great numbers from Pantellaria in the nineteenth century, and in the 1920s there were at least forty of these families in Kelibia, almost all owners of small vineyards. For years an Italian named Giovanni Conversaro, an appointee of the Tunisian government, was in charge of the Kelibian port, and when he died his son Francesco, took over. This post was an important one, as the abundant produce of the area was frequently transported by sea rather than on the often poor roads. He and other Italians, such as a sea captain named Centouze and referred to as er-Rais (the captain), managed to acquire land and real estate in conjunction with the older Kelibian families such as the Gharbis, the Najars, and the ben Cheikhs. Weyland remarked gloomily that except for the habous lands and one plateau "presques toutes les régions du Cap Bon voient peu à peu la colonisation italienne se développer"[20] (Weyland 1926: 71). (Much later, after World War II, the French, as might be expected, made it very difficult for the Italians to retain any land, and after independence, the Tunisians did likewise. Today, only one or two older Italians from the old families remain in Kelibia.)

World War I seems to have affected Kelibia only peripherally. There were a few *anciens combattants*, men who had fought for the French and who were paid a veteran's allowance, which they collected at the post office every month. People remember seeing sea battles off the coast. They remember especially the night that the remains of a supply ship washed ashore. They remember that the flour was so fine it slipped between your fingers if you closed your hand, and there were liquor (champagne) and cigarettes with a picture of a camel on each package.

It was around this time, 1914–15, that the first coffee shop appeared. The proprietor, according to Si Mohamed, would arrive and beat on his *darbouka* (drum) to wake up the neighborhood. The first arrival got free coffee because the "proprietor wanted company." Prior to this time, before going to work in the fields, people would eat at home a kind of porridge made of sorghum and a syrup of olive oil into which they would dip dried, halved figs. Other breakfasts depended on powdered hot peppers mixed with wheat in some form, bread or porridge, and olive oil—a precaffeine jolt, good to give strength to an older man with a young wife, laughed one raconteur.

Kelibia again was growing. By the mid-1920s, Augustin Bernard, a French administrator doing housing research in Tunisia and Algeria, reported that the Kelibia region had 156 tents, 105 *gourbis* (huts), and 1,057 houses for a population of almost 10,000—quite an increase from the 480 homes of 1885. The houses, like those in other parts of the Cap Bon, he observed, were mostly of stone, covered with flat roofs. Bernard, who considered any settlement with more than two hundred inhabitants to be urban, paused to point out the similarities among all such Mediterranean towns. He also pointed out that Tunisia was very urban—eighteen out of one hundred citizens living in urban settlements in 1924—while Algeria was comparatively rural—only six out of one hundred citizens being urbanites.

During World War II, Kelibia, as might be expected from its centuries-old use as a militarily strategic location, was in the line of fire. French North African troops were quartered in town, and later conquering German and Italian troops were stationed in the area. Consequently, the town was bombed by the Allies. Several people remember that when the Allies regained control the English-speaking soldiers went from door to door asking for Germans. Since "German" approximates "duck" (جرمان) in Tunisian Arabic, there are amusing accounts of old grandfathers innocently taking these strangers into their gardens to see the ducks. There is also a road outside town called the Americans' Road, since it was evidently built by American troops so they could gain access to the top of the highest hill around. Again, these accounts or signs of the foreign presence seem to be offered by townspeople as indicators of the cosmopolitan Kelibia. During this war many people moved to the countryside (story 21), or took temporary refuge in walis' shrines (story 20), confident that a local wali could not be hit by bombs. Everyone tells stories about the exodus to the countryside or farther to await the cessation of the hostilities. A close friend of Lella Nesria's tells of Nesria's childish delight in the fact that she finally was farther from town than the *makintijjir* (< *makina(t)* "machine" + *jir* "whitewash") a feat that seems to have taken precedence over concerns about bombs in her seven- or eight-year-old mind.

By the conclusion of World War II the French began to realize that Tunisia would become independent, and it did in 1958, with relatively little bloodshed. In Kelibia a kind of guerrilla warfare was practiced against the French soldiers (killing those who strayed too far from the group) with the idea that one man told me, if people in far-off France were losing their sons for a country not even their own, they would decide to leave.

However, Kelibia did have its martyrs. The local boy-scout troop evidently became a revolutionary group, and two of its leaders, a Gharbi and a Khoudja, were executed (probably tortured—the sheikh is whispered to have come home sick and "with blood spattered on his shoes") for plotting to assassinate a French administrator in town. Knowledge of the countryside was considered very important at this time, since it gave people one advantage over the French. Traveling only by foot or donkey, as most of them did, to Tunis, Nabeul, and neighboring towns, they knew every inch of local terrain—where to take shelter, where to get food, where to hide, and so on. "He [a Frenchman] couldn't know her [the town] like [the sons of the town]," one narrator said. "You would find him moving about as if he were blind. Never knowing if he was about to fall in a well, a cactus patch, or upon a wall or . . . ."

Paradoxically, the town that has experienced so many violent incursions also has been a refuge for outsiders. Of the families who settled Kelibia in the 1800s, several, like that of Si Mohamed, came from Algeria after the French invasion in 1830. Other families were fleeing internal disorders occurring during the Turkish domination, and others came from Tripoli, quite possibly to avoid conscription into the Ottoman army. One popular lullaby in Kelibia still speaks of a woman crying because "her son is in Istanbul." Another begins, "Soldier, my son, worker for the bey."

In later history at least one Spaniard came into exile in Kelibia after being on the losing side of the Spanish Civil War. This man opened a hotel on the beach at Kelibia and catered to colonialists until independence. Everyone in town knows of him, and we all remember when Franco, on his death bed, forgave all his opponents and invited them to return to Spain. Eager to see his son, the hotel owner got as far as Paris, they say, and then turned back, afraid of a trick.

Perhaps because Kelibia was a place of refuge for many of its inhabitants or their ancestors, and because as a town it is more vulnerable to outside attacks than are nomadic tribes, for example, accounts of the past do not include stories about factional fights or wars with outsiders except on a one-to-one basis. The town is the conquered, not the conqueror, and this very vulnerability has probably had the effect of quickly forging disparate groups in the town into a cohesive unit. It has also had the effect of compelling the community to assume a generally pacific stance toward the surrounding tribes as well as to be outwardly submissive to powerful groups such as the Ottomans, the French, or the Tunisian central government.[21]

By the time I first came to Kelibia, in 1967, the town had grown to some 2,500 houses and 15,000 people. Besides the influx of government and school officials, a study by Guy Paollilo indicates that 58 percent of the people coming to settle in Kelibia during the mid-sixties were actually Kelibians returning home. The town is also seasonally swollen by the students who come from nearby smaller settlements to attend secondary school. They comprised 40 percent of the lycée student body in the late 1960s according to Paollilo.

For most of the townspeople, the last thirty years—since independence and particularly since the break up of the habous land by the government—have brought an increasing abundance. When land could be sold, it was often the Kelibians, not the former owners or the people in the countryside, who had the sophistication, the experience, the foresight, and the savings to buy land and make it profitable. It was also the townspeople who had the proximity to take over land (and businesses) when the colonialists left their town. From being more or less restrained on one side by the inaccessibility of habous land and on the other side by the colonialists, Kelibians found all obstacles removed at the same time. Most of the Safis did not know how to work their land, were profligate, and were forced by financial need to sell. Hafedh Sethom writes that the Safi family is une population peu active, qui ne travaille pas par elle-même, qui a toujours bien vécu [sic] et qui a continué [sic] à vivre en dessus de ses moyens. Pressés par leurs besoins financiers, les Saafi ont vendu une grande partie de leur cheptil [sic], puis ils se sont mis à vendre la seule chose qui leur reste, leur terre. (Sethom 1976: 242)[22]

"The villagers of Kelibia," he adds, "those who possess capital, have already bought appreciable lands."[23] He refers to this phenomenon as *prolétarisation* of the land and sees it as a disturbing development. Nevertheless, it is the Kelibians, now no longer hampered by habous restrictions on the one hand and colonial superstructure on the other, who are coaxing the land to produce abundantly. Needless to say, this increased prosperity has favorably affected almost everyone in the town—seamstresses, carpenters, barbers, owners of Turkish baths, school teachers, merchants, bankers, jewelers, stone masons, architects, and fishermen.

Since the 1950s and Tunisian independence and the tremendous improvement in the circumstances of most Kelibians, the correspondence between Kelibia and the outside world has escalated rapidly. There are several reasons for this. First, educational possibilities for the Kelibian youth have increased. These young people, prepared by an older generation with a respect for learning, are taking advantage of these post-colonial opportunities in great numbers. In 1978 an official of the Tunisian Embassy in Washington, D.C., a man from the island of Jerba, told me that it was his impression that a greater percentage of students from the Cap Bon area than from any other area of the country, including Tunis, graduate from college. Needless to say, many of the work opportunities for these young men and women are not in Kelibia. The young people of the town are scattered from Tunis to Paris to London to various cities in Spain and to the United States, either continuing their education or working. Even those who do not pursue higher education often work abroad in Libya or France to earn enough to buy and import equipment to start carpentry shops or automobile repair businesses, for example. In 1970 alone statistics show fifty emigrants from Kelibia were working abroad under a government program to combat unemployment, twenty-five in France, fourteen in West Germany, and eleven in Libya (Paollilo 1972).

On the other hand, more outsiders have come to Kelibia. In 1965 the town had 2,427 houses and 14,000 inhabitants (about one-third working in agriculture), in 1972 around 18,000, and in 1984, 24,595. Since then the number has risen to at least 30,000 though exact figures are not available. The high school, which was built in the early 1970s, brought in the families of instructors and administrators. Police and other government administrators are by policy assigned to towns other than their own; so they swell the population. Further, many people are moving in from the countryside and the smaller villages.

Also, in the late 1960s the Swedes, now gone, built a maternity hospital, fishing port, and school for the town and brought in students for the fishing school and trainees and medical staff for the hospital. Kelibia has also built two tourist hotels on the beach.

Today, many people in town own cars, so four or five main streets of the town are paved—including the large ones running from south to north, continuing up to the tip of the Cape, and from west to east down to the seashore. A number of entrepreneurs have started summer taxi services to take people to the beach two and a half kilometers away from the town center. The roads are still shared, especially on souk, or market, day, with sheep, goats, donkeys, carts, and cows, as well as bicycles, motorbikes, and pedestrians. (Although there are more women on the streets, the younger ones unveiled, than when I first traveled to Kelibia in 1967, to truly arrive in town for a woman still means going through the door of the high-walled courtyard into the embraces and greetings of waiting women friends.)

The new, large, covered market in the center of town, which houses several small poultry, fish, meat, and produce shops, teems with activity all week. On Monday, souk day, the entire front and side of the market are surrounded by colorful displays of vegetables and fruits brought in from the countryside.

Although marriages between Tunisians of different towns are increasing, marriage outside the bounds of religion and/or nationality seems to take place at about the same rate as in the past. Muslim women are not supposed to marry non-Muslims, but some men who wish to marry Muslim women convert to Islam. Some townsmen have always chosen to marry women they met on their travels. For example, in one household, the parents, now in their fifties, each had a non-Muslim grandmother who later converted to Islam. One woman, on the mother's side, was Tunisian-Jewish from Tunis, and the other, on the father's side, was Italian-Catholic, the runaway daughter of a representative at the Italian Consulate in Tunis. Thus, what western scholars have perceived as the preferred marriages between cousins, especially the offspring of brothers, are nicely balanced in Kelibia by marriages between unrelated townsmembers as well as by these more exotic alliances. Two of the great-grandsons of the aforementioned women have married French Catholics, but one doubts that these women will become absorbed into the community to the same degree as those who arrived when money was scarce and travel difficult. Nevertheless, the practice continues and is representative of another and continuing contact that Kelibians have had with extra-community members.

This gradual homogenization of so many and varied cultures in a single place must have a profound effect on the structure and content of all Kelibian aesthetic culture forms—verbal and material. The long history of agricultural and cosmopolitan concerns, of frequent and varied cross-cultural contacts, of dominance by outsiders—absentee landlords to foreign powers—is deeply embedded in the Kelibian sense of self and community. As I write, I happen to glance over at my Kelibian market basket (woven by Si Hamdan, one of the storytellers). Worked into one side is, قليبية the Arabic spelling of the Roman "Clypea." On the other side is woven the outline of the Turko-Byzantine fort—the appreciation of which Kelibians realize they share with outsiders, scholars, foreigners, and tourists. So, in a humble item of material culture, history, artisanship, and language combine in service to a visit to the market.

It seems that the particular past of Kelibians has meant that the people of Kelibia, from housewives to carpenters to basket weavers, do a lot of home philosophizing, especially about the practical implications of cross-cultural contact. The study of human nature and human relationships has historically been a means of survival. One suspects that the same honing of interpersonal skills would be evident in any sedentary, agricultural, Mediterranean community, since such communities as these have always been vulnerable to incursions from north and south, from land and sea. A theme in many hikayat is of a "crisis" brought about when interpersonal proprieties have been neglected for impulsive or immature behavior. Rifts are then repaired either by the protagonist or the narrator, or both. Thus the dilemmas of a permeable town are addressed in hikayat, a genre of verbal artistry that is historical and that is about the people of Kelibia.

Notes

1. See, for example, Si Mohamed, field notebook 1.
2. The great Arab sociologist of the fourteenth century who completed much of his work in Tunis.

3. As a self-appointed mediator between one kind of western establishment or institutional culture, that of the social sciences, and one sort of Kelibian folk culture, that which pertains to the past and to stories about the past, I have drawn upon data from both institutional and folk, Arab world and western sources. As will be shown, for the main purpose of this chapter, which is the detailing of certain aspects of the Kelibian world view significant for hikayah-telling, they do not contradict each other.

4. It will become clear that, unlike Braudel, I do not see the community *mentalité* that emerges partly out of its geographical situation as fixed or confining. Traditions originate in creative actions, as Marshall Hodgson noted (1974: 80). Traditions are inventions. The aspects of the past chosen for the hikayah-telling framework today and storytellers' orientations toward those aspects can be freshly perceived at any inspired moment.

5. Information about the history of Kelibia is drawn from the following sources: H. Boulares and Jean Duvignaud (1978), Mohamed Fantar (1972), André Louis (1964a and 1964b), Guy Paollilo (1972), Hafedh Sethom (1976), Joseph Weyland (1926), the "Zone Septentrionale" dossier (1885), and the oral accounts by Kelibians.

6. See Moudoud (1989) and references therein for discussion of the very early and continuous urban character of much of the region that is now Tunisia.

7. See Abu-Zahra (1988) and references therein for description and discussion of this ritual in the Tunisian Sahel. See Webber (1969: 47) for a version of the Ummik (your mother) Tambu song different from the one Abu-Zahra quotes.

8. Abun-Nasr (1975: 52).

9. Abun-Nasr (1975: 65).

10. Abun-Nasr (1975: 77).

11. The last Muslims were driven from Sicily at the end of the eleventh century, but in the twelfth century the kings of Sicily still read and wrote Arabic.

12. See Moudoud (1989: 104 and 128) and references therein.

13. Term coined by the historian of Islam John Alden Williams to reflect the Muslim focus on proper practices as determinants of piety.

14. The relationship between wali and sufi, variations in the natures and behaviors of walis, and the functions and possibilities of habous lands (see page 41) need to be studied much more thoroughly in terms of local belief systems. What I have been told or have observed concerning the roles of walis, dervishes, sheikhs, or habous practices in Kelibia often does not correspond exactly to practices in other regions of North Africa (let alone elsewhere in the Arab or Islamic world). Neither does it fit precisely with what, for example, the *Encyclopedia of Islam* has to say, or with the precepts of orthoprax Islam. This text is not meant to be a study of these phenomena, but, inadvertently, the hikayat point up the richness and diversity of folk and establishment religious traditions and reveal how much there is yet to be understood about them in practice, as time-, space-, and, to some extent, class-specific phenomena.

15. "As for the episode of the Turkish occupation, it strongly affected the human

physiognomy of the tiny city of Kelibia, in its architecture as well as its craft and clothing tradition."

16. See Hodgson (1974: 2: 51) for a discussion of the relationship between habous (waqf) land and the iqta' system.

17. A large tax on olive trees in 1866 hurt the Cap Bon region a great deal, but in comparison to other parts of the country it weathered the disasters of the nineteenth century well.

18. One hectare = 2.47 acres.

19. "This motif, having ceased to exist, . . . to abandon this dangerous practice."

20. ". . . nearly all regions of the Cap Bon witness the progressive development of Italian colonization."

21. It is evident that many of the transformations that take place in Kelibia, which Kelibians must manage creatively, were (and still are) often, as Lisa Anderson points out, "fostered by, and in the interests of," outsiders (1986: 22). This has "always" been the case, as far as Kelibians are concerned, and the history-conscious, at least, are not about to abandon local and kin ties, including local patron-client ties (although even who is patron and who is client at any particular time also shifts as opportunities change in the outside and Kelibian worlds), for the uncertainties involved in alliances with outside, possibly fleeting, powers. Historically, the lesson has been to have kin and community ties on as many sides of a power struggle as possible (cf. Fernea and Fernea 1987: 340). As Anderson also writes:

Unlike the rural societies of Europe, those of the precolonial periphery were not exclusively peasantries. In many parts of the Third World there was no central administration until the recent past, and many populations permanently escaped the surveillance of those formal political institutions that did exist. Of the methods of distributing resources and guaranteeing cooperation in such societies, kinship was the most common. (1986: 27)

Outside bureaucratic states have come and gone many times and domestic social structures over the centuries have had to adjust to the penetration into and withdrawal from the town of outside administrations as well as the possibilities for involvement by the townspeople in the politics and economies of the outside world. Domestic powers may wane, but are respected and held in reserve because of the memory of what will come again. Historians often write of the maintenance by outsiders—conquerors, larger state bureaucracies—of indigenous forms of authority, but in Kelibia, even when those are dispensed with or made irrelevant by outsiders, communal agreement maintains them informally. As Michael Meeker and many others have pointed out, "The centers of civilization in the Maghreb have been especially vulnerable from very early times, to destabilization by foreign powers" (1979: 214). I would say that this is true of the Mediterranean region in general and that coping mechanisms are incorporated into basic units of world view. As Meeker's work also suggests, mechanisms such as habous, veneration of walis, religiously mandated protection of the weak, hikayah-telling, maintenance of economic and personal contacts far and wide, and an interest in foreign ways are practical communal responses especially, for those (like Kelibians) who are dependent on land production.

Definition or analysis of a town like Kelibia on the basis of class divisions is problematic and I have avoided it. Not only has a large segment of the upper and middle classes departed relatively recently, but there have long been sets of ties cross-cutting Kelibian "class" lines both within and outside of the community. Family ties, for example, crisscross occupational, standard-of-living, and political boundaries. Better-off relations attend the weddings and other rites of passage of poor relatives, and they have some obligation to try to help them find work or to help their children. Poor relations have talents to contribute. I think immediately of gifted jokesters or storytellers, of a brother of the family who was a fisherman and would drop off fresh fish in the morning, of an aunt who was a marvelous seamstress, of a poor sister-in-law whom all the women hoped to have attend their family weddings because of her beautiful dancing, and of an older woman a family "connection" whose organizational skills at large gatherings were considered priceless.

22. ". . . an inactive population, which doesn't work by itself, which has always lived well, and which continued to live beyond its means. Due to their financial needs, the Safi family had to sell a large portion of their livestock, and then they began to sell the only thing that remained theirs, their land."

23. "Les villageois de Kélibia, détenteurs de capitaux, ont acheté déjà des terres appréciables . . ."

The Structure of Male Storytelling Events[1]

Time passes—that is a constant: generation succeeds generation—and this simple, universal phenomenon can explain a large part of that history that is made locally.

(John H. Davis)

But of course what we are interested in is not the mere differences between the past and the present but the way in which the former grew into the latter, the social and cultural processes which connect them.

(Clifford Geertz)

Despite Kelibia's lengthy past, hikayah-past does not consider events much before the turn of the century, the time when many of the present core group of inhabitants, those of various Ottoman and Arab extractions, were given impetus to solidify and define themselves vis-à-vis the European presence. As we look back over two thousand years of Kelibian past, however, we see that the geographical *longue durée* has fostered certain social structural continuities from which Kelibians (and I daresay other similarly situated Mediterranean groups) have fashioned a certain *mentalité*, a particular set of world-view touchstones that recur constantly in the hikayah-tellings of short-term, local history. As historians inform their short-term narratives by reference to the historical "big picture," so do Kelibian hikayah tellers draw on communally shared understandings of Kelibia's lengthy past in the fashioning of both the social and the narrative aspects of storytelling events.

The social context in which men in Kelibia tell hikayat can be described and discussed using Claude Lévi-Strauss's "anecdotique et géométrique" approach. Generalizations about the geometric relationships among physical setting, temporal setting, participants and narratives are illustrated by

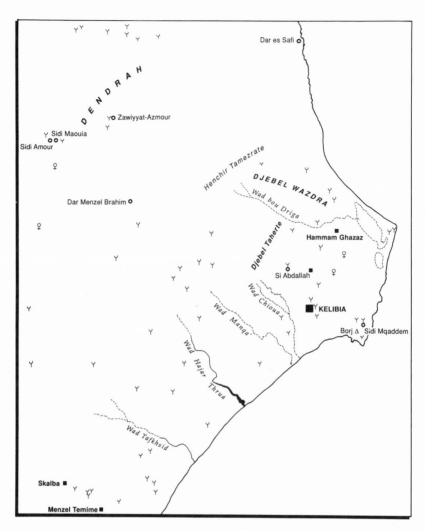

Map 3. Kelibian environs. Locations of Wali (Υ) and waliyya (♀) tombs or shrines are approximate. Sometimes, a small graveyard surrounds the holy figure. This map is extrapolated by reference to a series of very detailed maps done by the French army in the late nineteenth and first half of the twentieth centuries.

anecdotes from specific storytelling events. Close scrutiny of the common features of these events, combined with some attention to the participants' positions in the community, provides a perspective from which to analyze how the stories' performance[2] and genre features work rhetorically and give insight into the significance of the stories for narrators and audiences. Sociocultural referents outside of the events themselves will also be drawn upon freely as they become relevant to my analysis. For "the truth of the interaction is never entirely contained in the interaction" (Bourdieu 1977: 81).

The importance of analyzing verbal art forms within their sociocultural and particularly their situational contexts is now recognized by scholars from many disciplines. In this chapter hikayat will be treated "as situated communication, bringing together within one unified frame of reference artistic act, symbolic and expressive means, esthetic response, and situational and cultural context" (Bauman 1977a: 121).[3]

Of course "cultural context" implies contexts of both time and place (cf. Bauman 1986 and my Chapter 1). Here in the hikayah-telling events, attention to the intersection of time and space, the "chronotopic situation" to borrow Mikhail Bakhtin's term, is particularly rewarding for providing insights into cultural process and the place of history in story and vice versa. Within these narrative events at least four chronotopic situations intersect. There is that of the creator-narrator of the hikayah together with his work in creating and renewing his artistic construct with each telling. There is the chronotopic situation of each listener together with her or his individual and collective roles in both the creating and renewing his artistic construct with each telling. And, there is the chronotopic situation as fashioned in the narrative itself. The productive convergence of these three chronotopes is achieved largely by certain basic, shared community starting points, the units of world-view described in the previous chapter. The shape of these units continues to be adjusted, however, as narrators and audiences respond to and shape their own times and places.

Finally, of course, each of us—I as the author of this book, and you as the reader—looks at all of the above through our respective locations at the juncture of our own spaces and times. Our evocation of the Kelibian community must, as well, start from a look at its artistically and communally constructed, its "legendary," past from the inside out. For this is where so many of the community resources come from, for molding an aesthetically pleasing and thus a viable present and future.

Compared to the circumstances of many artistic works, the first three chronotopic situations are not separated greatly by space and time. Still, much of the generic and rhetorical work taking place, as hikayat are being told, moves toward leveling even more of the small, remaining cultural and spatial distances. First, collectively, hikayat themselves demonstrate that community values, community heroes, and walis stand community members in good stead, even when they are far from home—minimizing spatial distance. Kelibian "essence" is to be found anywhere that, at least in Tunisia, there are Kelibians. The difference between Kelibian and extra-Kelibian place for sons of the town is leveled, not by making Kelibia like other places, but by imposing its values on those other places in the person of Kelibian walis and heroes (cf. stories 2 and 12).

The collapsing of time differences is achieved as constant equivalents are found among story time and the storytelling time of both the narrator and members of the audience. Listeners are reminded of what it is like to be twelve years old or, less overtly, of the "timeless" admiration of certain heroic traits (story 7). At the same time, narrators take pains to bring up in their stories meta-commentary about landmarks, like neighborhoods, buildings still standing, natural formations; about people, like descendants of people in hikayat or ancestors of people in the audience or of the narrator; and about practices like hawking, travel, sportsmanship, even practical joking that are still current phenomena for their audiences.

Kelibia, as much as possible, is made in *essence* the same place for narrator, audience, and the dramatis personae of the narrative. These shared phenomena balance and put into perspective bygone and out-of-place aspects of the narratives. They frame the "strange" event in the narrative to give its seemingly time- and place-bound nature a chance at the same time to become time*less*—relevant to other times and places. Narrative time and place are the transparencies superimposed on past events and present situations to create the "timeless" place necessary to comment on the future. Narrative time can take the time to achieve this

tacit assumption that the audience and narrator can "stand in each other's shoes." The narrative is performed with an artful minimalization of artifice, and it is important that the narrator opens the text to the audience's statements of collaboration and confirmation. The best example of this type of realism is the personal experience narrative, which celebrates the idiosyncracies of personal experience at the same time that it calls forth examples of similar experiences from its audience. (Stewart 1982: 35).

Only we, the final set, writer-text-reader, are set off by a comparatively greater cultural space and time and by our medium. Mediation of that final distance is the task of a study such as this one. As we shall see, even the tension between the individual and collective or community roles is moved toward resolution in the storytelling event. This resolution is more ephemeral though. It is all well and good to portray a world as these stories do in which young people challenge the world and win, but in practical terms the successful may be lost to the family (and even to the community), and all cannot win. It is a self assured and gallant mother, to take an extreme example I remember, who, illiterate and confined for the most part to Kelibia, can allow her only daughter to spend years away from home becoming a lawyer when that mother knows very well that there is no present call for female lawyers in Kelibia. The benefit to the community of having a Kelibian lawyer practicing in Tunis or Paris is cold comfort to a mother whose daughter is likely to grow culturally as well as physically distant.

So Kelibians, along with us, are interested in "how the past grew into the present," and one way to explore the process is through discussion of certain striking events in their own pasts or in those of their friends or neighbors. I would argue we are interested in such processes for much the same reasons—to celebrate the phenomenon and to better prepare for the future.

Since the stories center around community personalities and representative highlights of town history (such as miracles by local holy people and triumphs of cunning, courage, or skill by community characters), special attention is given to those elements of time and place, of the storytelling event and the stories themselves, that are conducive to community-related talk or to those elements that can stimulate a sense of community. In order to illustrate the process of communal structuring of reality, I wish to emphasize the "shared" experiences and characteristics of the events rather than the idiosyncratic, psychological orientation of each individual narrator.

To understand how this structuring is achieved demands close attention to the contexts and to the genre and the performance (stylistic) possibilities of these stories. They are significant not simply as a descriptive outline, but because here we (and the audience) find overt or covert arguments for the particular interpretation of the text. Since verbal art is used rhetorically or persuasively (Abrahams 1968), it behooves a clever narrator to draw on all possible persuasive resources, the contextual and textural as well as the textual (Dundes 1964).

After describing these particular situational contexts and some of the sociocultural contexts in which the storytelling events I recorded took place, I will look at performance "keys" (Goffman 1974: 45) and genre markers. How are people verbally cued to the fact that a performance is taking place or is about to take place? And what are the genre markers by which a hikayah is defined? How are these instrumental in achieving a communal forum for the romancing of community past and present and for the negotiation of community past, present, and future?

Situational and Sociocultural Contexts

What are the general characteristics of situations suitable for the telling of hikayat? What influences, collectively, do these characteristics have upon the actual content and context of the texts? Setting is particularly important. Since men traditionally spend only eating and sleeping hours at home, they relax (and tell stories) in cafés or in *garages*⁺ or shops. Men know where to find their friends in these places, even if they do not know exactly where these same friends live. Some men consider it a status symbol to have a garage or shop at their disposal or the disposal of one of their friends—away from the "riffraff." But most like to spend at least some of their time in the more free-wheeling atmosphere of the cafés, where a variety of social groups are represented and new experiences are more likely. This, then, is the atmosphere in which many hikayat are told—in the summertime on benches or chairs, outside a particular establishment (café, garage, or shop), and, during the winter, inside. Other settings that come to mind are shady, sheltered outdoor places—beside a wall in the central area of town, or under a tree or in the shadow cast by the cactus fences in the country. The place, no matter how rural, is "domesticated" by a fire, or by the illusion of enclosure provided by a patch of shade, a straw mat, a wall, or a circle of friends, or by a pack of cards, a darbouka (drum), or the sharing of a meal.

Both verbally and through these cultural trappings, smaller groups are made to feel communal, and community is made to feel like family. Even in a café the individual is drawn into the table of "his" group—secure, though ringed by strangers. Emphasis on community is heightened too by the fact that father-son, brother-brother do not commonly attend the same cafés. For reasons of respect to be discussed later, younger brothers avoid smoking, swearing, and mentioning sex before older ones, as do sons before fathers. Since all of these activities are common in male, and especially evening, gatherings, male family members go their separate ways.

Hikayat can be told anytime, but certain times of the day are also particularly marked as times for sociability. After or during *Qaila* (the midday siesta period), is a possible time for men who work traditional hours in their own shops or in the fields, but many now have these hours available only on the weekends. After Qaila is more important for women's visiting—an opportunity to relax after the morning chores and the preparing and serving of the mid-day dinner. The time most marked today for everyday male sociability is evening, after supper, at dusk or after dark, depending on the time of year. At this time, called the *sahrah* سهرة , males, teenaged and up, leave home to go to a usual café or garage where people may be playing cards or board games such as dominoes, backgammon, or chess or simply drinking tea or coffee, smoking, and talking. The sahrah itself is an art form, with variations found under different names all around the Mediterranean, and particularly memorable evenings become stories themselves. For example, an especially heated card game during which a usually dignified older community member dispenses with *qaddir*[s] (the respect due him) in order picturesquely to describe to his opponent how many ways he is going to be sexually violated by the end of the evening is worth storying about over the next few days.[6]

"One story suggests another," the Kelibians say, so any gathering in which stories begin to be told is likely to be a lengthy one. Typically, a thick, sweet tea or a Turkish coffee will be ordered if the group is at a café. If the gathering is at a shop or garage, the waiter of a nearby café will come over for the order, or the proprietor or owner of the shop will have a brazier constantly going, and his friends will sometimes contribute tea or sugar.

Though verbal exchange of various sorts is definitely the central focus of male leisure-time activity, talk may center around the card or board games going on at the same time, with spectators adding their analyses during vigorous games. Nowadays, a television may be on and commentary may center around its fare. When the Americans landed on the moon, Malek said older men harumphed but remained silent in front of younger men, unsure whether these diplomaed youngsters shared their skepticism or would laugh at their doubts. In such cases, sensitive young men tend to be understanding and careful of the older generation's sensibilities, almost as if they value their elders' disbelief more than their own belief. In hikayat, the opposite often seems true—young men cherish their elders' beliefs and seem to find them the antidote to their, sometimes, worldly skepticism. Again, this mutual appreciation of age and youth, belief and skepticism, facilitates a sense of community, a collapsing together of chronotopes before a narrative even emerges. Finally, it is impossible to imagine any of these gatherings without a haze of cigarette smoke.

There are other differences between the café and the less accessible gathering places. Often, in the garages and shops, one or two of the men are working while talk is flowing. School-age children of both sexes who belong to one or another of the men may be present and sometimes listen to the stories. On the other hand, children and women never go into the cafés—unless a woman sends a boy in to fetch her husband or son. Consequently, talk there tends to be rougher. As mentioned earlier, fathers and sons or even brothers will not be found in the same cafés, since prurient talk, at least as a public value, is considered inappropriate among males of the same family. The presence of a close male relative would be inhibiting.

In searching for the significance of the hikayat discussed here, it is important to remember that hikayat are told in public or semi-public surroundings (shops or the outer, typically male, gathering-place of a household) in which men of diverse community backgrounds and ages are frequently present. Audience and narrators are the same categories of people with whom one is likely to travel to search for itinerant or seasonal work, to work in the fields, to hunt, to fish, and to attend religious and secular school. Tunisian men, for a multitude of reasons, tend to spend their time out of the home and in relationships with nonfamily. As a man grows out of boyhood, he spends more of his time away from home. He establishes his "territories"—certain cafés, certain cliques of men—but these are in constant flux as anyone with a connection to any of the group participants is likely to drop by. So, even in the semi-privacy of the garage or shop, men are exchanging stories and sharing experiences with numerous other men who, for lack of close family ties, will never come into their houses. And, though the absence of relatives and women permits greater license to talk about sex, *intra*-community gossip is stifled because, as an older woman told me, "if you search hard enough, everyone in the town is related to you somehow." In this community, women maintain extended family ties in their social interaction, mostly visiting relatives. Thus they are quicker to criticize even families of sons- or daughters-in-law if members of those families are not present, and they are the ones who spend time reviewing intra-community conflict, factions, and feuds (assuming that comments will be kept "in the family"), while men talking to unrelated men tend to maintain larger community relations.[7]

Sharing of talk and of past and present experiences is community-centered for men, rather than home-centered. Older men have come to know every nook and cranny of the town and every person in it, by family affiliation, if not by name. Like the rural American described by Richard Dorson, a Kelibian "regards his town as a second family and its history as scarcely less personal than his own genealogy" (Dorson 1952: 182). And the atmosphere of shared tea, cigarettes, the warmth of the brazier, a cutthroat card game, enhance the community and the community-as-family feeling created by the shared words. A certain limited range of settings thus creates the aesthetically correct atmosphere for hikayah-telling: the most typical setting recapitulates or reinforces the textual theme of sense of community and sense of place, and therefore that setting is an important component of the social document (speech event) representing Kelibian community thought.

In this interpretation "aesthetic" is given its broadest possible meaning. As the hikayat in this study are performances, they are open at every level to aesthetic evaluation. Every aspect of the event has an aesthetic, nonisolable dimension or component. Contextually, the scene is set for storytelling, and the more one can coordinate or integrate the event context with the structure and intent of the story, the more aesthetically pleasing the entire event will be judged to be. In fact, of course, all elements and therefore all aesthetic aspects of the storytelling are not at the command of the storyteller. For example, though he can structure his stories to suit a particular audience, he often has little control (the code of hospitality being as it is) over who turns up or the visitor's particular past and current attitudes toward the storyteller or others in the group or moods of the moment. He cannot control the weather—which sets a mood as well. But, as a good storyteller, he can effectively incorporate dramatic weather, for instance, as entryway into a story. For example, he might choose to recount an event that occurred, ". . . on just such a night as this. . . ." Found objects can be manipulated. A mug on the table is just like the one in the story. A box of matches can be used for sound effects. A member of the audience is the descendant of someone in the story.

So the stage is set.[8] Mostly unrelated men sit on mats or sheepskins around a steaming tea pot under a tree, or in a place of business, or at a table in a crowded, smokey café. It is a time of leisure (the typical Mediterranean "siesta" hours—especially during the hot season) after the noon meal and rest, or after the evening meal, when the evening stretches out.[9] Of course, telling hikayat is only one of the events, and one kind of talk, that may emerge from this structure but other types of conversation often lead into a story or stories. A specific story asked for usually is not told as well as those that occur naturally within the conversational context.

Other performance-centered behavior likely to take place includes playing cards, having one person read aloud to others in the group (who may be working), telling riddles, telling jokes or joke stories, telling khurafat (fantasy stories), or reminiscing about daily life in the past and comparing it to present-day life or describing in nonnarrative form an unusual past event. Some of these pastimes involve displays of competence other than aesthetic, for example, knowledge of past events or skill at backgammon or cards. Yet the ability to transform any of these activities into a performance is one that is appreciated and encouraged by participants.

One of the most significant aspects of the situational context for the hikayat discussed here is the juxtaposition of older and younger men. And many older men do take a proprietary interest in the younger ones and want their attention. After all, aren't they *awlad al-bilad* (sons of the town)? Younger men too tell each other little vignettes about their experiences with girls, at school, on vacation, and so forth, but their success is dependent on facts and not style. They are reporting, not performing. Besides the fact that they have not yet developed a personal aesthetic for hikayat, they have not the authority of age or the practice to talk about the town or townspeople, nor have they accumulated adventures to compare with those of the older men.[10] But older men enjoy certain younger men too—those who seem (almost) as clever and resourceful and adventurous as they once were themselves.

Certainly, not all older men want to establish these ties with the younger ones and when they do, they are selective; it requires a certain relaxing of qaddir which properly must come from the older man, and, naturally, to some this would be undignified. In many instances, however, qaddir is relaxed, and opportunity is made for a bond to be forged across generations of community members. These bonds can be forged in other ways as well, but with the tremendous amount of change taking place in the community, older and younger people literally do not speak the same language. Young adults have to ask their elders what they mean by sayings that refer to customs that no longer exist or that use words that are no longer common.

All of the stories discussed in this chapter were essentially a communication between an older and a younger man (or men), the older man narrating to the younger. During the narration of the stories most eye contact was between the narrator and one young man, Malek. He represented the constant presence. The hospitality we enjoyed was for his pleasure primarily—and mine only secondarily. Much more than I or other members of the audience, he was the one checked with to be sure that he understood who the characters in the story were and where the events took place. This particular younger man–older man relationship was most significant, in my opinion, in terms of influence on subject matter and on the structuring of these particular narratives although my own presence as westerner-outsider was also crucial to the story choice.

Addressing me directly would have been odd, especially at first. These are stories men tell men, for the most part. Even though young daughters may be present under certain circumstances, certainly an unrelated, adult female cannot be part of the group unless there is a sexual interest or until she can be reassigned status as a "daughter," "niece," or "sister" of a man in the group. Si Hamdan finally did speak to me directly one day while Malek was in the midst of a rousing game of cards. That was the day I heard about the prophecies of Sidi Bou Bakkir (pp. 38–39) and accounts of long-ago evening riddling sessions in Si Hamdan's uncle's store. To Si Hamdan, I think I was something like *bint al-bilad* (daughter of the town). This would be a variation on the Kelibian habit of addressing contemporaries as "brother" or "sister" and older or younger people as "aunt" or "uncle" or "daughter" or "son" to show respect and, in the case of opposite sex interaction, lack of sexual intent.

In many ways it matters who Malek is and who his narrators are as well. It is important to keep in mind, though it is not the main thrust of my discussion, that Malek and the various narrators (and I myself) were not just slots representing young men, older men, and a westerner. Each personality as well as each background in combination acted as catalyst for the speech event that occurred. Malek, as we will see, was not simply the oldest son of a sheikhly family in reduced circumstances, but an engaging, audacious young man, the kid who would make narrators think hopefully of their community and its promise and fondly of their own young manhoods. I was a teachable westerner, appreciative of the stories and their tellers with nothing to offer anyone, except what we all had to offer, our good companionship.

Before turning to look at the stories themselves, it is appropriate to talk about the actual conditions under which the hikayat were gathered. Malek was the central audience member for a majority of the stories recorded. Like many fieldworkers, I was influenced strongly in my perceptions of my research community by my friends and contacts in that community. Most of my approximately five years in the town (distributed over the last eighteen) were spent living with one family. An enormous number of my town acquaintances were made through the mother of this family, and she is my town mentor. But Malek, her oldest son and her favorite, was obviously the most important town influence on this study for not only were they *his* evaluations of the stories and storytellers that I most often heard, it was to him that the stories were usually being told. Let us, then, take a brief look at his background.

In 1978–79, when these stories were recorded, Malek was in his late twenties. He and his generation are transitional and thus mediating figures in the community. Having been children both before and after the tremendous impact of Tunisian independence, they can act as interpreters between community members older or younger than they. His was the last age group, for example, to play the games the older men played, and he remembers when soccer and volley balls were first introduced into the town and changed forever the play patterns of the boys. He remembers the time before independence when he and his friends would throw stones at the French soldiers' trucks (and how he almost got caught once), and, like the older men, he knows the names of the colonialists who were living in the town and the names of the French soldiers who were stationed there. A large middle class of foreigners lived in the town then. His mother had a Spanish seamstress to make clothes for him and his younger siblings. He remembers when the community center was a church and church bells rang on Sunday morning. Almost all these colonialists are gone now, and those younger than Malek cannot remember them at all.

He attended the *kuttab*, religious school, when it was the only educational opportunity for most young Muslims. Since there was no school in town for Muslims except religious school, at an early age he was sent to boarding school. Soon after independence, public, secular schools were established, and his brother, only two years younger, was able to complete sixth grade before he had to leave, and his sister, five years younger, could stay in town through high school. Now, if youngsters attend the kuttab it is only for a year or two as "pre-school." In his late teens, Malek rebelled in ways the younger generation still understands. He grew his hair long, went to French movies, romanced the girls in French and Arabic—whichever worked best—wanted to drop out of school, tried alcohol, refused to fast during Ramadhan, and generally worried his parents and aunts and uncles in the modern fashion.

Because Malek is the nephew and grandson of town sheikhs, the community has, perhaps, more of a proprietorial attitude toward him than it would have toward other youths—besides which, he is the oldest son, with

Figure 2. A Christmas present for Myriam from Nesria, December 1979. (In background are Fatma, Nesria's sister-in-law, spouse of Si Mohamed's younger brother, and Marie Thérèse, Nesria's daughter-in-law and mother of Myriam.)

all the Mediterranean-Middle Eastern attendant responsibilities and privileges. Further, like his mother, he is a keen observer, and therefore a master, of town life. As his mother says, "When Malek is here I know I have a lion in town." He knows everyone and is an expert among experts in the field of human relationships. He has a history of being a sportsman, a ladies' man, and an excellent card player. He can speak and write French well and has a solid grasp of literary Arabic. He is the kind of person people want to do favors for and, as is true of anyone who is a master of their cultural rules, he breaks them with impunity (as does his mother in her own way). Especially, he moves much more freely between the domains of women and men than do his brothers or, for that matter, most other males in the community.

In 1977 he married a French woman, Marie Thérèse,[11] whom he had known for five years, and at the time of this study, everyone knew they would be moving to France with their baby daughter. He said it was "only for three or four years to save the money to build a house here in Kelibia," but his family was worried, and his mother was often in tears that year. She would say, jokingly, "I don't care about you, but how can you take my grandchild?" His uncles took him aside and talked to him, and though he tried to hide it, he was nervous and irritable when he thought of leaving. Some years earlier he had won a hard fight to be assigned a teaching job in his own community. Now he would be giving up that position for France, land of opportunity, but also land of unknowns.

Besides being a representative "son of the town," to these older narrators, Malek could also represent, symbolically, one of their own sons. The two men by whom he was told the most stories and whom we visited the most, Uncle Gacem and Si Hamdan, also have sons who were mediating or, in the past, had had to mediate among French, Tunisian, and hometown lifestyles and values. Many of these young men were still "traveling" for work, education, or vacation and had not as yet come home and settled down. (As in many good folktales, the young heroes must leave their homes, find the "instrument of power," and return.) Of course, the underlying tension of "will they ever come home?" (and everyone knows of some who have not) conflicts with pride in sons, like Malek, who can "master" the outside world. And then, of course, Malek is a symbol of youth, the lifestyle of which the narrator can compare and contrast with his own youth and with his current situation and, indirectly, comment upon in his stories.

The hikayat were provided by seven men over the age of forty. In fact, all but one were in their sixties or older. (I have included comments and narratives by two women in Chapter 3.) I will refer to the men as Khali (maternal uncle) Gacem, Si Hamdan, Si Mohamed, Si ben Youssef, Si Hmida el Bedoui, Si Tahar, and the barber. Stories from all but the last two are included in this volume. Their storytelling contexts were as follows.

We could usually find Khali Gacem in his pottery shop across from the new central market in town. His visitors, including Malek and me, would bring in chairs and order tea from the café across the road—an appropriate and typical setting. Anytime one passed by that bustling center of town, one could see him holding court either in his shop in the winter or sitting just outside in the balmy summer dusk. In spring 1983, I was in Kelibia for a few days and stopped to see Uncle Gacem several times. Each time his shop was closed. A passerby finally told me and Lella Nesria, Malek's mother, that he was in a Tunis hospital, very ill, and not expected to live.

The barber was recorded in his shop by Moncef, Malek's brother. Moncef and his friends would spend almost every evening in the barber's shop, playing cards or talking. One evening he took the recorder with him and reminded the barber of some stories he had told him and his friends before. The barber knew the stories were being recorded for me, but I never met him since I could not go to his shop, very much a male preserve. He is over eighty and remembers that he shaved Malek's and Moncef's paternal grandfather on his wedding day.

Si Hamdan is the guardian at the local grammar school, where Malek coaches sports. He would often regale Malek with stories and jokes between classes, and when he heard that I wanted to know about the town's past, he invited us to come visit him.[12] He told Malek he had grown up in his uncle's shop and from a young age had heard stories from his uncle and his uncle's friends. He always received us in the large front room, cum shop, of his almost-completed new house. (Shops and garages were often a part of traditional, high-walled homes. In more recently built one-story bungalows a front room may be used as a quasi-workshop and gathering place for men or women. Women in town who are seamstresses or hairdressers, for example, use their front rooms as places to work and to greet customers and friends.) Si Hamdan's room is a large workroom where he stores his supplies and weaves his rush mats and baskets and where he also receives his friends. There is a television, and his five teen-aged children often gathered there with us. Young children and older boys could be with their fathers in these semi-private settings (as opposed to cafés), but the presence of Si Hamdan's two teen-aged daughters was a little unusual, a sign of the times and also the fact that they had three older brothers who were very fond of them. I have seen them both with their brothers at the Sidi Bahri coffee shop—frequented by both men and women in the summertime. Si Hamdan's older daughter was shy and a "little woman," but the younger, Sa'ida, just on the brink of adolescence, did not hesitate to speak up and her participation was welcomed. As might be expected, his wife seldom entered the room and never did so when guests other than Malek and I were present. If one of his girls was there, she would make us tea. If not, Si Hamdan or one of the boys would. His frame for weaving extended down one side of the room and sometimes he would be sitting on it working when we arrived.

We heard two genie stories from Si ben Youssef one day when he happened to drop in to visit Si Hamdan. I learned very little about him, but understood that he is distantly related to Lella Nesria.

We met with Si Mohamed, card-playing associate of Malek's in his mid-sixties, in a room off the courtyard of his traditional-style house. We would sit apart from his wife and grown children, though his wife would come in to serve us tea or coffee. Once, one of his sons joined us. Si Mohamed is missing a hand, having blown it off playing with dynamite detonators when he was an adolescent. He is considered a town spokesperson by the other older men, and was recommended to me and Malek by the former town sheikh. As a young man he organized a *malouf*[3] singing group that used to accompany wedding processions. Today, he and his old friends still meet at the town club (the former Catholic church) to sit and sing together.

The few stories of Si Hmida el Bedoui and Si Tahar were first heard in cafés; the former by a young doctor who only comes home to Kelibia on the weekends, and the latter by Malek. Malek searched out the two men and got their permission to record the stories. Malek took home with him Si Tahar, who is very poor, to make the recording. Malek met Si Hmida in the courtyard of a mosque about which he would tell a story.

Each of the men described above had seen more of the world than Kelibia—whether by choice, or need, or fortunes of war. Thus travel for them as well as for their young audience was a norm—not only because they are of a community made up of "travelers," having all come from elsewhere, but because they personally had traveled. Most had simply visited other rural and urban areas of Tunisia, but Uncle Gacem had gone off to Algiers by train (without a passport) during the French occupation to sell a basket of opium.

All the storytelling sessions were visits. As will become clear as the personalities of the narrators emerge in the course of their storytelling, any suggestion of remuneration by me for the stories would have been highly inappropriate. The primary social identities of these male narrators (and the two female narrators to be found in Chapter 3) are as family members, community members and friends—not as storytellers.

The most unusual contextual feature of these storytelling events was my own presence as a woman and a foreigner. Of course, the stories could not be taped in cafés because, even discounting the noise problem, most cafés are by custom only for men. But the narrators did decide the meeting places, and, as has been shown, most of the settings were fairly typical for their narrators.

My presence, though, must have limited the repertoires of some of the men, especially as they tried to avoid any references to sex (except, surprisingly, the venerable Si Mohamed, much to Malek's confusion and embarrassment) and attempted not to curse, not only because of the presence of a woman but because of the tape recorder. However, in the case of Si Hamdan and Si ben Youssef, choice of language and subject matter also was influenced by the presence of Si Hamdan's daughters and sons.

Stories were directed to me at first, and this fact destroyed the stylistic or performative value of the stories told. As a townswoman said when she listened to a trial tape, "They're breaking their words"; that is, they were talking in a simplified manner so I would be sure to understand. Therefore, Malek, enthusiastic about the project anyway, became the recipient of the stories. We agreed that it would be to him that the storyteller would address himself. (As noted earlier, it was awkward socially for me to be the recipient, anyway.) We would discuss beforehand what we hoped to elicit and the young man or one of the others present usually took responsibility for conversational interactions with the speakers.

It is more difficult to assess my effect on the stories as a foreigner. Si Hamdan once told Malek in my absence that I was "half Kelibian." Another time he told to me to consider what would happen if he sent "that one" (his younger daughter) to America at such an early age for such a long time (referring to my first stay as a Peace Corps volunteer in 1967–70). Wouldn't she become Americanized? In general, it seems that most of the narrators' hikayah repertoires were as available to me as they would be to a younger female relation of their own, but I will argue in Chapter 4 that my presence as "foreigner" consciously and unconsciously influenced the narrators to remember more accounts that treat community members' encounters with the outside world, especially the western and colonial worlds. My individual effect as a woman was on what was *not* told, while Malek and the other younger men and I, as a westerner, influenced what *was* told and how.

Since no two storytelling events can be the same, we must step back to a level of abstraction at which we can make generalizations about the events' structures. These generalizations will allow us to postulate ways in which the events comment upon and seek to influence community perspectives. In the events just described, the fact that an older man was telling a story to a younger man or set of younger men is particularly significant for defining and limiting what and how stories will be told. As will become clear, this structure, the representative positions of listener(s) and narrator in community context, and the ever-changing history and current status of the community, all contribute to the emergent[14] significance (the structuring) of a particular hikayah and of a storytelling event.

The makeup of the audience and what its members hold in common interest with the narrator are central to this equation. The audience and narrator share interest in and knowledge about their community and its inhabitants, their status as Kelibian men of established families, expectations about what a hikayah is, and a set of standards for evaluating one. Even more basically, both are male, one is young and one was young, one is old and the other will be. Drawing upon shared knowledge and shared expectations provides the delicate balance that assures the narrator that he will be attended to as he adds information his listeners are not familiar with and takes, at times, a not altogether agreeable rhetorical stance.

Of course, one can never know for sure how any other listener will respond to the narrator and his or her text. As Tzvetan Todorov points out in reference to readers, "we add and suppress what we wish to find or to avoid" (Todorov 1968: 100).[15] And audience reactions only hint at the spectrum of responses or missed cues. Nevertheless, meaningful communication between raconteur and audience must be achieved at some level. If there is not a basis for complicity established early in the story, or at least the introduction of subject matter potentially interesting to listeners, the story does not get told at all. The subject is politely changed, a previous engagement is recalled, a card game is suggested, and so on. Thus, the audience is critical to the narrator and his shaping of the story and the storytelling event; it provides him with an opportunity to tell *his* (side of the) story; but he won't be allowed to tell it, and they won't listen, unless it is somehow their story as well, something that they can relate to their own life experiences, whether anticipated or completed.

Taking the subject matter of these hikayat into consideration, we find respectable family men telling younger men about experiences they had as young men or recounting experiences seen through their eyes as youths. In the former's case, listeners cannot forget that the conventional wildness of youth has been tempered now to the requisite sobriety and responsibility of age. In the latter's case, a more direct bond is formed: "Look, even in my youth I found this person laughable or this event despicable or worthy of wonder," and, implicitly (since he is telling the story), "I still do today." Illustrated here are acceptable role models for youth and maturity, standards that change with age, and those that remain the same. In the search for meaning, then, various interrelationships of narrator, story, and listeners, must be taken into account. The narrator, mediating between and interweaving earlier community time and present time, maturity and youth, can bring the most respectable (often represented in his person) and most outrageous (usually represented by his story characters or his audience) aspects of male culture together. When the storyteller plays off his current plus his youthful (as a participant in the narrative) persona, the message becomes very complex. His impact is doubled, and in these cases one message is most clear, that is, "have adventures, break (certain) rules, leave town to seek a livelihood, save your life, or see the world, but come home to tell your stories and settle down with family and community."

Generic Markers and Rhetorical Strategies

The features of hikayah-telling events mentioned above—the settings, the times of day, the actors (narrators and audiences), are not exclusive to hikayah-telling. Other kinds of talk, or activity, could emerge from just such configurations. But I have stressed the community characteristics present in this particular configuration because that is the thread I feel is seized upon by the narrator when he decides to tell or his audience asks for a narrative of the kind I am discussing here. Of course, as Jonathan Culler points out, response is one determinant of genre. So, although my response to a narrative as a hikayah is determined by constituents in the text, in a real sense, especially after a hikayah or two is told, "the interpretive assimilation of a response is what gives certain elements significance within a work" (Culler 1981: 59). It works both ways. So, turning from discussion of speech community and the structure of the speech event to the structure of the hikayat themselves, we see that the hikayah's special generic features also emphasize community. What are the generic markers that distinguish hikayat?[16] They are true stories involving one or more current or past members of the community. They take place in the not-too-distant past (usually within a generation or two), and they are told in informal settings appropriate to a sense of community. The latter marker is one that exists external to the story itself. It would be inconceivable to sell these stories as café entertainment. Their semi-private nature would be destroyed, and their purity, and thus veracity, as a free gift would be open to question.

Other genre markers include: minimal and diffuse opening and closing remarks; heavy emphasis on the establishment of credibility by use of specific detail and enumeration of witnesses to the stories' events; audience participation; and generation of other stories around similar themes or subjects (for example, stories about miracles or stories centering around a town character). Individually, these markers need not be exclusive to hikayat, and not all of them need appear in every story or speech event. Essentially, the story must be offered as at least possibly true, and as having happened to the raconteur, or to someone he knows or knew, or to someone whom someone he knows or knew knows or knew. Conceivably individuals from two different towns could exchange hikayat, if a basis for complicity could be found. For example, I heard a story in Kelibia about two Kelibians who were to be shot by the French colonizers. It so happened that the execution was to have taken place in front of the zawiyya of the wali, Sidi Bahri, and so the French were rendered unable to fire their guns. I repeated this story to a friend from the Sahel region of Tunisia, and he repeated a similar story from his home town. (That is, our wali and yours were united in expelling the French.) Thus hikayat in times of stress might be used to forge extra-town bonds. More markers can be found in a story that is more centrally than peripherally part of the genre (see story 8 and discussion) and that is "more performed" than reported and, therefore, a narrative in which the narrator is more personally involved and has more of a stake in his audience's evaluation of his story.

All of these markers to some extent involve the hikayat with one of their community contexts: they minimize barriers between the story (recreated) world and the real world, bring narrator, narrative, and audience, as well as past and present, closer together, or build bridges between story and story. If the story form draws attention to the split between an experience and its reporting, form must somehow be minimized (though not entirely done away with) so that the event can be felt to be reexperienced. The structure of the speech events discussed in this chapter and the structure of the narratives themselves are such that the distinctions among the chronotopic situations of narrator, story, and listeners are blurred by the deft interweaving of time-past and time-present, the story events with current events.

The raconteur draws (his chosen) past into present, illustrating a Kelibian historical process that privileges both continuity and change. A central place, Kelibia, is a constant, and that helps blur time as well, but the result is not the "cyclic rhythmicalness" of "folkloric time" postulated by Bakhtin for his idyllic novel of place (Bakhtin 1981: 224–225). Even the idyllic aspects of these narratives—the beauty of the town, the abundance of resources from land and sea, the capacity of its people to win out over adversity—are subordinated to the real. Thus, the ideal, as shall be shown, is made more real. The continuation of the "timeless" aspects of Kelibia, its beauty and abundance, its generations of special occupants, depends on mediated acknowledgment of disruption, of change, and, ironically, of the fact that two hundred years ago the town in its current, idyllic "timeless" state did not exist.

The minimal and diffuse boundaries between story and the real world help blur the distinction between the two. The story is moved closer to "reality," to a conversational mode, and made less "storylike." Because openings are relatively boundary-less, access-egress by audience and narrator alike is relatively easy throughout the story, giving audience members or the narrator the option of dropping out of the story and into conversation and vice versa. And, of course, all of the genre characteristics that diminish the impenetrability of a story at least have the potential of integrating it more closely with time-present, with everyday conversation.

Thus the narrative is made more immediate and therefore, I argue, more believable and a more potent vehicle for commenting on present-day community life and prescribing for the future. The usefulness of the tendency of hikayah markers to minimize various sorts of boundaries will become more evident as we discuss them in conjunction with various performative devices used in hikayah-telling.

When a story or series of stories is *performed* rather than simply reported, certain stylistic devices (not necessarily exclusive to hikayah-telling) are employed by the teller that key the listeners to the fact that a story performance rather than simply a report of a story is taking place. These devices (or keys) may be referential, commenting on the relationship of the story to its cultural or situational (extra-story) context, or they may be reflexive, commenting on aspects of the narrative, narrator, or narrating itself. Whether referential or reflexive, it is these performative devices, used alone or in conjunction with generic markers, that enhance the power of a narrative to communicate effectively and thus render it capable of carrying special multivocalic strength and depth. At the same time, the performed story "elicits the participative attention and energy" (Bauman 1977b: 43) of the audience so that a well-told tale heard by an audience sympathetic to the teller is especially impressive and persuasive and seeks an understanding of the message far more subtle than a simple belief or disbelief in what the narrator says happened. For a Kelibian, perhaps, at least one close to the original event, the story can give the illusion of being complete in itself. But for me, even approaching an unattenuated understanding of the narrative demands conscious attention to where the various keying devices within the story point to certain analogous or completing details both within the storytelling event and in its sociocultural and historical contexts, as well as attention to Kelibian sociocultural and historical details that call one hikayah or more to mind.

Central to my consideration of performative devices will be an analysis not only of *how* but to what *effect* these devices are manipulated alone or with various textual markers to reinforce hikayah context and story-specific textual content. A narrative may be told, as William Labov and others have pointed out, for the purpose of self-aggrandizement. Certainly many of these particular hikayat may be expected to have as one characteristic the projection of self as brave or good or tough or mean. (Although some storytellers, to the contrary, take care to transfer credit for a particularly impressive deed to a wali or waliyya and not give the praise to themselves or their protagonists, the aggrandizement, of course, is also always lodged in the storyteller's ability to tell a good story.) In the entire set of hikayat under study here, though, another characteristic is more significant than that of self-aggrandizement or its absence. The narrators are particularly interested in achieving audience-narrator complicity, in establishing within the storytelling event a shared feeling of community pride and commitment, as well as in manipulating attitudes and aesthetics to be structurally consonant both with ideals of the community at large and with the content of the actual story being told.

Many of the hikayat told in Kelibia are "personal narratives," stories told by narrators about experiences from their own pasts. The performance style of personal narratives has been labeled "rough," not fully developed, by scholars who perceive them simply as early steps toward more sophisticated productions such as legends.[17] But a polished, professionally elegant rendering would be an inappropriate aesthetic for the informality and intimacy of this type of story and occasion, as would a paid performance in a café. The narrator does not want to distance himself too much from his audience. The prestige of his years and his credentials as a witness of the past suffice. Too, he does not efface himself from or subordinate himself to the account, as might be considered desirable in another type of performance. It is as if the narrator invites his audience to watch and evaluate the actions of the actors in the story along with him, be those actors fellow community members past or present or himself as a younger person.

All this is not to say that good performance is not important to the audience and the narrator, only that high polish, as we think of it, say, in the smooth, stylized, formulaic performance of a Yugoslavian epic, would be out of place here. There is an aesthetic protocol for these stories. Listeners do evaluate a performer's communicative competence and pay special attention to the act of expression. And, too, there is a great deal of variation in style in the area of what Jan Mukařovský calls unstructured or individually systematized aesthetics (Mukařovský 1964: 61–62). He observes that these aesthetic touches are intimately linked with the comment the narrator is making: "We must also note again that in communicative speech the unstructured esthetic shares its roles with the extra-esthetic intent" (Mukařovský 1964: 36). These unstructured or individual aesthetic touches, as well as more standard performative devices, are actually important indicators and supporters of the intent(s) of a certain type of story. In the case of these hikayat, the techniques often add a kind of conspiratorial, "down-home," or intimate rapport between narrator and audience: the narrator incorporates a relative of an audience member into the story; he mentions a story landmark that is still in evidence; or he reminds audience members of how they all felt as twelve-year-olds longing to do grown-up things.

Since hikayat, as opposed to other town narrative forms, are told as true stories, much of their potential persuasive power depends on whether the male narrator can convince his audience that he is telling the truth. (If he can't persuade them, they may say that what he is telling are khurafat, fictions.) If hikayat are, for example, to persuade an audience of the "specialness" of their community and effectively to negotiate town mores, they must be believed by the audience. And it is obvious from the effort the narrator makes to establish his own and the story's credibility that he sees a barrier to belief. This perceived necessity for extensive proof stems partly from the audience's temporal and experiential distance from the events in the hikayat. Although most of the events took place only twenty to fifty years ago, the world was in some ways very different from the one younger audience members live in today. Because of the enormous changes that have occurred, the time might seem longer. Younger listeners lack a great deal of cultural information with which to judge the story, and so stylistic competence must be brought into play in order to equate the landscapes and people of yesterday to the circumstances of today, to "familiarize" them—not simply on an intellectual but on an experiential level.

Second, the experiential distance necessary to an hikayah must be mediated if the story is to be believed. Experiential distance is necessary either in the process of what Roger Abrahams calls "making strange"[18] or in what William Labov calls "reportability," making a story unusual, special enough (by artistic reperception of a common event in the first case or presentation of an unusual event in the second) to be worth listening to. Referring to what he calls the "history *legend*," a genre resembling the hikayah as discussed here, Richard Dorson writes that it must be "salted with some humor or tragedy or mystery, it must be human and personal, tied to a familiar name or a landmark, and yet slip over into a realm of mystery and wonder" (Dorson 1952: 11). "Mystery and wonder," though, would seem to be polar opposites to "human and personal." Thus, there is a delicate balance that must be maintained between "making strange" and making believable, human, and personal. What is susceptible to being narratively framed, those "interesting and energizing topics" or characters that will work rhetorically in a community actively to involve the audience

(Abrahams 1968b), are often those bordering on unbelievable. The more improbable a story (and therefore often, perhaps, the more spellbinding), the more difficult to make believable. Here again, culturally and generically appropriate performative devices are employed by skillful narrators to maintain needed balance. There are two means by which veracity is most frequently established in these hikayat. The first is by strict attention to specific detail—that is, to whom, where, and when the particular event occurred, situating it in time and space. Then, there is something akin to what in classical Arabic is called *isnad*, the system or chain of verification whereby a *hadith* (anecdote or narrative about a prophet and especially about Mohamed) is given authenticity. Traditionally this isnad (literally "documentation" or "building [a chain of] authority") is a list of names starting with that of the eyewitness to the words or deeds. Each link in the chain is the name of the next historically reliable person told, down to the present. One example of this handing back of responsibility is Si Hamdan's assertion, "This one was told to me by my paternal uncle, God have mercy on him."

In these hikayat, though, the list of witnesses is just as likely to be a number of people synchronically rather than diachronically associated, people who are still alive and can be consulted as to the truth of a particular account. Si Hamdan was especially good at that. As I and Malek and Si Hamdan's sons and daughters settled back on low mattresses and sheepskins absentmindedly sipping our tea and listening intently, he would take us on a mental tour of the town. He would push his red sheshia back on his head, thoughtfully pull on his cigarette, and begin to link people to places, present to past.

Before beginning the following story, Si Hamdan pauses and says, "Who's still alive from that group? [stops to think] Jebali [a barber in town] is still alive." Malek confirms that he understands that this is "Jebali, the barber," and Hamdan again emphasizes that they heard the story from the protagonist, "and from Jebali, too." (The implication is that such a strange story needs verification from someone besides the admittedly flighty protagonist.) Then, after establishing the approximate time of the incident ("four or five years before independence") and the name of the protagonist, "Ahmed Qmira," he continues:

(2) SI HAMDAN
The group was going to Tunis. There wasn't . . . There was only the TAT [bus system] at the time. At quarter to two that national bus left

from in front of the post office. Standing room was not allowed then. It was forbidden. Everyone had to sit down. Everyone sat and of the seats, the half in front were one price, and those in the rear another. [laughter, comments] The seats were numbered starting from the rear. Say, from number one up to twenty were one hundred francs, and the others were eighty francs. The twenty at the rear went for one hundred francs. Understand?

They went to Tunis. It was spring at the time.

When they had gone from here to near Menzel Hur [a small town nearby], there was that Stefan or whatever his name was. A colon.

Malek: A French colon?

A Frenchman . . . you see. He got on. He met the bus to hitch a ride [but] there wasn't a place.

Malek, Sabra: [being served tea by Sa'ida, Si Hamdan's younger daughter] Thank you. Long life.

Malek: That Stefan got on?

Yes, he was going to Tunis. He met the bus to get a ride. So . . . Who came to make [Qmira] give up his place? The ticket collector and the driver. They made Ahmed Qmira get up.

Malek: [laughing] So Mr. Stefan could sit.

Yeah.

Malek: Because he was French. They got the man up so a Frenchman could sit down.

Right, right—that Ahmed Qmira . . .

We have that Sidi 'Ali Qsibi here. Who knows if he's a wali or not a wali?[19] The shrine was built for him by Mohamed Haj 'Ali ben Youssef. And I also knew him because he was the grandfather of 'Abd al-Karim. I knew him when I was young because his son was married to my aunt and I would go to their home.[20]

Well, Si Ahmed Qmira. . . . We used to "push the pawn" [have a good time] with him. Si Ahmed Qmira when . . . The man was like an actor.

He could laugh or cry on cue! [laughter] Listen! If you wanted him to cry, he'd cry and if you wanted him to laugh, he'd laugh. Whatever you wanted . . . They say he got out [of his seat] and said, "Oh where are you, Sidi 'Ali Qsibi, witness of my disgrace. [more laughter] If you call me 'my son' I want it to happen between Korba and Beni 'Ashour." Now what's between Korba and Beni 'Ashour? It's no distance at all.

Malek: They run right together!

Between Korba and Beni 'Ashour, I want the right front tire to blow! [laughter] Both the tire and the tube.

Malek: What's that again?

He said, "Where are you, oh Sidi 'Ali Qsibi, witness of my disgrace? If you call me 'my son' I want it to happen between Korba and Beni 'A-shour!"

Malek: Ah!

Everyone swears that the minute they got through Korba and left the Korba bridge and got up the rise [the wheel] blew like a cannon shot. TOFF! [laughter] The right front wheel just as he had said.

Malek: Just as he said!

Si Ahmed Qmira fainted and they had to sprinkle his face with water. That Frenchman got up, "Move, move [pushing his way to Qmira]. [He's a] marabout, a marabout" ["marabout" is the French term for "wali."] and paid for [Qmira's] ride. And he is just a hashishi,[21] poor guy. He's said it for the heck of it—not thinking it would really happen. [laughter]

I like this story because Ahmed Qmira and Sidi 'Ali Qsibi so nicely balance each other—even in their similar names (three syllables, starting with "q," ending with a vowel). Qmira is a community member who is not to be taken seriously. He is just a "hashishi" who calls on Qsibi "for the heck of it." Qsibi is, at least in this story, a similarly non-serious character, a debatable wali. Together, however, they get the best of the colonialist, who, by simple virtue of his Frenchness, has ousted a Kelibian from his seat. Town strength is such that two foolish townspeople of dubious credentials can best one colon. In fact, the Frenchman in turn becomes foolish by jumping to the conclusion that Qsibi is a "marabout." The gesture he could have made for a displaced fellow traveler, paying Qmira's fare, he makes only after he becomes fearful.

Besides balancing town "saint" and town "sinner" to achieve a communal strength by tying together opposites, the story balances past and present—both in terms of landmarks and in terms of people. The shrine of Qsibi is still in town, by its presence representing at least two generations before that of the narrator, and the descendants of the builder of that shrine are in town as well—living reminders of the stories about Sidi 'Ali Qsibi. Korba and Beni 'Ashour still run together. So, temporally and spatially, from living townsmen who serve as repositories of knowledge and living "icons" that call to mind events of the past involving their ancestors, to constructed and natural landmarks that also serve as reminders and bear witness by their presence to the truth of an event, a spectrum of town resources is marshaled to surround a small insult and stifle it. Of course, the story is an example of a thousand small (and larger) humiliations that Hamdan and his generation lived through. By trivializing and joking about one incident he shows his young audience a way to deal with domination—colonial or otherwise. The dominator is made a figure of fun. The outrages to (relatively) powerless youth can be treated similarly. In this same session Hamdan later tells the story (4) of just such dominated youth—his unfair treatment at the hands of his older brother, who negates Hamdan's hard-earned day of fasting in his mistaken understanding of religious law. In that story Hamdan and his young audience gently laugh at the older brother. Laughter, in these stories, often becomes a catharsis for remembered anger and frustration.

Herein lies a basis of complicity for narrator and audience. The colonialists are gone, but the situation of domination by "foreign" powers such as representatives, like police, of the national government or older adults or "wealthy" westerners remains.

In one way the hikayah is not about change but simply about a technique or attitude that could be adapted to work as needed for a new generation. This technique helped Kelibians endure, even creatively combat, a potentially culturally degrading, destructive occupation and emerge fairly intact culturally. As Geertz notes for Moroccans, so for Kelibians: "Beyond the economic and political, the colonial confrontation was spiritual: a clash of selves. And in this part of the struggle, the colonized, not without cost and not without exception, triumphed: they remained, somewhat made over, themselves" (Geertz 1968: 64). What remains unsaid, of course, are the times when insults could not be stifled.

One triumph was preservation of important community (and Arab) values of generosity and hospitality—even toward the former oppressor. Now Kelibians voluntarily make room in buses for foreigners, "visitors." After all, westerners do not have the stamina of Kelibians, as I was told by Lella Nesria more than once in various stamina-requiring circumstances from all-night wedding celebrations to scrubbing floors or doing laundry by hand. And so a kind of whimsical resistance through narrative is one way that defeat of the colonizer did not become the almost Pyrrhic victory it became in the greater- and longer-suffering Algeria.

Finally, the story within its various pre- and post-colonial contexts demonstrates that Kelibian circumstances are better than they were and thus that change is possible and (can be, at least) very positive. In several ways, then, Hamdan's hikayah has community import that spans generations and ensures the interest of his young audience.

In this short story are all the genre markers mentioned above: the easy slide into (and out of) the story and the distribution of audience and narrator interaction throughout the whole story, the plethora of detail—even to the season of the year and the workings of the old bus system. Finally, as we will see, this story suggests others similar in one way or another.

The balancing of past and present does not stay confined within the narrative framework. When Hamdan describes the old colonial period bus-riding routine, he and his listeners are implicitly comparing that to what they know today. All of us were forever riding buses and we all knew that the system had changed. All seats were now the same price, leveling the old hierarchy. And foreigners were very often voluntarily made comfortable on the bus—seated, given food—offered the very sorts of hospitality expected of hosts in Tunisia, but forced upon reluctant hosts during the colonial period. The way the past is remembered (or transmitted) by community members like Si Hamdan, I submit, has a good deal to do with the ability to treat past and even present oppressors generously. Stories such as the above are part of the process of managing community and cultural self-respect so that a younger generation can emerge relatively unscarred—generous, secure, confident.

Also, stressing the community aspect, through the presence of both a pan-community jokester and a pan-community "religious" figure, narrators demonstrate the necessity of group cohesion over the *sauve qui peut* impulse of which many Kelibians were probably guilty at one time or another, but that is never mentioned, except obliquely.

Again, none of this significance of the hikayah can be transmitted unless the male narrator can make it clear, drawing upon the generic features at hand and his own rhetorical strategy, that the story is true in its essence and that its truth has implications for today and tomorrow.

Sometimes the proof that a hikayah is true is more covert, subtly embedded in the narrative. In the following hikayah Si Hamdan mentions a landmark, the barber shop where it was proved that Mohamed Zakrawi could not find lost hawks through consultation with his genie wife. Then he adds that its proprietor "Mohamed is still alive 'til now, the brother of Haj Hamda ben Hmid." (On the other hand, lack of living witnesses can be suspicious. "Humph," said Malek, referring to Si Tahar's story, not included in this collection, about drowning a genie in a goblet of chicken blood. "You can tell it's a lie when the witnesses mentioned in the story are all dead!")

(3) SI HAMDAN

Malek: Well, what's the story about that Zakrawi?

Yes, that Zakrawi, yeh Sidi [oh, Sir], who says, "I'm married to a genie," and he'll tell you all about it.[22] As I see it he was just looking out for himself . . . We had . . . Mustafa Sha'r, God have mercy on him. Do you know Monji Sha'r? Zah [his nickname]?

Malek: Yes, I know him.

His father died in '46 in this month. He [Zakrawi] was a reckless bastard. I mean, a devilish, wide-awake son of a gun not uh . . . And whoever lost things, say someone lost a pack animal, he'd go to 'Aam [paternal uncle] Mohamed Zakrawi, give him two francs in those days or a duru [.25 of a cent today] and he'd ask, "Where was the last place you saw it?" and this and that and he'd put his ear to the wall, thus, and you'd hear his words but wouldn't hear the other [person]. Like a telephone. [laughter]

Si Mustafa Sha'r . . . At hawk time [spring], they were always losing their hawks. Everyone was raising the hawks. Those who lost them and searched and searched with no luck would go to Uncle Mohamed Zakrawi. Where did they find Uncle Mohamed Zakrawi? [pauses, lights a cigarette] Sitting in a store of Khmais ben Hmid. That store at the time was where Mohamed Larnou barbered. Mohamed Larnou is still alive 'til now—the brother of Haj Hamda ben Hmid.

Sha'r said, "I'm going to 'push the pawn' today. Tonight I'll show his game to you, expose his lies." (That's who exposed him, see?) [Sha'r's] hawk was at the house perched on its perch. He went home and after he ate dinner, he went to Mohamed Zakrawi and went in. "Peace to you, where's Uncle Mohamed?" "Oh Uncle Mohamed today I lost my hawk. Here are two francs . . ." (At the time a package of cigarette tobacco . . . There were two brands of tobacco. There was a package whose cover was white that was a franc and a *surdi* [a small piece of money] and the blue pack was a franc and seven.)

"Where did you let him up?"

He said, "By our well," (called the Barley Well), "about a kilometer or more from here." He said, "The last time I saw it was above the fort." ([Sha'r] couldn't even see that far! Near the quarter of the town beneath the fort, he meant.)

That's all. [Zakrawi] leaned up against the wall and began mumbling. [laughter]

Sabra: What?

He started mumbling—talking to himself.

Malek: As if he were talking to genies.

Yeh. The guy [Sha'r] didn't even wait for results. He said, "Oh, Uncle Mohamed."

He said, "Yes?"

He said, "Why don't you look for another job. Stop this nonsense. My hawk, I swear, is at home." [laughter]

The subject of genies (*jnoun*) comes up often in these stories. Especially in the stories of Si Hamdan there will emerge the kind of ambivalent attitude toward them that can be seen in this story. Hamdan's point seems to be that genies exist, but not to make a profit for townspeople and not to interfere visibly in the lives of Kelibians. All his stories about genies, as will be shown (except, perhaps, 5), are stories of people falsely claiming a relationship with, or encounter with, or interference by, a genie. As I will argue in more detail later, genies appear so often in such contexts because attitudes about them are in the process of renegotiation in Kelibia. There is a growing agreement that a person who is visited by genies is most likely either superstitious and ignorant or a "reckless bastard," a "devilish, wide-awake son of a gun," like Zakrawi, taking advantage of the ignorant.

Carefully establishing the truth, and distancing it from falsity, is especially important in a story like this Zakrawi narrative, which contains characters (genies) that can so easily slip across the border between fact and a *One Thousand and One Nights* fiction. Thus we are even told how much Zakrawi was paid to find each hawk, and then everyday, nonexotic details such as the fact that he charged more to find one of them than the cost of either a blue or a white pack of tobacco. Notice the ambivalent attitude toward Zakrawi in this story—sneaking admiration for his audacity coupled with a warning to the young audience about the fate of popular musicians.

For, in his youth, Zakrawi had been a musician playing for popular audiences. As in many parts of the world, musicians are culturally suspect—powerful, dangerous but necessary. Zakrawi falls into the category of "town characters" to be elaborated on in Chapter 3. Musical skill is potentially a dangerous talent, one peripheral to community mores. Properly curtailed, it is positive and necessary to community well-being like extraordinary physical strength, sexual virility, or a lusty appetite. The culturally peripheral, whether a musician flirting with the underworld or a foreign visitor, must be attended to, even selectively appreciated, but carefully.

Again, to begin to achieve an interpretation like this, narrative-narrator-audience chronotopes of time and place must mesh as closely as possible, the audience and narrator should feel they can "stand in each others shoes." Hence, the existence of Zah (descendant of Mustafa Sha'r), of the still living Mohamed Larnou, of landmarks—the store where the unmasking took place, the Barley Well, the fort—and of other iconic representations of the story that all participants can know in common and that attest to the truth of the story are important pointers toward understanding the story in a certain way. As in the first story, reported dialogue also adds to the feeling that we are very close to the events that occurred.

Other means of proof are possible. In the following story about the dervish 'Abd ar-Rahman, Si Hamdan personally knew al-Jerbi, the man who saw the lion. Hamdan assumes his own veracity will not be questioned but must give his endorsement to al-Jerbi's story. "Now, that al-Jerbi I knew well," he emphasizes and adds, "Now, the man swears, an older man's binding oath." Sometimes, as in this example, a performer's grasp of an audience's criteria for proof is obvious. An "older man's oath" is more trustworthy, it would seem.

(4)   SI HAMDAN[23]

Time went by and another occasion arose. There were, they say, lots of taverns in the community.[24] He'd ['Abd ar-Rahman would] go and drink. Drink and not pay. And later he'd pay, not uh . . .

Well, there were [animals] promised [to a certain wali].

Malek: Um hum.

So a farmer, for example, a rancher, would say, "That bull calf there is going to be given to Sidi Hmid when it's grown."[25]

When ['Abd ar-Rahman] was completely broke, he'd go to the zawiyya and knock on the tomb and, they say, he would be told for example, "Go to such and such a person and tell him. . . ."

Malek: "Give me your promised animal."

"Tell him to give it to you." Understand? "Go to, for example, Malek and he'll give you such and such a calf that he promised to me." Yes, and it was specific. Pack animals are named.[26]

Malek: The Mottled One, for example.

Understand? He'd go and they'd immediately give it to him. He'd take it, sell it, and pay his debts.

Until . . . there was a person called Mohamed al-Jerbi who has been dead twenty years now. I knew him when he was old. He was an employee of the bartender. The bartender ordered him (an Italian bartender) instructed al-Jerbi, "Don't pour drinks for this person ['Abd ar-Rahman] if he comes in. He's a pest. I don't want to deal with him until he pays up his old debts."

In the afternoon he came in, around dusk, went up to al-Jerbi standing at the counter and said, "Pour."

Figure 3. "Well, there's Sidi Hmid here. . . . Here is the door to Sidi Hmid and there's a small cupola near it. Know what that is? . . . That is called Sidi S'eed."

He said, "Sir . . ."

He said, "Here, I'll pay. Come along with me." Well, there's Sidi Hmid here [gestures with his hand]. Here is the door to Sidi Hmid and there's a small cupola near it. Know what that is?

Malek: No.

That is called Sidi S'eed.[27]

Malek: Sidi S'eed?

Yeh, Sidi S'eed. He said, "Come along with me and I'll pay you."

They went out and along. (Now, that al-Jerbi I knew well. His father was . . . [to Malek] no, you don't know him. He lived in the neighborhood we were in yesterday. In that very alley.) No sooner had they opened the gate of Sidi Hmid and gone into the center of the graveyard there then . . . (Now the man swears, an older man's binding oath. He said, "I witnessed it with my own eyes—not at night or in a daydream.") All of a sudden there was a lion lying head raised, paws in front of him. ['Abd ar-Rahman] said, "Go over to him. He'll pay you." (He swears a binding oath, not . . .)

Malek: By that little cupola?

Yes. Sidi S'eed. In front of it—lying paws outstretched. He said, "He said to him, 'Go on. He'll pay you.' "

Malek: Was that Sidi Hmid?

No, that was Sidi S'eed. That little cupola there is called Sidi S'eed. The surname is S'eed but he transformed himself into a lion or who knows? That's all.[28]

After that ['Abd ar-Rahman] left and the next day, God willing, he came in and paid. Not the lion paid. No, 'Abd ar-Rahman. That's what I've heard about Sidi Hmid.

Now, 'Abd ar-Rahman, everyone knows, was a descendant of the wali Sidi Hmid. As such, he was a likely candidate for dervish status. Irresponsible community behavior, like drinking alcohol, could be excused as dervish behavior, and people would hesitate to cross him because he is (partly, as will be seen later) protected by his wali forebearer. Of course, the Italian does not know this, or does not believe it, so he inconsiderately puts al-Jerbi in some jeopardy. Al-Jerbi is stuck between the dictates of his boss and his fear of crossing 'Abd ar-Rahman. As it is, 'Abd ar-Rahman lets him off with a good scare. (Note that Sidi S'eed seems to be a watch-lion for Sidi Hmid. As will be shown in Chapter 3, story 11, there is a hierarchy to wali-ness, and Sidi Hmid does not need to become directly involved in this little incident.) As is foreshadowed at the beginning of the story, after the scare, 'Abd ar-Rahman collects from a rancher an animal promised to his ancestor, sells it, and pays his drinking debts, thus getting al-Jerbi off the hook.

A holy person is making it possible for a Kelibian to buy alcohol, prohibited by the Koran. Of course, according to an account by Uncle Gacem (story 15), the alcohol is transformed before 'Abd ar-Rahman drinks it; so he is also protected from sinning. In his story, Hamdan in no way implies that drinking is acceptable community behavior. In fact, though not stated in the story, listeners would assume that al-Jerbi, who works in the bar, is probably not Kelibian. His origin is the island of Jerba off southeastern Tunisia. It is so common for dry-goods stores to be run by Jerbians that another word for "grocer" is Jerbi. These Jerbians spend years away from their families, living simply and saving so that they can provide well for those families and retire to the island to live out their days in comfort. Thus, even a bartender is distanced from the community. And, in fact, al-Jerbi probably would not work in a bar in his town of origin.

Behind or juxtaposed to this story is the unverbalized knowledge that even though Europeans are gone, for the most part, from Kelibia, there are still bars in town and still Kelibians who have trouble with drink. There is no legitimizing of alcohol, forbidden by the Koran, or even opening up of discussion of the possibility of such, in this story. This is true despite the fact that most Kelibian males participating in these storytelling sessions have sampled alcohol on certain, controlled occasions (cf. Webber, forthcoming). Hamdan is simply, here and elsewhere, surveying a range of Kelibian inhabitants in a tolerant manner, and aberrant behavior by a dervish is more tolerated than similar behavior by others. And yet, if this story is combined with the account by Uncle Gacem, who himself, remember, went off to Algiers with a basket of opium, even the dervish has his alcohol transformed before he can drink up.

As is again illustrated in the discussion of the al-Jerbi story above, the clues to understanding a story such as this are not all contained within the structure and content of the story itself. One must also share cultural "facts" besides those explicated in the text, such as the religious prohibition of intoxicating drink, the colonizers' need for taverns and people to staff them, the implications of the name "Jerbi," and other stories about dervishes, especially about 'Abd ar-Rahman. Also, the young audience and Hamdan share the knowledge that Europeans expect one to "pay right away," whereas Kelibians are more patient, and this misunderstanding triggers the small crisis. Nevertheless, the performance or rhetorical strategies employed by Hamdan and the generic markers of the story and the event make room for more detailed understanding, enabling both narrator and audience to "be there" in the story world and thus perceive the relevance of the story for today—pride of place and past—in terms of dangerous but potent substances like liquor, or people like dervishes, or animals like lions that are controlled here by the story. (See Chapter 4 for development of this theme.)

Now, with Kelibians working abroad in unusual numbers compared to the past, especially in Europe, and sometimes working at jobs that would not be acceptable for them to do at home, and being exposed to unfamiliar and sometimes unpleasant cultural practices, the story has points of comparison between past and present that can emerge if the teller can manage to collapse time-past, time-present, and story time enough to make what happens in Kelibia relevant to other places as well. This latter strategy can be seen more clearly when hikayat-specific contents are looked at as a corpus in Chapter 3, but almost every story, if looked at carefully and culturally, points in some way, if only by implication, to cross-cultural contact, to a wider world. Here, the Italian and the Jerbian are the most indisputable examples. To begin to interweave the three dimensions of time, transition from conversation into story is minimal. The narrator, who has just told a story about Sidi Hmid and his descendant 'Abd ar-Rahman (story 4), indicates that after a time a new deed of the dervish came to the ears of the townspeople. All through the story present time and story time flirt as Malek interrupts to finish a line ("give me your promised animal"), to elaborate ("The Mottled One," for example), or to ask questions. If he does not step into the story, Hamdan steps out to ask him if he understands how it is that 'Abd ar-Rahman gets money, or if he knows what the small cupola is outside the zawiyya of Sidi Hmid. These community stories are as permeable as the community itself. Believability and a feeling for the currentness and relevance of the narrative are again sustained by the offer of proof from witnesses, the detailed account of the dedication of animals to walis, the quotes by the Italian, by al-Jerbi, and by 'Abd ar-Rahman, and the report of the exact position of the lion. These all serve to offset the strangeness of the event so that it can be believed. Again, the strangeness is just as important both aesthetically and culturally as the familiarity in the teller's rhetoric, just as process and change are the counterpoints to tradition.

If the subject is the narrator's personal experience, usually less proof by witnesses is required, but most stories put a great deal of effort into establishing the veracity of an occurrence by liberal use of place and time and actor specificity, and more background is provided. At various times, the sorts of cigarettes available and their price, the system of promising one of a group of farm animals to a holy man's shrine, and the old bus system are all described. This context is needed to situate the younger listeners by relating the past to the present, since, though different, there still is a bus system, almost all men still buy cigarettes, and animals are still promised to holy men. Not only does this practice make the story more understandable, but the tremendous overload of detail makes it more real (believable) to the listener and also implies an immediate relevance by equating it to common, present-day situations. For the same effect, terminology is also explained (for example, "The town deputy [now] is like the sheikh was [then]"). Explicitly or implicitly, in these stories we are frequently reminded of continuities or links between past and present.

Landmarks, both natural and human-made, are mentioned to add veracity: 'Alaya ben Kdous's house, the Zawiyya (shrine) of Sidi Hmid, the wasteland near Menzel Temime (a nearby town), and so on. Again, the mysterious or wonderful or special event is being anchored or brought down to earth by fixing it to a familiar location.

The audience is also provided with names of distant cities and towns that are relevant. Dates are usually included and, of course, the names of participants. People outside the town are most often only named by place of origin, religion, or ethnicity, for example, the Kerkanni, the American, the Jew, the Black. Closer to home, even nontown members begin to be named, for example, "that Stefan or whatever his name was. A colon." In these hikayat, anonymity achieves polarization not necessarily between protagonists and antagonists, but between people more or less attached to the community and its environs. In terms of veracity, names of outsiders are not important.

Any of the above means of establishing the veracity of stories can be presented more or less skillfully by the narrator. Of course, skill here refers to the use of stylistic performance devices that are appropriate for the performing of this particular genre. A device can be skillfully used in these cases to enrich the meaning of a single utterance so that it will economically and powerfully transmit an array of messages. Dates, for example, can compactly give a sense of the cultural or social scene rather than simply marking the time period. Notice the skill with which Si Hamdan begins his genie visitation story:

(5) SI HAMDAN
There's something else. [starts talking quietly] This happened to me not so long ago in '47. '47 . . . , Ramadhan . . . , and it came in the summer that year, in the hottest part of the summer. The time of prickly pears and figs and grapes and watermelon . . . in August.

I'd sit up, sit up at the Jebali store. We'd sit there in front of the store playing cards until there was half an hour or thirty-five minutes until the morning prayer and I'd go home. Now, my oldest brother, dead, God have mercy on him, held that if the drummer could no longer be heard in the town, the time to eat was over.[29] That was the religious law as he saw it. What did he do to me? He declared that I had broken the fast [for the new day].

When I went home . . . (At that time they were building, he and that brother of mine that's still living. They were sifting the sand getting it ready for the workmen who were coming the next day.) I found them sifting the sand, I put down the meal and sat down to eat.

He said, "Go away and sleep and get up in the morning and eat." [laughter]

Malek: "You're not fasting."

"You've broken the fast."

"But sir, it's still early, sir . . ." Nothing.

He said, "Forget it."

Well, what could I do? And I . . . (That entrance hall of ours, the door was in the middle and the rest [of the wall] was made into a storage place with lots of reeds, not small armloads but enough for four or three truckloads. The small ones [trucks].)[30]

[Brief interruption as a friend comes into the room]

Well, Si Malek, the reeds were stored, piled up as far as that T.V. antenna over there. All around the walls like this [points to an unfinished wall surface] above the reeds, well, the entrance hall wasn't smoothly finished, poles were sticking out from which hung, no offense, braided onions.[31] Braided, braided, braided thus and hung over the poles. And, nearing the end of Ramadhan when the night was dark . . . Well, even in summer the night is dark at the end of the month!

After I sat for a while and washed my mouth and smoked a cigarette . . . A sheepskin like that [points] and a piece of a straw mat, and a pillow—I brought them far from the door. (The door of the entrance hall was open.) Why did I make the bed there? So in the morning when the sun would rise over there [in front of the door] I'd still be in the shadows until it got higher.

I was still relaxing there, still not sleepy . . .

Malek: Still awake.

Still awake and I hear as if [rustling sound as he drops a full box of matches]. The next instant, BLUT, three or four bundles of reeds fall down. We didn't have any children around [to disarrange the bundles of reeds]. It occurred to me . . . did some kids come over from my uncle's house and play on them, sit on them and make them fall? Now it's dark, and I'm going to get up and put them in order? I'll get up in the morning and do it.

[In a very quiet voice] When I got up in the morning I found not one out of place. Now, between me and the door was as far as from here to my son Hafidh.

Daughter Sa'ida: Oh!

Understand me? Like from here to Hafidh my son and I hadn't gone to sleep and awoken in other words. I wasn't drowsy from sleep. No. I swear I was still awake.

Malek: Still awake.

Awake.

Malek: And from time to time you heard BLUT? [laughter]

As if a bundle had fallen. I could hear it perfectly well. Now, between me and the reeds . . . [gestures] like where Hafidh is. When I came in the door, as soon as I turned to the right I'd find the reeds—three or four meters between me and them. When I got up in the morning, not one piece was out of place.

Malek: Each was in place.

All stacked up.

Malek: Maybe your brother got up in the morning and replaced them or . . .

No, no man! I . . . The reeds . . . Since I worked with them, my brother when I came home with the reeds wouldn't lay a hand on them. I'd get up and stack them and he'd pass them on to me. Even in the dark if I wanted to get one I'd know where to find what I wanted. You see? [silence] Now, my brother is still alive and if I called him . . .

In a few words at the beginning of the story, we are told that people were fasting, observing Ramadhan, during the hottest part of the year. (Ramadhan, based on the Muslim lunar calendar, moves around the seasons and is much easier to endure during the colder months when the days are shorter and one gets less thirsty.) Tempers are likely to be short but rigidly controlled because a display of temper can also invalidate a fast. Without further elaboration, the audience can assume a great deal about the young Hamdan's state of mind as he tries "respectfully" to argue with his older brother, who has accused him of eating after daybreak. And then we have the exact time of year stated twice, once by the harvest, which is available then, and once by the western calendar. The former method conjures up rural images of the bountiful harvest of fruit that the region enjoys while the latter shows a facility with the precision of the solar calendar. In a very limited fashion we have here a display of community members' (ideal) mastery of both rural and urban speech modes and traditions.

The effectiveness of this orientation rests on Si Hamdan's manner of presentation as well. Taking advantage of his momentum from the previous story, he can start talking softly, and in doing so not only capture the interest of the audience in a way that out-shouting everyone cannot but evoke at the same time with his low speech and frequent pauses a feeling of mystery, hot, hot langourous summer time and the lassitude induced by Ramadhan. From there, too, he can build up to the confrontation with his brother, a confrontation in which, incidentally, the narrator places himself in the position of sharing with his younger audience a frustration with older authority.

Other ways used to establish time also serve to comment upon the story to come. In the story where Qmira is made to give up his bus seat to a French colon (story 2), we are told that it happened "maybe four or five years before independence." Before the confrontation even arises, we have been deftly prepared for a story involving a colonial incident. In the story of Zakrawi's unmasking (story 3), on the other hand, though we are not told exactly when it took place, we know the protagonist "died in forty-six in this month" (i.e., in December), which situates the event not later than 1946 while at the same time making the account more immediate and believable by its specificity and its cyclical connection to the present, "this month."

Si Hamdan dates another story (25) by indicating that it happened in the year Bourguiba (then a young leader of the Tunisian resistance to the French and at the time of this telling President of Tunisia) came to town and tomatoes were thrown at him. By dating the story in this manner, he indicates not only the year it occurred but, with no further comment, is able to convey why the newborn baby in the story was named Habib (Bourguiba's first name). He also manages to startle and amuse his young male audience by his audacity in mentioning Kelibia's early hostility to the President. "You are going to say that on the tape?!" his son interjects.

A review of these time orientation or verification techniques, points up another device used in the context of these stories. The style here might be called "inadvertent." For example, the narrator couches some observations in a naively appealing way, or the younger listener thinks he has. Because of the changes that have come about so rapidly in the town, young men expect to be and frequently are amused by older men's pronouncements, seeing them as endearingly naive or old-fashioned. The practice of identifying a season by its products (see above) is one of these. In these cases, the appeal of the phrasing would be diminished somewhat if the listener thought it were deliberate. Its persuasive power would be undercut. Perhaps some of these phrasings *are* naive, but most, I think, are more conscious choices in performance than the audience members or I realized at the time.

Finally, another device Si Hamdan uses while orienting his audience to actors, places and times is one that again helps break down audience—narrator—narrative distance. That is, he will ask a rhetorical question of a listener, thus stepping to an extent out of the story context. In the Jebali story (5) he asks, "Who's still alive from that group?" And, in the following story (6), "Who was it," he asks Malek, "who leaned over to [the cadi] (Muslim judge) and whispered to him?" It turns out it was Malek's grandfather, a former sheikh of the town. So not only does the narrator step *out* of the story, he incorporates the listener *into* it, giving him or her a stake in it by using a family connection. Not only do devices like this highlight the next clause, the answer, and involve the audience, but even without expectation of an answer, the question form retrieves audience attention and reemphasizes the listener-narrator alliance with its implied need for a response.

(6) SI HAMDAN
Well, to continue, there was, it is said, this Habib Jaluli was the administrator in Nabeul and he would come maybe once a week. Our souk used to be on Friday and he would come on Friday. Where did he govern?

Malek: Govern?

Rule on rights or disputes. In the second story of the house of 'Ali ben Kdous. The house of 'Alaya ben Kdous. Where that house is now. There. They say that one of the descendants of Sidi 'Alaya [that is, Sidi Hmid] named 'Abd ar-Rahman was always . . .

Malek: The son of Sidi 'Alaya that lives [goes on to describe where he lives].

No, no. I don't know that one.

Malek: Oh, a long time ago.

No. No. Not such a long time ago—probably during my time but I didn't know him. When Habib Jaluli came as cadi in 1930 he was still in his prime. They say . . . I don't know who filed a complaint against him ['Abd ar-Rahman]. He owed . . . He had come to you, say, and taken something of yours—borrowed from you, and promised to repay you shortly—not intending to gyp you or renege or whatever. When they brought him [to the cadi] he came in drunk. He always drank. He was always drunk.

Malek: Who? That Jaluli or who?

No, no man, this son of Sidi 'Alaya called Si 'Abd ar-Rahman! He went in, up the stairs, through the whatever . . . As soon as he went in they say [the cadi] smelled the odor [of alcohol]. He said, "Get him out of here," and started cursing him. "Can't you return people's money, you dog?" And cursed and humiliated him.

That's all. Who was it who leaned over to [the cadi] and whispered to him [that Abd ar-Rahman was a wali's descendant]? A.N. [Malek's grandfather].

Malek: A.N.?

Yeah. He said, "That one is someone to beware of. He's the son of a zawiyya." What more is there to say? He ['Abd ar-Rahman] cursed him [the cadi] and was still on his way out, they say, when he [the cadi] started moaning, God knows, and clutching his stomach and gave himself up for dead. Do you see the misfortune?

They left him like that and the doorman went to bring him ['Abd ar-Rahman] back. It was no good. "By God, I'll not return. It's too late," he told him. And so, sir, he went on his way.[32]

As can be seen from the examples above, there are many stylistically appropriate devices through which isnad or specific story details concerning actors, places, and times can be presented. And all of these devices can be used with varying degrees of skill. The revelation that the town sheikh (A.N.) is the one who warned the judge about the power of the dervish 'Abd ar-Rahman is an important device for several reasons. First, the specific names help tie down the veracity of the story. Second, Malek is in-volved; so, as mentioned earlier, past, present, and story time are telescoped, again illustrating, as William Faulkner is supposed to have said, that the past is not gone, it is not even past. Third, however, we see that it is the very proper, scholarly sheikh who is warning the judge about the power of a drunken dervish. So two men who are at the opposite ends of a community religious spectrum in every way are, in Si Hamdan's narra-tive, placed in a situation where they are constrasted to the outsider, the judge. This unlikely "alliance" is made more likely by Si Hamdan's reminder that the dervish is a descendant of a respectable community wali. The in-terweaving of generations is threefold: a wali and his dervish descendant (both found in the narrative), a sheikh and his grandson (one in the nar-rative and one, Malek, in the audience) and Si Hamdan and his sons (nar-rator and audience members). Thus, Hamdan uses a variety of literary devices and resources-on-hand, "found objects" to surround his historical narrative with the present. Notice that even in the midst of the narrative Malek is drawn into the past, and the past thereby is pulled into the pres-ent.

Other criteria used for verifying the reputation of the narrator as a truth-ful person, and the ability of the narrator to retell a story without "chang-ing" its essential details (in the audience's judgment), require knowledge external to the narration of one particular story. For example, the audience must already know, in the first instance, that a certain narrator has a repu-tation for truthfulness. In the second instance, the audience, or some mem-ber of it must have already heard the story from the same narrator.

Some performative devices mentioned above in connection with the verification markers of the stories: voice pitch or loudness, asking rhetori-cal questions, judicious use of pauses and giving an impression of guile-lessness can be used along with other generic markers in a narrative, or they can stand alone. Use of dialogue or special sets of vocabulary are two more examples of this sort of device. The dialogue, "actual" words of the actors in the stories, may appear story-wide and so unite the reality of the story with community reality and that of the storytelling event. The pres-ent tense of the dialogue forces the story out of the past and gives it im-mediacy, enhanced experiential impact.

Special vocabularies are adopted as rhetorical devices by individual nar-rators to varying degrees, and for purposes that may or may not have to do with verification. As discussed earlier, because classical Arabic is the repository of "correct" public Arabic, speakers can manipulate their private, colloquial speech with creativity and impunity. In many verbal art forms the townspeople shamelessly appropriate foreign words to mix and match them with colloquial Arabic. One man in town spices his stories with curses. Delighted young men will tell you that he "can't tell a story without swearing." Another, the barber, sweetens his stories with phrases from classical Arabic.[33] "Ah," volunteered Malek, appreciating this man's juxtaposition of the two language versions, "I think he might be the best storyteller!" Either technique creates a group intimacy. In the former case it is conspiratorial, achieved by clever use of "taboo" language (especially when an older man uses it with a younger), and in the latter it is intellectual and aesthetic, created by shared knowledge and appreciation of an intricate language, correctly used. The achievement of an in-group perspective, of course, contributes to the feeling of an aesthetically special community among those listening to the stories. Since community equals trust, it also serves to enhance the believability of the hikayat.

Performative devices are frequently reflexive as well—commenting on the male narrator, the narrative, or the narrating process. Not only do such devices comment upon the narrative, they also tend to break down audience—narrator—narrative and past—present boundaries by involving the listener in an exchange, even if it is only a nod of agreement. Or they separate the narrator from his story as if he, along with his audience, were simply an objective observer and evaluator of the story performance and story events. For example, in the following long narrative, the elderly Uncle Hmida deftly allies himself with Malek, his only and much younger audience member, by turning with him to comment on the protagonist's actions and thoughts (his own, as a child), as if he were simply a part of the audience watching that long-ago child. "I was young," he reminds him, thus ensuring that Malek judges the protagonist's comportment as that of a child, not an adult. In the same story he opens with, "Now we are going to talk about the story of Sidi 'Ali Qsibi." He is telling Malek, "This is such and such type of story and should be understood and judged accordingly" (Babcock 1977: 71). This comment is particularly striking in Uncle Hmida's story because Sidi 'Ali Qsibi isn't even mentioned in the story until it is more than half told.

(7) UNCLE HMIDA
Now we are going to talk about the story of Sidi 'Ali Qsibi. My father was crazy about falconry and I would be his lookout for the gendarmes.

(Because falconry was forbidden. The gendarmes would arrest falconers.) I'd ride on the donkey and he'd hunt.

Well, he had a wonderful falcon, I mean, any quail that flew up, it would catch. Honestly, not one would get away. And I got caught in the same mire. I became more obsessed with it than he. I was young. So when I saw such a good falcon . . . [My father] would sit with the falconers, sit on the ground, roll cigarettes, and feed the falcon a little. Well, I would beg him—tell him, "Give me the falcon to throw on a little quail." I knew the falcon was so good that anybody could catch something with it.

Malek: How old were you?

I was twelve.

Malek: Still young.

Yeah, young, trailing along after him. He'd tell me, "Not now. Wait 'til the falcon can hunt even better and I'll let you." (He was just keeping me hoping. He wasn't going to give me the falcon because father would say, "The falcon is something apart from my family." Anyway, a great obsession. He was keeping me hoping.)

I asked him three or four times on different occasions when the falconers would be gossiping together and the falcon next to him on his perch.[34] I'd say, "Give it to me, let me take a turn [hunting with it]." He'd say, "Let the falcon molt a little and learn to hunt better." I thought to myself, "Anyway, I'll wait 'til a night when he isn't [going to be] home and take it out secretly early in the morning. (Just like I'd see him get up at dawn.) I'll take it and go hunt with it."

Things went as planned. One night, the eve of the souk[35] . . . . (He was going to the souk to bring back that twine used [for making] the warp for the mats from Menzel Temime so we could line up the warp on the loom. We were weavers together, he and I.) I thought, "I won't find a night better than this. In the morning he's going to the souk on the donkey. He's going and I will take the falcon and go hunt with it and after, . . ." (It didn't occur to me that the falcon might get away. I just counted on my getting a quail with it or two, watch it, and go home with it.)

Yeah, well, [my father] on the eve before he was going to leave for the souk said, "Hmida!" I said, "Eh?" (Now he loved me a lot but he was strict, tough.) He said, "Well anyway, I'm going to the souk in Menzel Temime. You aren't to touch the falcon." (Now if he hadn't told me, I could have pretended I didn't know and done the deed and he would have forgiven me. But after he'd instructed me, there was no way out.) He told me, "Leave the falcon alone while I'm at the market. When I get home if we hear there are quail, I'll take you and we'll go hunting." I said O.K., but I was still determined to go.

Well, Sidi [sir, to Malek], he got up early and I saddled the donkey with him. The little moon was still shining, thus [points to the moon]. It was early morning. He started out to Menzel Temime, but the wind wasn't right for hunting and not right for quail. It was Corsican[36] [blowing in from the north] and so very strong that the grain crops were being bent to the ground. Not for hunting. No one would go out in it.

Well, he left and I took the little hawk[37] and the beating stick. (Mother still hadn't awakened. Because mother wouldn't have let me go.) I went out toward Sidi 'Ali Qsibi and kept going until the Jdud farm and came to the Sharif's farm and headed down [towards home]. I didn't flush out one quail and I wanted to raise even one to throw [the falcon] at so I could watch and then go home. Nothing doing! When I got near the door of the house—the house wasn't far away anymore, about four or five plow widths is all, not very far—the caraway was in front of me and I saw in the middle of the crop a little bird—a tiny bird. Under similar circumstances my father, if he was hunting and there weren't quail and he didn't have any feed would on his way home cast [the falcon] on a couple or three birds [to feed it].

I thought, "By God now here's a bird that has flown into the caraway and I'm about to go in. . . ." And I hadn't seen, flushed out any quail, "I'll just toss it on the bird. Let me catch even this. I'll see how [the falcon] catches it and go home with him." I never took into consideration that he might fly away from me at that time. (And the falcon was really strong and I had listened when the experienced falconers had said that if the falcon flew off from the owner that person must immediately follow it, track it with his eyes as it keeps on rising in the air, rising and rising until the instant when the sky swallows it. When it looks like a gnat, and then disappears, when it disappears, fix his position. We might say, he disappeared by an olive tree or near a certain farm. Watch where it disappears from your [sight], he'll come down there or to the right or the left somewhat, but in that general area. In that spot there, he'll come down.)

Well, I went up planning to shake the bird out. It had ducked into the middle of the caraway bush. I remembered where and started over, went like this with my stick [disturbed the plants] and it came out saw the falcon on my hand and returned! As soon as she popped up she returned because of the falcon on my hand. By that time I'd already thrown the falcon.

The falcon, when it left my hand, . . . (he'd been used to finding a quail but he didn't find anything). Like a shot he took off into the sky and the wind was Corsican so he'd drift to the back [inland]. He would go out of the town. Well, the falcon started to spiral and rise, to spiral and rise. . . . "God damn what had I done?! After I had almost gotten home! Oh God, what a deed!! What am I going to say to my father? If only he hadn't warned me!"

Anyway, at least I remembered listening to the falconers talk about how when they had lost a falcon, how they followed it with their eyes. Well, I'm watching it with the light in my eyes [demonstrates shielding his eyes from the sun] the light in my eyes and the falcon is circling and rising and [with] every turn he moves away five or six kilometers. Yes! so every turn he took he went higher and farther and I follow him, follow him, follow him, . . . until he was like a gnat, until the sky swallowed him.

When he went into the sky and I had been tracking him thus when the sky ate him up I fixed the position (as I had heard from the elders—people obsessed with falcons). I calculated it [to be] from the Hamura neighborhood, for example, from the Hamura neighborhood near the Zmirli farm. There was a kind of jujube tree there in the Zmirli farm and the Limam gully next to it belonging to the Samouds. It would come down in the Limam gully or in Zmirli's farm. He was maybe five or six kilometers behind the town.

I took up the stick and started running after him. But my idea was to go to the Zmirli farm to look there for signs of him. I ran directly to the Zmirli farm (and it was far, the Zmirli farm lies about six or seven kilometers [away]). I got to the Zmirli farm. (The point where I felt the falcon might have landed was there.) I went around the bushes and around the ben Majlif orchard, but those I asked had not seen a falcon. I couldn't hear jingling. [Falcons had little bells on their tails.] I went to the Kordoghlis' land looking everywhere. Nothing.

I ran to all the landmarks like that. When I got tired and the important places I was counting on for finding the falcon were exhausted, I no longer knew where [it could be]. I was out of control and thinking about my father, who was about to come home. It was mid-afternoon and the sun had gotten hot. I ran this way and that way. I asked people. I asked workers. No one said he'd seen it. Not a one. It was getting hotter. My legs were scratched. My clothes were torn . . . "I'd better go home. [But] what would I tell my father? If only he hadn't ordered me. Damn that act [of mine]." (And my father was a little strict and he really loved the falcon so.)

I was heading home and desolate. Going home I passed Sidi 'Abdallah Taherti there—started going down and came to those olive trees of Qsibi until I came up to [the zawiyya of] Sidi 'Ali Qsibi and Sidi 'Ali Qsibi faced east and the door on the east side was open. It crossed my mind to go into Sidi 'Ali Qsibi. I just went in to take a look. Now, I knew Sidi 'Ali Qsibi was a holy man.

I went into Sidi 'Ali Qsibi and came up behind the tomb like this facing the grave marker. [gestures] Here [to Malek], I'll show you. [gets up and shows him how he stood] There now, the marker was in front of me. I said to him, "Oh Sidi 'Ali Qsibi, I've come to you and if you're sleeping, get up," and I pounded the marker once. "Get up, Sidi 'Ali Qsibi, and listen to me. I want to tell you something." (Well, I was young. See what I had in mind?) "If you're asleep, wake up, and if you're awake, listen to what I'm going to say. I, in any case, I can't do anything for you [but] I'll weave you two rush mats and bring them and lay them out in your midst and here is *al-fatiha* for you."[38] If you really think you are Sidi 'Ali Qsibi and you claim, 'I am Sidi 'Ali Qsibi, a holy righteous man,' well [when] I go from here and go into the orchard of Mohamed

Kalash that has date palms in it, I'll get into the olive trees and I'll find my falcon perched there. I'll take the falcon and go home without having to search at all I promise I'll make you two floor mats and bring them and spread them in your midst, and here is al-fatiha ("Praise to God on high . . .").

I went out of the dome and cutting across country I went along and came to that orchard of Mohamed Kalash that I had told you about. There were olive trees there. I went in and followed the little path by the cactus fence and the planted area. I was going along the path thus. (Now, I was out of my mind, "What will I tell my father, and father is going to come any time now.") I arrived and went into the middle of the olive trees. I ran into the leash. It hit me here [gestures to his face], thus. The leash of the falcon!!! I raised my eyes and found the falcon perched rubbing his head on his shoulders, ruffling his wing feathers, opening his wings and going like this [demonstrates] . . . puffing himself up. He didn't run away from me, didn't run from me. He wasn't stuck, wasn't tied up. Just perched and the leash swinging down and that's it. I went like this to the leash [pulled on it] and grabbed him and started home, as happy as if I'd found the Prophet, and I hugged it with happiness— safe from the wrath of my father.

What can I say, I got to the house, went in and found mother at the door. "My son, my son, why did you take the falcon?" I said, "Oh mother please don't tell father. See, I took it and wanted to watch it with a bird, throw it on a little one, but there weren't any. Well, I came home with it, is all." (I didn't tell her anything except, "Please don't tell father.")

"Come on get in here—don't do that anymore. Your father would have a fit."

Well, I perched the falcon and paced back and forth in the entrance hall. Mother got down [from the stove] cous-cous made with *droa*[39] and put out the dinner. She put my father's dinner to one side and put mine out. "Come on and eat." I said, "No, I'm not eating. I'm waiting for father." Father arrived, he arrived and I went out to meet him, helped him unload the donkey baskets, tied up the donkey, and he went into the house. Mother set out the low table, she put out a pottery dish of cous-cous made from droa' (it's like I'm seeing it all now) and pumpkins and fava beans. . . .

He sat down there and she put the low table before him. And I went there [gestures] a little distance from him in the middle of the room and sat. I decided not to tell him until he had eaten. Maybe he'd get mad and not eat. Well, he sat down and ate. After he had finished (I was peeking over at him) . . . After he had finished dinner he pulled out the tobacco pouch and started to roll a cigarette. I said, "Oh father!" He said, "Eh?" I said, "I'm going to tell you a little something. Don't get mad at me." [He tells him the story and they make the mats for Sidi 'Ali Qsibi.]

Like Si Hamdan, Uncle Hmida here creates a bond between himself and his audience (only Malek, in this instance, although many people in town know this story), but his technique is quite different. While Hamdan shows his disquiet only outwardly, first by his protest over his brother's ruling, ". . . but sir!", and the account of his unquiet night, his internal dialogue only denies that anything is wrong, "did some kids come over . . . ?" Hmida narrows the distance between us and his twelve-year-old self by drawing us little by little right into that agitated mind. He turns from reflexive comments, "He was keeping me hoping," to more direct encounters with the youthful mind, "I thought to myself . . . ," to, as the crisis hits, an unmediated staccato of thoughts, "God damn what had I done?! After I had almost gotten home! Oh God, what a deed!! What am I going to say to my father? If only he hadn't warned me!"

In the midst of panic, however, the youth remembers what he has learned from his elders and step by step takes us through the tracking procedure. When he does all he can—looks everywhere, asks everyone—he finds and tries Sidi 'Ali Qsibi, and rather amatuerishly, as he lets us know ("Well, I was young . . ."), he asks his help. Skillfully, drawing upon a range of generic and performance possibilities, including reflexivity, Hmida displays and invites his listeners to appreciate the positive aspects of community—a warm father-son relationship in which they work and hunt together, a youth's knowledge of the geography of his community and of the people in it, his ability to listen and learn from the talk of his elders and to take constructive action in the face of panic, and the resource of walis to fall back on. Even the young Hmida's controlled defiance is part of the community ethic and aesthetic. Then and now is evoked as Hmida describes the evening meal. "It's like I'm seeing it all now," he reflects.

All of this does not lead to any indication that the young Hmida should not have "borrowed" his father's hawk. In fact, a good deal of the reflexivity in the narrative is directed toward justifying his deed. His father promised to let him try, he knew he was simply putting him off, and so on. "He was keeping me hoping," he repeats twice. All of the positive, "idyllic" aspects of the story, even the happy ending, surround and mediate the disruptive element, that is, a prepubescent boy's violation, direct violation ("If he hadn't told me, I could have pretended I didn't know . . .") of his father's instructions. At no time is there a hint, except for the panicked boy's "Damn that act," in the midst of the crisis, that he has done wrong, though he is fearful of his father's wrath. From Hamdan's point of view as an old man, even for a youth obedience is not always preferable to disobedience. He does not say if his father lets him go hawking after that experience, but acts of defiance of authority, if done with finesse, even if they do not lead to change, are part of Kelibian strength. (See story 21 as well.) A partly domesticated hawk from the north (Europe) and a partly untamed boy on the threshold of manhood combine to shake up the ordinary, to enlarge life's possibilities—a behavior celebrated by the story and rewarded by a town wali. All through the narrative one must ask what the story is about. It certainly is not about a boy who does wrong and learns his lesson. Is it really about Sidi 'Ali Qsibi's benevolence when he does not even enter the story for so long? No, I argue that it is a story about becoming and being a man in Kelibia and the calculated risk-taking that that sometimes entails, the making of a judgment contrary to that of others, including the older generation. When the hawk is found through the *barakah* (blessing) of the wali, is not that endorsement of the appropriateness of the original act within the Kelibian context? Kelibia, carrying on so often a discourse counter to that of outside powers, cannot help but nurture that "countercultural" spark, carefully framed, of course, within its own youth. Ironically, the community's continued maintenance as a viable culture depended, and may again depend, on it.

Some reflexive devices comment on the actions or thoughts of specific actors. For example, they often appear next to the deed of an actor to ensure that the audience shares the narrator's interpretation of the deed and the actor. When Si Hamdan tells a story about a man who ran for asylum to a holy man's tomb, running away from the authorities, he emphasizes that the man was not really a criminal. "[He] owed money, government taxes, or something. He hadn't killed someone or anything." Neither was a descendant of a holy man who was being put upon by the authorities a true villain. "He owed. . . . He had come to you, say, and taken something of yours, borrowed from you, and promised to repay you shortly, not intending to gyp you or renege or whatever." Numerous examples of this sort of simultaneous interpretation of the text can be found—often serving as well to delay the progression of the text and thus heighten suspense. In these Tunisian hikayat, opening and closing markers are often conspicuous by their vagueness. Tunisian fictional stories, by contrast, have very definite formulaic introductions and closings. In hikayat, though, where the narrator is trying to meld his or her story with reality, it is sometimes difficult to decide where a story begins and ends. Where does the discussion about the story actually stop and the story start? As in Emanuel Schegloff's and Harvey Sacks's discussion of telephone conversations (Schegloff and Sacks 1973), closing comments are often overridden and story details amplified, discussed, or explored. In the following story the indefiniteness of story boundaries is especially evident:

(8) SI HAMDAN
[General talk—everyone at once]
Should we make some tea?

Malek: There is still some.

[Si Hamdan starts talking loudly, then gradually lowers his voice as he dominates the conversation and other people gradually stop talking.]

Well, the group that spent the evenings at our shop was also an older group and the Sidi 'Ali Qsibi terrain was frightening.

Malek: Was what?

Frightening. They were afraid of it. [It was "haunted"—like, for example, a cemetery.]

And money was dear. People didn't used to have money and especially at that time [of year] in the winter. You'd find everyone just sitting round. They didn't [have] work. Nothing.

Well, among the group who "pushed the pawn" together, "Look, who will go now to Sidi 'Ali Qsibi and pound in, God forbid, a peg [the kind

used to tether animals—as proof he had actually gone] and come back?"
(He'd come back, and we'd all go together, take the lantern and go together to see. If he put the stake where we told him, he would get a
duru, as we would say.) [A duru is now worth about .25 cent.]

Malek: A duru was a big thing?

Yes, a duru would buy two sheep or more.

[Digression about how much coffee cost in those days, and the kinds of
money that circulated.]

Hafidh: Go on [to his father].

Well, a guy called Mohamed Qurbusli started off. (He was during my
time.)

Malek: You knew him?

I knew him—the father of Jamal who lives on the hill. That's all. The
man was wearing a heavy cloak. He was apprehensive, scared to death.
[low laughter] When he got there, he knelt down. The cloak. . . . He went
to hammer, and he hammered his cloak [to the ground]! [laughter] And
the group found him. They had been following him, and if they hadn't
been, he would have died—died of fright. [laughter]

Malek: Did he yell?

Yell! What do you think? The man was struggling. He thought, he
thought he was going to die!

Malek: "They've got me! They've got me!"

If [his friends] hadn't been with him—ready quickly with "I'm so and
so," "I'm so and so," and "My son, don't be afraid," by God, he would
either have gone crazy or died fom shock.[40]

Now I'm going to tell you something else. . . .

As can be seen, the audience is involved at the beginning of the story,
only gradually relinquishes the floor to the narrator, and gradually joins in
again as the story nears conclusion. In between times, it is not too difficult
to interrupt, either. Right in the middle of the story Malek asks about the
value of a duru in those days and Si Hamdan joins in a discussion of the

former buying power of that coin. In fact, it is another member of the audience, Hafidh, who calls an end to this discussion and asks his father to "go on."

Amid all the commentary coming after the resolution of the story, there is no definite concluding phrase. The story just winds down, until the author picks up momentum again, introducing the next story with "Now I'm going to tell you something else," which effectively ends the story by starting the next one. The final remarks are not offhand on the part of Si Hamdan, though. Sensing that the audience only grasped the humor of the account and not the communal significance of the fact that friends were there to back Qurbusli up, he reiterates the importance of that point by using two devices. First, he switches to dialogue to repeat what was actually said to Qurbusli, and second, he reemphasizes strongly that if his friends had not been there Qurbusli would have gone crazy or died. Frequently, then, as more stories are told and audience and narrator become more animated, as in this case, story boundaries become less and less clear.

In contrast to the diffuse ending above, concluding remarks in other stories are so short and so rapidly fired off that one fails to grasp them at all except, in retrospect, as a bridge to another story. Si Hamdan observes at the end of one story, "And from then on he could no longer walk right." Immediately he slips into another story, "Yeah, there was another person from the descendants of Sidi 'Alaya." Then he finishes that story with a quick, "And so, sir, he went on his way," and at once goes on to say, "Time went by, and another occasion arose." In these cases, contrary to what might be expected in storytelling, the narrator does not relinquish the floor after one story. Rather than give up his turn, he hardly pauses before he launches into another story. It isn't until Si Hamdan says, "And that's what I know about Sidi Hmid," after completing a series of three stories that Hafidh, his son, asks for a story: "And the story of Ahmed Qmira?" Interruptions occur everywhere in this series of stories except at the conclusion of each. It is as if the narrator has deliberately contrived a very short, abrupt conclusion for each after the resolution of the plot so she or he can finish and take off on another story that has come to mind. Thus, the technique seems to be used to avoid interruption at a place where the audience would be most likely to intrude. This rather personal device can be used effectively if the narrator is attempting to stress similarities of structure or content across a series of hikayat.

Another genre marker of the hikayat is their interdependency. The precise meaning of a performed story depends not only on conversational context but on past and future stories in the same storytelling event. The townspeople say, "One story suggests another": the telling of one story provides inspiration and brings to mind other stories thematically similar to the first. Almost every storytelling event I recorded produced stories that were (up to a certain saturation point) progressively more inspired, that is, tended to draw more heavily and effectively upon stylistic resources, to be more intensely performed (Bauman 1977b: 24), and positive audience feedback visibly energized the speaker.

It is not surprising that a series of stories would address itself to a single subject or theme, and it is of interest to observers from outside of the culture to see which range of subjects is considered relevant to a certain series and how performers connect the stories stylistically. For example, the day that we heard the story in which Sidi Hmid had caused a man to go lame (see Appendix) the subject for some time had been miracles of local holy men, and Malek had specifically asked about Sidi Hmid. Si Hamdan had told a second story in which Sidi Hmid had wreaked revenge on an unjust district judge (story 6) and a third (story 4) in which the holy man took the form of a lion in order to protect a rather reprobate descendant of his. Si Hamdan ended that section by concluding, "That's what I've heard about Sidi Hmid." His son says, "And the story about Ahmed Qmira?" At which point Si Hamdan indicates that the story is not appropriate here, and why. "No, that's like a joke. It was just a coincidence." But then after showing his awareness of the difference, he allows himself to be persuaded to tell the story (2). Afterwards he returns again to more serious events and tells a story where Sidi Maouia, not Sidi Hmid, was the protector. Again, he draws to conclusion that series of stories: "I know lots of similar stories, but they haven't been verified."

Here we have an instance where Hamdan gently brings up the notion that Sidi 'Ali Qsibi is not a true wali, something he might not bring up with an older audience. Who are or are not considered walis does change over time, but this subject is a more delicate item of negotiation than, say, the presence of genies in town (see stories 3 and 9). In fact, I never heard anyone say that he or she personally rejected the claim of other community members that such and such a deceased person was not a wali. What I did hear people say was, "They say he isn't a wali anymore," or, like Si Hamdan, "Who knows if he is or isn't a wali?" In this story, Hamdan is presenting us with a very different point of view about Sidi 'Ali Qsibi than

that expressed by Si Hmida. The same youths listen to both stories but the
narrators do not meet. So possible change in the status of one wali is not
even debated in carefully couched fact-to-fact stories. This situation underscores sharply the observation by Richard Bauman that

considerations of truth and belief will vary and be subject to negotiation within
communities and storytelling situations. This would suggest that if we are interested in the place of narrative in social life, it is the dynamics of variability and
negotiation that we should investigate; the issue should be tranformed from a ty-
pological comparative one to an ethnographic one. (Bauman 1986: 11).

In this case, the two hikayat cannot be juxtaposed without one of them
coming to be understood at least slightly differently from the way its narrator intended.

Series of stories tend not only to stay with the same subject matter but
to comment in the same way about the subject at hand. Four out of five
stories in the series above dealt with the humiliating or unfair treatment of
a townsman by an outsider or person of power and the subsequent inter-
vention of the Kelibian wali, Sidi Hmid. Thus, Hafidh's requested story
about another (questionable) holy man was deemed inappropriate to the
series not because the Frenchman did not get his comeuppance—he did—
but because, in the opinion of the narrator, the incident had nothing to do
with Qmira's call to Sidi Qsibi but was strictly an amusing coincidence.

Emphasis on a certain point by the narrator does not seem to come so
much from repetition within one of these stories (considered by many ana-
lysts to be characteristic of verbal stories since they cannot be reread like
written ones) as from use of a string of stories that can make that same
point—being similar not only in content but in how the content should be
interpreted in light of other stories in the series or in a corpus. "One story
suggests another," but in addition, while succeeding stories are generated
by previous ones, they also reinterpret what has gone before. Succeeding
stories may cause previously related events in a storytelling session to be
freshly perceived and reinforced, or to be interpreted differently.

Whereas a series may be simply an elaboration or an opening up or ex-
pansion of one person's philosophy of personal and community life, if
two or more people are narrating (or at least commenting), it may also
become a "discussion" through narration. By this process the focus of an
exchange emerges, and an aspect of social or cultural reality has been analyzed and perhaps altered as well.

For example, when Si Hamdan starts telling stories about genies, at one point in his session, the stories, although told seriously, are met with skepticism and even laughter. His son Hafidh asks for another genie story from an older visitor present, 'Abd el-Karim ben Youssef. (Hafidh has obviously heard this story before and finds it funny.) In fact, ben Youssef seems to tell his story in order to be funny, in the pseudo-naive manner we discussed above (compare above, p. 98). At one level, the younger members of the audience have to believe that he is serious, or the story is not funny. But, simultaneously, they have to know they have the license to laugh without hurting the narrator's feelings. So to suit the purposes of both narrator and audience, the ostensible reason for the laughter is the recollection by ben Youssef of his agitation at the time of the story rather than the belief per se that the man had been attacked. After all, no harm was done to him. In fact, though, the younger listeners are laughing because, on that sunny afternoon of storytelling, surrounded by friends and family, they do not believe in genies and are amused by ben Youssef's assumed naiveté. Looking at the story from the narrator's side, we should ask whether ben Youssef is interested in establishing the truth of his story. Notice that he claims no witnesses, no dates—only a landmark (a house with which some of the participants are familiar) and details of his preparation for sleep. In fact, he emphasizes that he was alone in the house, which could indicate that there was no one around who might be playing a trick on him, but also that there was no one around to corroborate his story.

(9) SI BEN YOUSSEF
Hafidh: Now 'Abd el-Karim has a little story.

[Jumble of talk, laughter, as people urge him to tell his story]

Malek: [to 'Abd el-Karim ben Youssef] You mean it happened to you, yourself?

Sa'ida: Oh! That one about the genies when you were in your house!

That one?

Si Hamdan: Ah. Ah.

This is it. There was a night when I was alone in the house. When I got home I wasn't apprehensive or afraid or anything. Nothing. That's all.

Si Hamdan: As usual.

As usual. I went to my room, lay down, and pulled the covers up to my face and commended myself to God against the devil and read a little, for example, from the Koran and slept.

Well, when I went to sleep, no one was home, as I said, I was alone with my head. All of a sudden the covers over my head went like this. [gestures] They were pulled off my head and down around my feet. [laughter] When that happened, I immediately sat up and turned toward the middle of the room and what did I see but two apparitions [silhouettes], grey things this size [short] in the middle of the room. When I caught sight of them, without knowing what I was doing at the time [two unintelligible sentences] . . . As if, God forbid, nothing, as if I were naked. As if I no longer had control over myself. I was so afraid. I went to them and asked, "Tonight, what are you going to do to me tonight?" [laughter] [But] when I dashed for the door in fright, they, those apparitions, were watching. I could feel them at my side and then they ran back into the middle of the room.

When they went into the middle of the room, I pulled on the door. I pulled on the door and opened it. What did they do but start pulling on my clothes, pulling on my clothes. One pulled from here and another pulled over here and another pulled from there. And the world was flying around my ears. All you could hear, God knows, was a din. [laughter]

That's all. I went outside with one pulling from here, another from here, and another yelling over here.

Back in the courtyard I had felt like I was being eaten up on all sides until I got out. We had two thick entrance halls, rough finished like an
. . .

Malek: Arab?

Arab house. That's all. There, a darbouka [ceramic drum] had started playing [laughter] and there was clapping and something pulling on my clothes, by God.

Sabra/Malek: Were you afraid?

Afraid? I no longer knew anything. They pulled my hair so I almost fell on my face. I moved my legs only in desperation, and didn't know what I was doing. I felt like my *sheshia* [skullcap] was flying until I got out the door of the house. And I, what can I tell you? The darbouka and clapping and ululating and the world was upside down. A party was [taking place] in the house. I pulled the outside door and they pulled on me by my clothes—pulled and pulled. In conclusion, by God, when I got outside I felt like I was dead—like I'd come out dead from the house. I never in the world saw such a thing.

[Discussion of where this house is located]

Sabra: Did you go back?

Are you kidding? [laughter]

After ben Youssef's more frivolous performance, Si Hamdan does not think of stories to bolster his previous assertions about people encountering genies but chooses to recount two stories where people mistakenly thought they were being visited by genies and became sick with fright. And here he comes much closer than usual to lecturing his audience. He knows that young men will play pranks to give supernatural frights to older ones. But in his examples, although he points out that older people are more susceptible—"the group that spent the evenings at our shop was also an older group and the Sidi 'Ali Qsibi terrain was frightening"—he does not go so far as to show younger people victimizing older ones. Also, he seems to be admitting that some stories of genie visitations are the result of misunderstandings or pranks and, perhaps, implies that ben Youssef may indeed have been tricked.

Ben Youssef replies with another story in which he, as a child, and his aunt were grabbed away fom his uncle by a type of genie. Again, though he is specific about times and places in the account, he makes no effort to produce witnesses to the story's validity. The point of this story is his uncle's lack of courage in the face of his absolute belief that the attack on his wife and nephew was supernatural. Also, ben Youssef emphasizes his own youth, the onset of night, and their passing by a frightening, wild, genie-infested area. The audience can easily see that all three of the actors were susceptible to believing that they might have a supernatural encounter.

Si Hamdan then capitulates, in a sense, by telling a detailed, funny (rather than serious) story about a young country boy who was stealing grain from his father's underground seed cache after dark. The cache was near the grave of Sidi Bou Bakkir. A townsman, a friend of the boy's, follows him and frightens him by telling him that he is "Bou Bakkir." The young man runs away so fast they say he ran "right out of his shoes." Here, Si Hamdan offers no more warnings against causing undue fright, warnings that had been ignored by his audience in the previous two stories in favor of the humorous side of the stories. Si Hamdan even goes so far as to imply that supernatural visitations, even of saints or holy men (whom we have seen are taken far more seriously than genies), can be imaginary, conjured up in one's mind by a dark night, a guilty conscience, and a mischievous friend.

In Tunisia most people avoid passionate arguments, seeking to express and settle differences more obligingly. The story sequences in storytelling events are a feature that can be used for a group to explore together a controversial subject (such as attitudes toward the supernatural) that might cause ill feeling between individuals or generations. The basis of agreement after this exchange between the two storytellers and the listeners seems to be that at least some supposedly supernatural events result from trickery or misunderstanding. Also, there seems to be agreement that genies are inconvenient and mischievous rather than harmful (not a general town belief). The old men in the town have another compromise theory about genies: the old sultan of the genies has died, they say, and the new sultana, his daughter, has forbidden her genie subjects, under threat of punishment, to appear to human beings. So, of course, only the old timers have ever seen genies.

The town's hikayat, by drawing on incidents from the community past, have the potential to comment powerfully on current town situations and to illustrate obliquely areas in which community consensus on a certain subject has changed or is in flux. Some stories such as 8 do not achieve this goal. The graveyard story was actually unsuccessful to a degree insofar as the audience refused, at least overtly, to take it as seriously as it was intended. Whether or not the narrator is able to exploit the hikayah's potential for comment and thus persuade others to his (narrated) perspective(s) depends on how well he has developed his storytelling talents as well as on how divergent audience and raconteur's views on the supernatural are: what is important is to set the story firmly in a community context and to use referential or reflexive, personal or standard, performative devices. The devices must of course be appropriate for their community, situational, and generic contexts. The result, in terms of the hikayah-telling situation discussed in this chapter is a means for older men and younger men to draw upon stories of the community past to both juxtapose past and present and collapse past into present in order to talk about change and tradition and the process of interweaving and balancing the two for the present and future good of the community members.

Notes

1. Use of the terms "structure" and "structuring" in this chapter is intended to remind the reader throughout that it is not only the individual pieces of content and context that determine the meaning of a storytelling event but the systemic interrelationships among texts (subject matter, content), texture (performance devices), and context (setting, participants). A structural relationship also implies one that is not necessarily a linear or forward-moving, cause-effect relationship. Movement toward an emerging understanding can take place in any direction at any, or the same, time. "Structuring" implies here manipulation of the event (negotiation of reality) by the participants whereas "structure" focuses on the given—structurings of the past become culture (cf. Mehan and Wood 1975: 192).

2. "Performance" is used here to indicate a type of verbal communication that "calls forth special attention to and heightened awareness of the act of expression and gives license to the audience to regard the act of expression and the performer with special intensity. . . . The implication of such a concept for a theory of verbal art is this: it is no longer necessary to begin with artful texts, identified on independent formal grounds and then reinjected into situations of use, in order to conceptualize verbal art in communicative terms" (Bauman 1977b: 11).

3. Much of this chapter has to do with the aesthetics of hikayah-telling—proper setting, proper audience, proper delivery, response, and content. During my years in Kelibia, I did not attempt to elicit directly a unified emic aesthetic theory for the hikayah or other verbal art forms. I felt and feel that such a question popped into a conversation would inspire as fragmented and contrived an answer in Kelibia as in an American setting. I was, however, grateful when unsolicited aesthetic evaluations were offered and have incorporated many of them as appropriate.

4. Kelibians use the word "garage" to mean any garage-like structure (i.e. street level, without a fixed wall on the street side). The space is not usually used to store a car or truck, but as a commercial establishment in which to sell various food products or construction materials.

5. Qaddir is the term used for the proper respect shown to an older man by a younger one. For example, a man will not curse or smoke or make sexual jokes or allusions in front of his father or older brother or other older men. If, on the other hand, the older man is willing to waive qaddir, he indicates his willingness by

swearing, joking, or smoking. This is noticed and appreciated by the younger man, but does not mean that he can then do the same.

6. Margaret Mills (personal communication) raises the issue of the degrees of transiency/durability of topics, stories, and so on. I do not systematically address this question but do include some indicators to endurability that might be useful.

7. Of course, men visit with family as well, especially on holidays. Women have ample opportunity to visit with nonfamily at large gatherings (weddings, birth celebrations, celebrations at shrines), at the homes of neighbors, at the baths, or during early morning visits to the tombs of parents, siblings, children, in the graveyards. They can meet possible marriage partners for their sons that way and keep abreast of community-wide news. In these contexts they might bring home gossip (the unspoken message in the repeated tale often seems to be that our family does not behave like this), but difficult family matters or the gaucheness of certain neighbors should not be broached in these wider settings.

8. Hikayat are not told only in this context. Men also tell hikayat to their peers (or to older men or to their own children). Some hikayat are told by women. In general, though, men seem to tell more hikayat whereas women tell either khurafat or little family vignettes couched in terms of small incidents or general observations with specific examples from their own pasts (the consistent kindness of Lella Nesria's now deceased mother-in-law, the time little Malek broke his arm while teasing a chicken), usually closely tied to the present situation as an example, an object lesson, or a way to please or tease a member of the audience. Men also do this. I was on a bus once when it happened that the bus driver learned that a young man passenger was the son of a man with whom he had been very close when he himself was a young man. He proceeded to enrich the young man's appreciation of his father by giving a running account of their earlier adventures. These sorts of reminiscences seem to depend for effect more than hikayat in knowing the characters involved. However, genre lines here can be blurred. Women also tend to recite or sing folk poetry and/or sing popular songs.

Women in other cultures are also considered less likely to tell these stories than men (Tallman 1975b; Cothran 1972). Tallman and Cothran opine that the nature of men's tasks (which in agricultural communities encounter slack periods during the year) has led to this situation. One could also postulate that Kelibian women have traditionally been confined to the home and so have been afforded a limited range of adventures to relate. (But see story 14 in Chapter 3.) Thus, they are more inclined to tell imaginative stories, khurafat. One could argue that, as women are thrust more into the world, through school, outside occupations, and changing mores, they, like men, will find that hikayat suit their performative, communicative purposes. I heard, for example, two amusing hikayat from women, told spontaneously when only women were visiting together. Both concerned personal experiences in which the woman goes outside the home, in one case with her son to visit a doctor in Tunis and, in the other, alone, to sell a piece of gold jewelry. The stories were humorous accounts of the manner in which the women use men's stereotypes of their naiveté and unworldliness to outwit them (Webber 1985).

9. Typically, the after-lunch rest period lasts until the mid-afternoon call to prayer—especially in the summertime. Women take this time to change clothes and go visiting or receive visitors if other obligations or domestic problems do not intervene. Or it may be a time simply to relax with other, especially female, family members. Evening work then—supper preparation, washing up, distributing bedding and making up beds—might last from three-thirty or four-thirty until eight or nine o'clock, at which time, ideally, another period of resting, drinking tea, roasting peanuts, and visiting with friends and family will occur at home, paralleling male activities in the more public areas.

10. Language skills, especially in the area of artistic communication, are not fully developed simply because adulthood has been reached. Some older men do, however, encourage younger men to tell stories and make it clear to them that among equals hikayat are to be exchanged.

Both Bauman (1972) and Tallman (1975) discuss the ratio of speaking to listening among older and younger men. In both cases the older men are clearly the performers though Tallman reports that at Forsyth's store the younger men "occasionally" tell personal experience stories. In Kelibia, as at Forsyth's, the times are changing so fast that the younger men possess experiences that their elders never will have; so what they have to say interests their elders. In fact, older men invite the younger ones to talk. But when the younger men "perform" a story, often, they are just practicing. They do not take the steps necessary to involve their disparate listeners, and their stories tend to be very "self" centered as opposed to those of their elders. On the other hand some younger men are very good at riddles, jokes, and short, humourous anecdotes.

On this same subject William Labov writes, "An unexpected result of the comparison across age levels is that the use of many syntactic devices for evaluation does not develop until late in life, rising geometrically from preadolescents to adolescents to adults" (Labov 1972: 355).

11. After reading a draft of this section, a friend asked if Malek's parents would resent Marie Thérèse for taking him away. I think his mother knew he would have a good life with her and had encouraged him to marry her. They had known each other for a long time when they married. She already had learned Tunisian Arabic, had learned to cook Tunisian food from Lella Nesria, and was altogether an intelligent and agreeable individual. They could understand that she would want to be near her parents, but I think it was assumed that the man would make the decision.

12. Questions of social status with regard to occupation are evened out here due to Si Hamdan's other occupations, the educational promise shown by his teen-aged sons and daughters, and his status as a member of an old family.

13. Malouf is traditional North African music thought to have been brought from Andalusia at the time of the expulsion of Muslims and Jews around the fifteenth century.

14. "The emergent quality of performance resides in the interplay between communicative resources, individual competence, and the goals of the participants, within the context of particular situations" (Bauman 1977b: 38).

15. My concern is with a particular compositional mode, the hikayah. After all, as Eric Hobsbawm points out, the history that becomes "part of the fund of knowledge or ideology of nation, state or movement is not what has actually been preserved in popular memory," and, in fact, all historians "contribute, consciously or not, to the creation, dismantling and restructuring of the images of the past" (Hobsbawm and Ranger 1983: 13). (See also Crapanzano 1980: 6–9 for a thought-provoking discussion of historical texts and personal history.)

16. Genre markers are a cluster of traits that (most) hikayat share. Other genres of folklore may have one or more of the same traits. For example, just as hikayat generate hikayat, Tunisian trickster tales (Jha stories) generate more trickster tales. Tunisian proverbs, on the other hand, do not usually generate more proverbs and Tunisian riddles though they may generate more riddles, remain close structurally, but not (except very broadly) thematically constant. As a contrast to hikayat, with their minimal and diffuse opening and closing markers, khurafat are rigidly framed with a "once upon a time" and "happily ever after" sort of formula.

17. For example, "It will not be possible to make very much progress in the analysis . . . of . . . complex narratives until the simplest and most fundamental narrative structures are analyzed. . . . We suggest that such fundamental structures are to be found in oral versions of personal experiences" (Labov and Waletzky 1967: 12).

18. Not precisely the equivalent of Shklovsky's ostranenie, which is also relevant to what hikayat do. As Hawkes writes:

images and all other purely literary devices such as phonetic patterns, rhyme, rhythm, metre, the use of sound not to "represent" sense, but as a meaningful element in its own right, were assigned by Shklovský to one central use that of "making strange" (ostranenie). According to Shklovský, the essential function of poetic art is to counteract the process of habituation encouraged by routine everyday modes of perception. We very readily cease to "see" the world we live in, and become anaesthetized to its distinctive features. The aim of poetry is to reverse that process, to defamiliarize that with which we are overly familiar, to "creatively deform" the usual, the normal, and so to inculcate a new, childlike, nonjaded vision in us. The poet thus aims to disrupt "stock responses," and to generate a heightened awareness: to restructure our ordinary perception of "reality," so that we end by seeing the world instead of numbly recognizing it: or at least so that we end by designing a "new" reality to replace the (no less fictional) one which we have inherited and become accustomed to. (Hawkes 1977: 62)

Together, narrator and listeners slow down, and focus in on what is for them an especially richly significant incident from the past.

19. See story 7, where Sidi 'Ali Qsibi does prove himself—as far as one town member is concerned.

20. Roland Barthes discusses shifters, the markers for transitions into and out of the sui-referential mode in historical discourse as a means of desimplifying "the chronological Time of history by contrasting it with the different time scale of the discourse itself" (Barthes 1970: 148). As in the aside referenced here, these kinds of meta-statements, categorized by Barthes as monitorial (evidential) and organizational, are used liberally in hikayat, perhaps much more liberally than would be appropriate, in what Barthes calls "the discourse of certain classical historians." His

postulation about one purpose shifters might serve is especially relevant to hikayat. They help

"de chronologize" the historical thread and restore, if only by reminiscence or nostalgia, a Time at once complex, parametric, and non-linear. . . . The organization shifters reveal . . . that the historian's function is a predictive one: it is because he knows what has not yet been related that the historian, like the myth-bearer, needs a two-layered Time, braiding the chronology of the subject-matter with that of the language-act which reports it. (Barthes 1970: 148)

21. Smoker of hashish, a cleverly eccentric man. It is not necessarily meant that he literally smoked hashish.

22. Zakrawi had been a musician, an occupation traditionally thought to attract the attention of genies (*jnoun*). He had gradually gone blind and some believe that the cause was the blows he had received over the years from displeased jnoun when he played a wrong note. Now, when he could no longer work, a *jiniyya* (female jin) was, in a sense, supporting him. He had a human wife and children and a jiniyya wife and jnoun children as well. I was told that sex with a jiniyya is said to be not like the human sex but like "electricity," an electric jolt. For an account of a similar jiniyya-human situation consult Crapanzano (1980). Injuries caused by jnoun to humans are mentioned on pages 17–18.

23. This story actually follows story 4 (also about 'Abd ar-Rahman) immediately.

24. Due, the implication is, to the non-Muslim, European population dominating the town.

25. Dedicating one good animal to the zawiyya (ultimately to the poor) ensures wali protection of the rest.

26. See page 94 for a discussion of the implications of naming.

27. "S'eed" means "lion."

28. "Even through the 1930s tribesmen popularly attributed to Shergawa marabouts the capacity to change themselves into lions" (Eickelman 1976: 181).

29. Ramadhan is the Muslim month of fasting. Believers are asked to fast from that time in the morning when a black thread can be distinguished from a white until that time in the evening when the two no longer can be distinguished by color. The drummer is the town alarm clock—awakening those fasting to eat a final sustaining meal before the first prayer time of the day. Notice that in the story Si Hamdan does not directly contradict his oldest brother, worthy of much respect (qaddir); in fact, he obeys him, even though his interpretation of the religious law is incorrect.

30. Malek later mentioned his amusement at the preciseness of the description here. Not only does Si Hamdan indicate the number of reeds by the truckful; he tells us he means small trucks. (These are the small, flatbed Japanese-made trucks recently seen all over the Cap Bon.) The rushes, used mostly for woven mats and baskets are fine and plentiful in the region. The funcus maritimus, juncus acutus, or scirpus holschoenus (Reswick 1985: 29–30) would have been cut in early summer and dried in the sun for a month. Now, in August, they are ready to weave—an occupation Si Hamdan still pursues part time.

31. Onions stored in this attractive way so the bulbs would stay dry and last longer. Anything "unsavory" (like onions) or more serious (an illness or death or scandal) gets a similar polite phrase indicating that you do not want to remind the listener of unpleasantness or, in the case of illness, that you hope it will not happen to him or her.

32. According to Pitt-Rivers:

There are many Saharan stories about horrible diseases coming upon those who abused men of religion, . . . diseases which the inflicting cleric removed only after full repentance and recompense.

Sometimes inflicted illness was not the defense of the pious in danger but simply a weapon of in-fighting among the faithful, as for example when the Eastern Sudanese saint Walad Abu Sadiq, whose marital irregularities had been criticized by a judge, cursed the judge with skin disease. (Pitt-Rivers 1963: 28)

Just so, in Kelibia a wife (still living), descendant of a wali, cursed her beautiful, philandering husband with horrible-smelling boils, from which he eventually died. There are other stories in which a Kelibian dervish curses someone, but I do not recall that the curses are ever removed. Non-Muslims, Jews and Christians, are also considered by some to have powerful curses that may be taken seriously by God even if they are not meant. When I asked a woman friend why, she laughed and joked kindly, "Well, we Muslims are always cursing, so God knows we don't mean it!"

33. See Mukařovský (1964: 37–39) for discussion of the aesthetic effect of invectives, archaic expressions, foreign expressions, and dialect words in communication:

the role of the esthetic function is clear here, especially in all those cases where in borrowing an alien element its exotic nature is emphasized, as given by the geographic or social distance of the language, or functional form of language, from which it is borrowed.(Mukařovský 1964: 39)

All of these devices as part of the unstructured or personal aesthetic achieve their effect by surprise, unexpectedly foregrounding the linguistic sign over (or beside) the message it is being used to convey.

34. Hunters traditionally do a round with their birds and then sit for awhile before doing another round.

35. Weekly open-air market.

36. Coming from Corsica.

37. Lit. السوَيَّف , a diminutive for hawk. The hawk is not literally "little," but use of the diminutive indicates "dear" or "precious."

38. Koranic verse.

39. A grain.

40. This story is Aarne-Thompson Tale Type 1676B, Clothing Caught in Graveyard. A man thinks that something terrifying is holding him and dies of fright.

An interesting note is that in the western version of this tale type the person who is caught dies of fright, whereas in the Kelibian version the person is saved by the timely appearance of members of his or her community.

Chapter 3

Dramatis Personae: Walis, Dervishes, Heroes, and Clowns

> Let someone else be hungry, let someone else be cold. Let someone else make sure those lies and stories all get told!
>
> (Mel Tillis, "There Ain't No California")

In a single telling the thrust of a hikayah must be readily accessible. After all, hikayat are often told in circumstances where distractions are present— in a room in which a television is blaring, in a crowded café next to exuberant card players, or outside in the town square where interruptions are common. Also, they are rather long and do not have fixed forms and, thus, are not particularly memorizable in fine stylistic detail. This is not to say that hikayat do not often bear multifaceted meanings, but a single telling of one hikayah will not fully convey these meanings. To appreciate the complex significance of hikayat the listener must have heard more than one, more than once (and told by more than one person). The stories must

Key to Map 4

1. Sidi Ahmed (Sidi Hmid) and Sidi S'eed (4,18,19,29)
2. Jenhani's store (17)
3. Small Mosque (16)
4. Post office (2)
5. Hassine Zouari's store (18)
6. 'Alaya ben Kdous's house (6)
7. Khoudja's store (1)
8. Jebali's Store (5)
9. Turi's tavern (4,18)
10. Café Slim (32)
11. Ben Youssef's house (9)
12. Haj Hamda ben Hmid's house (27)
13. Si ben Slimène's (Si Hamdan's) uncle's store and house (5,25)
14. "New" nursery school
15. "New" bus station
16. Ouild Si 'Ali's house (22)
17. Big Mosque
18. Sidi Bou Dhaoui
19. Remains of town walls and gates (26)
20. Min Sahli's store (greengrocer) (23)
21. Sidi 'Abdallah Taherti (7)
22. Sidi 'Ali Kharfash (11)
23. Sidi 'Ali Mqaddem (11)
24. Ahmed Hammami's house (14)

Map 4. Kelibia. Some locations referred to in the text are indicated.

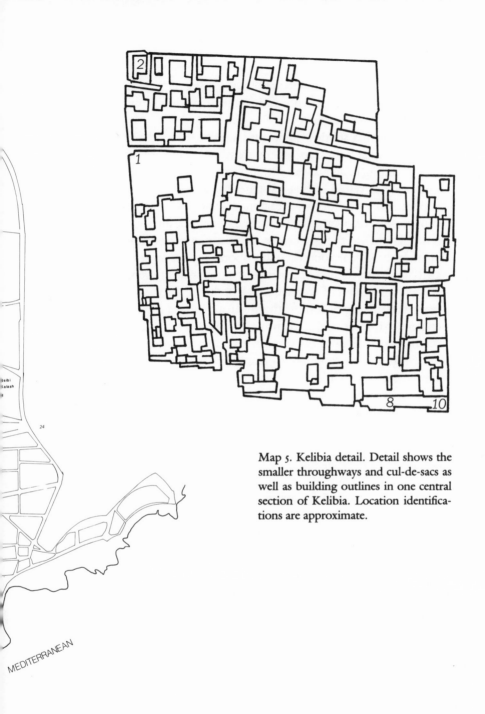

Map 5. Kelibia detail. Detail shows the smaller throughways and cul-de-sacs as well as building outlines in one central section of Kelibia. Location identifications are approximate.

MEDITERRANEAN

be absorbed within the context both of a string of "related" hikayat and of a lifetime of town experience and familiarity with hikayat and other traditional expressive culture forms.

It is thus that subtle insights into a problematic area of life can still be conveyed, even if listeners cannot absorb every nuance contained in a single recounting of an hikayah within a particular storyteller's repertoire. Hikayat may be retold so that a listener has a chance to notice more of the implications of a story with each new telling. And, very often, as in the examples above, hikayat are serial, one story inspiring another that is somehow "related" to the one before. Thus, a number of stories may examine identical or similar concerns and elaborate upon, or discuss, and perhaps arrive at a reperception of a particular social issue or event.

At a higher level of abstraction, all of the stories in this collection share important aspects of context (both situational and communal), form, and content so that looking at them as a group continually reemphasizes certain central perspectives of any single story. Each narrative contains clusters of indicators that are continuously rearranged to reflect the social and cultural concerns of community members. Indicators themselves are multivocal so that, for example, a wali can represent at different times or simultaneously the town essence, a religious or ethical ideal, or a personal loyalty of the narrator. Similarly, the cluster of indicators within one story may represent a recipe for living, a call for a certain collective attitude, and so on. The advantage of these narrative messages is precisely that this ambiguous or multivocal substance alone allows them to reflect accurately ambiguous, evolving, and potentially conflict-causing concerns in the social and cultural life of the town.

In this chapter, stories will be considered as they refine upon each other. The analysis is focused on the interrelationship among hikayat and their shared and differing contexts rather than on the often fascinating minutiae of the individual hikayah. It is important to make this distinction because the stories, looked at as a whole, may signify something(s) quite different from the individual significance of each separate text. Also, examination of the meaning of a set of texts, told by several narrators both men and women, must lead us away from the special social and personal concerns of one narrator toward concerns shared by various strata of the community.[1] Collectively, they are the common heritage of the townspeople and revolve around people, places, or events of mutual concern. Groups of narratives can surround certain communal dilemmas offering a variety of perspectives—insider or outsider, young or old, supernatural or unabashedly down-to-earth. Just as the townspeople by virtue of their place of residence are "vitally integrated," so too are these stories since they center on that rural town, its local "crises and the neighborhood characters" (Dorson 1952: 11). This is not to ignore the tensions that exist between social and individual perceptions of experience, but in the storytelling settings I have portrayed, I do find community interests overriding personal interests.[2]

In this chapter I have included comments or narratives from two women. These two women, Aunt Jamila and Aunt Fafani, are very different. Khalti Jamila, when I first met her in 1967, was a poor widow in her mid-thirties living in the zawiyya or qubba (term used for these shrines, denoting the domed roof) of a waliyya, Lella Khadhra, and trying to raise her children by cleaning at the nursery school. Gradually, she took on the task of preparing brides for their weddings—applying depilatory, henna, and *harcous* (a black, clove-scented, lacy hand and foot decoration) and dressing them—a task that is low-status but fairly lucrative. She told me about many of the lesser-known walis and waliyyas in Kelibia. Tellingly, one was a poor widow ancestor of hers (Lella Myriam) who had no way to make a living but who was blessed with the power to help women who were unable to nurse their babies. Her small grave is now visited by women with this special need. The last time I was in Kelibia, in 1983, Khalti Jamila had saved enough to have a house built.

Khalti Fafani, whom I met only in 1979, is a member of an upper-middle class family of Ottoman origin. Her daughter's two children were students in our nursery school in 1967–69. She is a kind of matriarch living in a very spacious but simple, almost austere, traditional-style house with a large central courtyard and room for brothers, sisters and brothers-in-law and their children and grandchildren to live in or visit.

The hikayat in this corpus for the most part involve four types of towns-people: town heroes of various sorts, town "characters," town holy men,[3] and town dervishes. Together and individually, these stories add definition to the town as a whole. Local pride in the community's recent history, underlined by these colorful and powerful town symbols, is directly linked to personal dignity and worth. Implicitly or explicitly, through the actions of these dramatis personae, acceptable community behavior is delimited. Thus, storytellers invoke the actions of these personalities to make statements about their hopes for the present and future of the community. The mention of a particular town wali or other personality inevitably triggers a story, other factors being appropriate.

This defining or negotiating of perspectives is achieved precisely by reference to characters who each in her or his own fashion is most able to break rules and transcend boundaries. These characters constitute the community other—different enough to become narratively central. As familiar, yet different, they are agents through which the unusual can be approached and dealt with in a foregrounded manner. Together, the four types are indicators of a broad range of potential and possibility, both individual and communal. They are theatrical figures who have won the right to be other even at home, and thus are able to move from real life into narrative (Bakhtin 1968: 159) as well as between cultures, states of being, and geographical locations. In a broad sense, they are picaresque-like: the storyteller or an associate engages herself or himself with the larger world—natural, cultural, or supernatural—and, in and through these stories, comes out ahead.

The local walis are especially adept at this—they can transcend death, space, and time and move between the supernatural and the natural, the animal and the human. They seem to mediate various sorts of hierarchical exchanges whereas, as we will see, local heroes mediate exchanges among "equals." In life and after death, walis' special, mystical closeness with God allows them to defy acceptable social conduct and to ignore religious law, though not, as we shall see, the laws of common humanity. In addition, attendance at their zawiyyas or shrines, cuts across the internal town boundaries of quarters and neighborhoods, and thereby helps to integrate the town actually and symbolically. Thus, they are the ultimate town mediators—the most multivocal, versatile human signifiers for a community. Dervishes, too, have special access to the supernatural, have oracular capabilities, and are expected to break rules of prescribed community behavior.

Heroes cross more limited, literal boundaries. They are adventurers, travelers, risk-takers, and challengers of human hierarchies and values. The town "characters," the tricksters or the clowns, are only semi-socialized, with prodigious appetites for sex or food, for example. They break down boundaries between nature and culture, behaving sometimes like animals and sometimes like machines, out of control in a way that a cultured Kelibian may find amusing but personally unacceptable. Their behavior is to be avoided.

Anecdotes about all four categories of remarkable town characters can be fashioned by narrators and audiences into subtle statements about the community-in-process and its ever-changing love/hate, attraction/repulsion relationship with the noncommunity, the rural or urban other, and with the supernatural. As demonstrated earlier, both the country and the city feed the town—literally and figuratively or intellectually. Religion and the supernatural also provide practical as well as spiritual benefits. Yet the town's easy access and easy egress bring problems as well—danger of outside control, threats to community values, and the loss of human resources. In short, a loss of acceptable community identity or an actual loss of community members may take place. These hikayat identify the personality resources traditionally available within the community and use these resources to put the other in both its negative and positive guise into perspective. All four characters found in the hikayat here represent links—between nature and culture, city and town, countryside and town or supernatural and human. (And looking at the accounts from another angle, we will find implied in them the dark and the light sides of town life as well. But drawbacks and community differences can be minimized in a hikayah that contemplates a common asset or faces and outfaces a mutual threat—symbolically, me, a semi-acculturated, female, western Christian. Shared laughter can be effective as well.)

Central to the townspeople's sense of history, of religion, and of well-being are its local walis, descendants of walis, and dervishes. Across the Middle East and North Africa the terms "wali" and "dervish" are used to define individuals who have varying attributes, but who share at least two features. First, they are men or women who have a special, close mystical relationship with God that allows them an autonomy not acceptable in others and various abilities that other mortals do not possess. Second, this special barakah (and thus their popular support and following) has made them desirable allies and undesirable enemies. They have at times been susceptible to being cast as leaders of popular movements, and therefore being perceived by political leaders as threats to be neutralized, contained, or eliminated.

Kelibian walis, since they are all dead,+ are particularly adaptable and thus ideally suited to symbolic manipulation in stories. As we shall see, they represent a challenge to both religious and secular political authority. Their powers are not territory-restricted (that is, perhaps because they often come from afar, they can act as protectors to their people when they travel afar), and their social linkages are non-specific (except to that specific region or to the town). Anyone seeking justice can turn to them. Because they are not living and because they are region- or town-specific they are also rather effectively immune from co-optation or elimination by extra-town political powers—whether Ottoman, French, or Tunisian.[5]

To say that supernatural phenomena are expected and taken for granted by community members is an overstatement, because evidences of super-natural interference or intercession are obviously newsworthy, the stuff of stories. But people are comfortable with more permeable boundaries be-tween the natural and the supernatural than are most westerners. Even younger adults, who may be rather cavalier about religion, are *culturally* comfortable with the idea that genies as well as past holy men can intervene in human affairs and that certain key members of the town, especially the descendants of a holy person, are able to communicate with these beings or to solicit their aid. The young Kelibian doctor who first told me about Uncle Hmida and his hawk story did not question the fact of Qsibi's assis-tance in finding the hawk. He told me the story as a true story—although it was true for him in a cultural, or community, rather than in a religious sense.

The supernatural is an integral part of everyday town life. In and around the town, poor families actually live in the less visited of the twenty or more zawiyyas. When I first came to Kelibia in 1967, Lella Khadhra's shrine housed a poor widow, and the waliyya's tombstone had become a low shelf on which cooking pots rested. Earlier, this shrine was used to house young men from the region who wanted to continue their religious education with a scholarly man in Kelibia. Lella Nesria remembers that households volunteered to feed those visiting scholars. She recalls a young student who would come to her father's house to pick up his meal and later return with the empty pan. Today, a family lives in Sidi 'Ali Qsibi's shrine also and a television aerial protrudes from the side of the dome. Visitors to the walis are shown around by a member of the resident family.

Sidi Bahri's shrine has been expanded into a beautifully terraced open-air café on the sandy slopes above the beach. Naturally, alcoholic beverages are not served, as the wali would disapprove. Thus, people are familiar with their walis but are not disrespectful. In Sidi Amor, a shrine where people sleep and eat while visiting Sidi Maouia, small children have even carved out hollows in the center of the floor so that they can play a favorite game (*bagra ouildit*, the cow gave birth) in which stones are moved from hollow to hollow.

The anomalous quality of local walis and their ability to break rules and traverse boundaries are underscored by accounts that emphasize their eccentric actions and miraculous deeds. As seems to be the case throughout the Middle East, important Tunisian walis often are not native to their chosen towns (or they are natives who have traveled extensively and returned). Thus, part of their ambiguity from the townspeoples' perspective is that the walis are "of us, but not of us." Whereas in many places an immigrant family would not be accepted into a town for generations, walis, by the time they die, are accorded a central position in the hearts of the townspeople. This fact is most significant in a town such as Kelibia, where, as we have seen, even the old-timers are well aware that they and their neighbor's great grandparents were almost all immigrants or migrants.[6] Structurally, the walis' choice of Kelibia underscores the belief that the ancestors of town members were intelligent in choosing Kelibia.

Sidi Maouia, the most well known of the local walis, came from a small village perhaps thirty or forty kilometers south of Kelibia. His descendants continue to inhabit that town. He is a holy man of regional reputation. The entire upper two-thirds of the Cap Bon is in fact called Dakhlet al Maouine (homeland of the descendants of Maouia). Sidi Maouia's grave is on a hill ten kilometers behind Kelibia. Significantly, he chose to remain buried near the town rather than return to his home village. He is known by the nickname Bou Qabreen (the man with two graves), since there are two gravemarkers in the center of his shrine.[7] Why? They say that when Sidi Maouia died he was buried behind Kelibia rather than returned to his hometown. Since it is very important for a town to have walis, his people traveled up to get him. However, after a night of altercation with the residents of the area, they were persuaded to pray and sleep there and resolve the situation in the morning. Upon awakening they found two graves side by side. They could not tell in which one Sidi Maouia was buried. Clearly, he wanted to stay among his later friends and followers.

Here, in the person of Sidi Maouia, are encapsulated two of those fundamental components of Kelibian world view vis-à-vis the outside world that I mentioned in Chapter 1. First, Kelibia is a desirable place in which to settle, a place chosen by Sidi Maouia (who had seen alternatives) as well as most Kelibians' ancestors. Second, if dealt with correctly, the town can be enriched (rather than simply harmed) by outsiders and outside ideas. After all, Sidi Maouia and the other walis brought religious wisdom and protection to the townspeople.

The indicators of Sidi Maouia's wali potential that began to appear gradually while he was still alive are traded among the townspeople. Again, the incidents dwell on his power to manipulate boundaries. For example, he could leave his sheep grazing safely simply by drawing a circle around them and ordering them to remain inside and predatory animals to remain outside. In that instance, he miraculously set boundaries for other beings. Maouia himself miraculously transcended just such natural boundaries. He had the ability to travel enormous distances in a day (for example, to Cairo to hear the sermon at the famous mosque and university al-Azhar). And he could make his presence felt in two places at once.[8] The following account tells of how Sidi Maouia was able to be both in Kelibia and in Meknes (in Morocco) at the same time.

(10) KHALTI FAFANI

They say a long time ago Sidi 'Abdelqadir was in his town in Meknes in Morocco sitting, teaching. He sat teaching and Sidi Maouia was irrigating his crops [in Kelibia]. [Sidi 'Abdelqadir] was teaching and Sidi Maouia when he bent down [to change the course of the water in the ditches] splashed the kids and they said, "What? Where is the water coming from?" [Sidi 'Abdelqadir] replied, "It's from Maouia, that crazy man . . . He's watering. Wait, I'll hit him with this switch." He hit out with his fist and the children were splashed again. They said, "Oh Sidi 'Abdelqadir, why is it that we are in Meknes and Sidi Maouia among his followers and he splashes us?" He answered, "Because Maouia is careless."[9]

The emphasis in the story is on the way a wali (or waliyya) can carelessly, almost in spite of himself (herself), collapse space and time. There is no cause, no righting of a wrong, behind Maouia's action. Both he and 'Abdelqadir are engaged in home and community tasks, the education of children and the irrigation of crops. The exchange between the two walis unites the everyday folk of western Islam and gives them a commonality with each other and with the holy people both in terms of life's mysteries and in terms of everyday concerns. As well, the incident and its recounting make a religious mystery seem natural, taken for granted, and everyday life in turn takes on a bit of mystical mystery and charm.

The day in March that Malek and I went to visit Khalti Fafani in the central courtyard of her big old traditional Arab house, she narrated to

Malek account after account of the doings of both the town's walis and its dervishes. As an older woman from an old and respected family, she had every right to teach the son of a sheikhly family about their "shared" past; the dimension she adds to this study is a highlighting of the fact that common community concerns are those not only of older and younger town males but of community women as well. Khalti Fafani's stories speak affectively about religious figures and life in the community to townswomen *and* townsmen.

To a certain extent, the stories told about the miracles and wise sayings of the walis carry on a continuing negotiation of both the walis' proper statuses in the hierarchy of walis and their place in town tradition. In the above incident, for example, Sidi Maouia's association with one of the best known of the North African holy men augments his reputation for supernatural travel and his connection with the wider world of Islam.[10] As the following story illustrates, wisdom is also a sign of a wali who is closer to God than other walis. Khalti Jamila told us this story one May afternoon when she came by to see me and Lella Nesria. Sidi 'Ali Mqaddem is an ancestor of Khalti Jamila's, as is a waliyya, Sidi Mqaddem's granddaughter and Khalti Jamila's grandmother, Lella Myriam. If I recall correctly, when Lella Myriam's husband died leaving her with small children and no living, her grandfather, Sidi 'Ali Mqaddem, appeared to her in a series of dreams and gave her the power to heal women who could not nurse. Both she and Sidi Mqaddem are buried near the old fort.

(11) KHALTI JAMILA
There were Sidi 'Ali Muqaddam and Sidi Kharfash, who lived next to each other, were neighbors, and were always sitting together in the shadow of the fort in the fort area. And Sidi 'Ali Mqaddem was the more advanced, more advanced than many walis, the more advanced of the two of them. And Sidi Kharfash wanted to be his equal . . . [Sidi 'Ali] said, "All right, we'll be equals."

There were two ships fighting in the sea. One unfortunate was about to sink. [Sidi Kharfash] was sitting pounding with a wooden mortar and pestle, pounding up tomatoes to use to cook dinner. He was pounding and watching how the one ship was about to sink. The poor ship. He felt sorry for it and didn't want it to sink. While he watched he went "uh *huh*! uh *huh*! uh *huh*!" [in rhythm with his pounding] and sank the other ship.

The unfortunate Sidi 'Ali Mqaddem didn't like that at all. He said, "It's not for you to sink them. I gave you an obligation. You should have petitioned God. God could have made things right between the two of them. It isn't for you to sink one or the other. [God] loves all people the same."

Among the townspeople, Sidi Hmid and Sidi Maouia are the holy people most commonly invoked when an individual wishes to avoid misfortune. Thus, during a crisis or a fright, the victim (or a friend or relative of the potential victim) will call out to these walis for help. In 1966, the rebellious teenaged Malek threatened to quit his boarding school in the town of Beja. His mother vowed to Sidi Hmid that if Malek would return to school, she would bake bread for the poor of the town. He did, and she did. (I first learned about this upon returning from teaching one day and finding loaf upon loaf of round bread stacked in the courtyard, in the kitchen, and in the hallways.) Sidi Maouia was invoked in the summer of 1979, when Malek took a sheep to his zawiyya as fulfillment of a promise he had made a year earlier. When his daughter had been born, the baby was not breathing, and quickly and much to his surprise (considering himself rather irreligious), he had promised Sidi Maouia a sheep if she lived. Many such promises are made in moments of stress.

Sidi Maouia also can protect a Kelibian outside his or her home boundaries.

(12) SI HAMDAN

But, there's another story. This one was told me by my paternal uncle, God have mercy on him. They [both participants in the story] are dead now. They were working at an olive press in Sousse, an olive press, about this time of year and this press had three grinding units to crush the olives. Its owner was a Jewish guy and the man in charge of the oil was a Kerkanni, from Kerkanna.[11] Well, al-Makki 'Asul and my uncle were among the laborers there at that particular grinder. Al-Makki 'Asul was a slight guy—like his brother but taller than Mohamed 'Asul.

Sabra to Malek: Do you know his brother?

Figure 4. "Sidi 'Ali Mqaddem was the more advanced, more advanced than many walis, the more advanced of the two of them. And Sidi Kharfash [above] wanted to be his equal."

Malek: The one that lives down by the beach?

Yeah. He was older than al-Makki. [pause] Night . . . and the man . . . What was his job? He threw the olives into the squeezer.

Malek: Into the grinder?

Yeah. They'd work those eight hours [at night] and leave when others came in. They'd alternate . . . [aside to some listeners who had finished drinking their tea] (Health, health to you). Well sir, al-Makki was getting chilled (since the olives were outside) chilled and freezing. He went over near the clay oven. (See, there was an oven to heat water. They build something to heat water on top of because when the press is rotating they pour hot water on it.).[12] From it [by its light] he was going to roll a cigarette. (Most people rolled their own.)

Malek: Ah, they didn't buy cigarettes, they rolled them themselves?

Yeah. I among them . . . You see, he came over to it to mourn for his father while moaning for his lover. [laughter]

Malek: What's that mean?

To mourn for his father while moaning for his lover.[13] From it he'd warm up a bit as well as roll a cigarette. You see? Mister Supervisor went up to him and humiliated him, cursed at him and ordered him, "Take off that work apron. You're not working anymore." And continued to humiliate him in front of his friends, in front of the workers from everywhere, and he an outsider among them—not even from that area.

Malek: And he was Kelibian?

A Kelibian . . . And he ordered him, "Now, get away from this factory." (And that was also where they slept—there in the middle of their work.) Here it was night.

Malek: And where could he go at night?

They say he turned toward Mecca, and said, "Where are you, oh Sidi Maouia?" (And tears were running down his face.) "Where are you, oh Sidi Maouia? Here I am in a strange town among strangers and that dog, son of a bitch, was humiliating me with no justification. Revenge me on him—that dog there."

Malek: Ah.

He swears, my uncle, God have mercy on him (I knew both of them). (And it [the machine] ran on electricity. We at the time didn't have electricity at all [in Kelibia].) Al-Makki said, "God be merciful, you're my commander," and he took up a saw and thus [makes a chopping motion] chopped through all the belts at once. Only the cams were left turning alone in space until they gradually came to a halt—their momentum run down. As the saying goes, "the wind ran out." Then there was nothing. Only the light was still shining.

Malek: Everything cut off.

Everything was cut off. Not one belt was left turning.

Malek: Wow, your uncle saw the whole thing?

My uncle was with him.

Malek: He worked with him?

Yes, they worked together, you see.

That's all. The Jewish guy who owned the press came and started questioning the workers and threw out that supervisor. That very night he promoted al-Makki to foreman.

He said, "Where are you, oh Sidi Maouia, oh my ancestor. If you call me 'my son,' that dog wronged me and pushed me around." See? Without any right on his side. ['Asul] had done nothing. Neither was he a thief. See? Simply tired and cold, he wanted only to warm his fingers and roll a cigarette. That's all. The one who was going to fire him was fired himself that very night.

Notice that in the above story no promise of reward is made but doubtless the travelers appropriately recognized Sidi Maouia's help upon their return home.

In stories like this one and story 18 it almost seems unnecessary to attribute the powerful act of the townsmember to the aid of a wali. But if an individual attributes his or her decisive act to reliance on the backup of a wali, that individual aligns herself or himself (or the storyteller aligns the protagonist) with the community. The entire community, through one of their walis, possesses or shares a part of a powerful act.[14]

Sidi Hmid's shrine is located in the center of Kelibia. As mentioned, he is particularly popular with women. One woman held a feast there to give thanks because her husband was not badly hurt in an automobile accident; another gave a feast because her son successfully recovered from an operation in Tunis. But men love Sidi Hmid too. As Uncle Gacem observed to us one day as Malek and I sat with him in his pottery shop:

we love the children [descendants] of Sidi Hmid and we love Sidi Hmid. Go to Sidi Hmid. There isn't a day you'll find it empty, not a day you'll find it empty . . . either outside or inside.[15]

In addition to the zawiyyas for local saints, shrines have been built in Kelibia to three Sufi mystics famous not only locally but all over the Middle East. Some of these shrines served in the past as religious lodges where

praises were sung to that mystic and to God; others were practical com-
memorative structures. As Si Hamdan observes:

> They, sir, were built in earlier times by people. They would make them
> public water faucets and Koranic schools and mosques and zawiyyas to
> glorify them. Now, Sidi 'Abdelqadir is from Baghdad . . . and is buried
> in Baghdad. . . . Sidi ben 'Aissa is Meknes, from Morocco. But they
> make them stations everywhere. Sidi 'Abdesselam . . . probably Libya.
> Understand? [See page 39 for historical references to these same holy
> people.]

Such shrines were established by followers of the holy men—either Kelibians who encountered a particular brotherhood on their travels, or by a
stranger who came to proselytize. Once again, this phenomenon illustrates
that certain serious aspects of the outside world are expected to be used
selectively to enrich town life.

It is from descendants of Sidi Hmid,[16] who, unlike those of Sidi Maouia,
live in town, that many dervishes come. They are, in a sense, his living
icons. (Dervishes are often, but not necessarily, descendants of the walis.)
All living wali descendants, whether overtly "dervish" or not, are considered religiously "potent" and therefore dangerous. Thus, young men and
women who can do so avoid marriage with the descendants of Sidi Hmid;
for no one can avoid marital disputes, and the curse of a descendant of Sidi
Hmid has been known to bear bitter fruit. (See note 32, Chapter 2 and
story below.)

Walis and dervishes seem to fall along a hierarchical continuum so that
in Kelibia, some dervishes, perhaps because of their closer connection with
"humanness" and lesser supernatural status, have more of a tendency to
human failings (such as a desire for vengeance) than those who have become closer to God. It is because of this volatile quality that there is fear,
as well as respect and love, in the townspeoples' attitudes toward the dervishes.[17]

(13) UNCLE GACEM
You've got Shadli. Shadli, also. He doesn't seem the type [to be a der-
vish]. [When] Shadli was still a bit young, see, they were working with
drilling equipment on their farm and he was a devil—wanted to play,
see. He wanted to put [the drill] down, wanted to sink it. And the drill

was down about sixteen, seventeen, eighteen meters to the floor of the well. Workers were working on it. When they didn't want to let him interfere, he said, "May God prevent you from succeeding." He finished his phrase and the drill broke. 'Til now it's still there because they made him mad not letting him.

Dervishes, in town parlance, are men or women who lead "aberrant" lives in the community. They seem simple, childlike, ignorant of what is expected of a "reasonable" person. They do not seem to have self-protective mechanisms, and they thus leave themselves open to exploitation, ostracism, or ridicule. Yet one has the feeling that God or their wali ancestor insulates them from harm. With this endorsement, townspeople too are forced to sanction their actions and protect them.

(14) AUNT FAFANI

And—the son of my paternal aunt was the son of [a descendant of Sidi Hmid]. (My aunt was married to [a descendant of Sidi Hmid], the brother of the wife of Qabura . . . .) Well, sir, he would come to my mother and he would say, "Give me, Mna, twenty francs or thirty francs" (a franc meant something in those days, not like now). He would tell her, "Mna, I want twenty francs."

My father told us, "If 'Abd ar-Rahman comes, don't turn him away empty handed, you hear? If 'Abd ar-Rahman comes, don't turn him away empty handed."

It got so that when we would bring in olive oil (father had a lot of oil) he would sometimes bring in a can or glass bottle [to fill up] and sometimes. . . .

One day mother said, "Damn him,[18] here's a can, here's a bottle, here's twenty, here's fifty [francs], by God, by God!! . . ."

Father came in and found her [angry]. He said, "Why, [what's going on]?"

She said, " 'Abd ar-Rahman said this and that." He said, "Are you giving it to him from your father's fortune then? I want you to give to him. I want you to give to him what is his uncle's. I'm telling you, give to him when he comes. When 'Abd ar-Rahman comes, don't send him away empty handed." I swear to God, Malek, I know this like I know there is one God.

We left for the orange grove. (We have a bitter orange grove near that Ahmed Hammami's house.) We went to the orange grove. (We locked up, locked up and we had a room that we called *zantana* [a room where olive oil was stored]—with clay olive oil jugs and nothing else in it.) We went to the orange grove. We were gathering orange blossoms and father was picking up fava beans. We sat shelling them. (We cook over there. The pot is over there so whenever we go to gather blossoms we cook there.)

All of a sudden Hamud Mraga showed up and said, "Run, the olive oil is coming under the door of the house!"

"How can that be—oil coming out the door?"

He said, "Out the front door. I swear the oil is almost up to the front of the grocer's." Oh Malek, by God and this afternoon [I'm telling the truth], father got me up on the donkey and we took off. (Mother stayed behind to gather those blossoms.)

When we got in we found our entrance hall . . . (We have a patio higher than the entrance hall.) The entrance hall was full to the brim and so was the patio, and the kitchen, which has a floor drain for water, was full of olive oil.

Malek: What happened? Did the oil spill?

Father thought that the clay jars had knocked each other over. He pulled over the rainwater container, spilled the water and filled it with oil. He emptied the big drinking water jug and filled it with oil. He emptied the jar . . . We didn't have a single container not filled with oil. And the oil was still gushing out.

And here comes Mother saying, "Did the clay jars break?" He said, "God, I don't know. No one could have come in." I was getting up the oil, and father came in from behind [around the oil] and stuck a burlap sack under the door of the house and my cousin forced it under the door so the oil could no longer get out—so even if some of it were lost it would be only a little bit stealing out. We filled, we hadn't one container left. We hadn't . . . whatever . . . we hadn't one piece of pottery left.

We didn't leave a thing unfilled with oil and my mother went running in [to the oil storage room] and what did she find? (She swore, mother, "May God paralyze me") the [oil] jar was standing in the corner. She said, "I found it throwing oil up, slapping it against the wall like an oil pump—as if a gutter were throwing it out against the wall." Thus, it was hitting against it.

And I swear we filled and we filled and we didn't lose anything. On the contrary we gained [more oil] and all because of what [my father] said to her, "Give to 'Abd ar-Rahman, don't turn him away empty handed." We were visited by Lakhdhur.[19] He's ['Abd ar-Rahman is] like that—a little bit dervish. Like you would find him . . .

Not all simple people are dervishes, but all dervishes seem to have "simple" ways of behaving that transcend the ordinary. Emphasis in stories about dervishes is on their violation of traditional social expectations and their departure from the ordinary rules of human conduct by their drinking, disrespect for authority, sloppy dress, and so on. Paradoxically, part of the recognition of dervish status derives precisely from their deviance, especially their religious deviance.

(15) UNCLE GACEM
We have Sidi Mohamed, the husband of Lella Huria. A dervish. But a dervish was very important and [he was] always quiet and he drank, but you wouldn't see him dizzy or falling over or so on. Nothing. He always drank, is all. Until one time he drank and left his glass on the counter [of the bar] with a little still in it. Al-Khnissi, father of Hassine—he came to my father. (I was there.) He came to my father and said, "Oh Si Khalil, those walis have limitless credit."

He replied, "Certainly."

He said, "It's not to be taken for granted." Said, "Sidi Mohamed the dervish, son of Sidi 'Alaya," see, "Well he drank down his glass and left around two fingers in it." Said, "Upon trying it, I didn't know if it was rose water or cologne or orange flower water or . . ." He said, "I can't describe how sweet it was and its fragrance was unimaginable. People want to say he drinks and he doesn't."

Dervishes do not manifest their deviance in one prescribed way. One dervish in town whistles like a bird when he wants to call his wife, ignores the products of his harvests so that his brother must sell them for him, and spends his days making jasmine bouquets and gleaning seeds for the birds from among the wheat stocks. Another always has candy in his pockets to give to children. These dervishes are fairly well off, but others are poorer and will gain food or money in the same way as 'Abd ar-Rahman, or by turning to their wali ancestor.

(16) UNCLE GACEM

It used to be the case that when somebody was in trouble he'd say, "Oh Sidi Hmid," see, "I'm offering a bull." Or [if] a cow was going through a difficult labor, he'd say, "If she delivers a male calf it will be for Sidi Hmid."

There was this Shadli—ouild Salha—Shadli ouild Salha of Temzerat. Well now, he has a son Hamuda, [pauses to think] and Mahmud and Mustafa. He's called Shadli ouild Salha. Do you know them?

Malek: No, I don't.

He had lots of cattle. He had a colossal bull—really colossal—and wild cattle in the forest. Know what I mean? No one knew how much they were worth or anything. They were born and weaned there in the forest of Temzerat. Well, among them was that colossal bull. He was always mooing, see, that one was promised to Sidi Hmid.

Si dervish Mohamed ouild Sidi 'Alaya was broke, sir. He hit the road and started walking. He was wearing a turban—a turban of silk. He kept going, arrived in Temzerat, immediately went into the farm and directly up to the cows, see. Then he went into their midst until he came to that colossus, and little by little grabbed it by its ears, see, pulled off his turban, wrapped it around its horns. He did that, and it followed him. He kept bringing him along, see. No one got in his way or asked what he was doing. They watched him silently. A son of Sidi Hmid had come to take his own [property], see. They sat with their mouths open and got the clubs ready in case it turned on him, see, to rescue him, see, to grab him away from it.

Malek: It might gore him.

Of course! See, like a wild bull. [They watched] until he walked out of sight.

Its head down, it followed him until he brought it . . . (I swear to God—I was there.) When he brought that bull, where did he tie it up? He tied it on the door ring of the Small Mosque with his turban cloth, and went to call a guy named Lalla. Who is this Lalla? Tahar al-Bedoui. He called Tahar al-Bidwi, see. He told him, "Take that bull and go sell it."

Lalla took the bull, see, and sold it to the butcher and brought him back the money, see. He put it in his pocket, see, and went to the tavern to drink, see, and every kid that crossed his path he gave [some money].

Again, as Uncle Gacem illustrates, some dervishes are pictured as always clean, and exempt from "animalistic" bodily functions:

(17) UNCLE GACEM
Malek: What about Sisi [Sidi Mahmud]?

When he'd come spend the evening at Jenhani's store during Sidi Ramadhan. . . .[20] And we'd always spend the evenings there, see.

SW: You and. . . .

Yeah, I love him a lot and he loves me a lot. He and I have been friends over fifty years. Over fifty years, see, and he's old now. He's over sixty now, see?

It was winter—the town hadn't put in tar at all and when it rained, see, there was mud and there's that passageway that he came from, you see, to Jenhani's store. They had put down stones, stones so one could . . . see? If one missed the stones he'd fall up to here in mud and water and . . . Almighty God's truth—Sidi [Sisi] Mahmud—the rain would be pouring from the sky, he'd come with an umbrella (he has an umbrella) and except for the umbrella (which would go "shrr" [noise of water running off]) well, [you'd] look at his clothes and not find even one drop of water and look at his shoes and find them so polished you could see your face in them. He neither stepped in mud nor had anything on his shoes. You'd say he had been walking not on a tarred surface [even] but on boards. Thus.

Figure 5. "When he brought that bull where did he tie it up? He tied it on the door ring of the Small Mosque with his turban cloth, and went to call a guy named Lalla."

Malek: And the rest of you?

I . . . if you were wearing shoes they had to get in the water (or bulgha [backless, slipper-like leather shoes] or whatever). Once we got there we'd take off our socks and get a jar of water from the water cooler and wash our legs, see and sit down, see. And we'd go wallowing home. And he'd stay up until more or less midnight, one o'clock, two o'clock. But if we got involved in a game of cards. . . . (He likes cards. Sisi likes cards. He *likes* belote and likes rummy, see, and he plays rummy very well, see.) In the winter it's cold here. Its not a big deal to get up two or three times and pass water. He never gets up! By God you'd say it's as if he doesn't have [to]. Never do you see Mahmud ouild Sidi 'Alaya go out of the store and go next to the wall and squat to pass water. . . .

But, other dervishes are disheveled, and, while some are sweet-spoken, others are rude and coarse, and drink. So dervishes do not so much neatly invert the social order as ignore it, as they do cultural order, religious and civil laws, and the laws of nature.[21]

Taken together, the above stories of walis and dervishes tend to focus attention not only on the miraculous nature of some town members (living or dead) but, by extension, on the special, unique, perhaps powerful, position of a group—that is, the townspeople—in their privileged associations with these friends of God. In many of the preceding accounts, the other, the outsider, who is not associated with this grace or barakah, has only been implied—partly by my presence. In the following hikayah, however, the outsider actually is present, and in an adversary relationship to the town member(s). Often, when the wali (or dervish) steps in, he seems to do so because the townsperson is at an obviously hierarchical disadvantage with the outsider (see, for example, the olive press incident, story 12). In the following story a powerful cadi (judge) is wrongly sentencing an obviously less powerful townsman:

(18) UNCLE GACEM
There was Mohamed Farjallah. He had lots of sheep and in the past if you didn't give . . . [tape changed—probably referring to a tax that Farjallah didn't pay for his animals]. On that pretext [they arrested] that Mohamed Farjallah. (The sheikh at that time was called Sadoq, Sheikh Sadoq Samoud.) They tied his hands behind him and tied him by the

neck to the window. Which window? Where was the place? Here [points] this store there that belongs to Hassine Zouari. Where Hassine Zouari is, there, that store. That one originally was Haj Shaban's.

Our cadi was called Hedi Slim. Where was the cadi? In Soliman. [Goes on to explain that under colonial rule the contrôleur civil for the region was located in Soliman for a time.] When does he come? He comes from Friday to Friday. Because this town's souk was on Friday not Monday like now. The old souk was on Fridays.

Where did [the cadi] come? He'd come to the sheikh's shop and sit there. Whoever had a complaint would complain and whoever was going to bring him things would bring them. . . . And the sheikh, you'd find having a sheep prepared and prepared fish and prepared this and that. And everyone was bootlicking.

The Farjallah family went to Sidi Mohamed, the dervish. "Oh Sidi," they said to him, "For the good name of your ancestor, go to the cadi," see, "so he'll release Farjallah," see. "His hands are tied, and he has been hung up by the neck from the window," see, "for nothing."

He said, "If you give me a sheep."

They said, "It will be your reward. We'll give you a sheep."

He headed out and started going over. He was wearing a northern jebba, it's called, a northern jebba of white wool, see, and he had a turban. He strolled over and as soon as he got there he immediately went in. As soon as he saw [unclear] he went in. The spahis [guards] were standing guard. He neither spoke to the spahis nor spoke at all. What did he do but go straight in. He said, "Oh Hedi Slim [the cadi], let Farjallah go!" You could see him approaching him wearing a jebba dragging and all of a sudden he went in. He didn't ask permission or anything. He didn't call him "Oh Sidi Cadi," not even "sir." Just like that he called him, "oh Hedi Slim," not "oh Sidi Hedi," [but] "oh Hedi Slim, let Farjallah go!"

He replied, "Get out of my sight! Get out of my sight or I'll put you in jail! What's this improper behavior you're showing? No greeting, no . . ." whatever. You know what I mean. "Did you eat 'assida[22] at my birth?" The spahis grabbed him and threw him out.

When they threw him out he went around a corner next to Tayyib Samoud's house and there he was met by Farjallah's people. "What did you do, man?"

He said, "He chased me away and wouldn't hear a word from me. May his anus fall out."

"Would they go see him again?" They wouldn't meet him again.

The whole thing didn't take long. A quarter hour, half hour, twenty minutes, you know, and Hedi Slim's stomach started hurting. There weren't cars in those times. There weren't cars. He would come in a carriage drawn by two horses from Soliman to here. He came to the carriage, looked at the driver. [to Malek] (What was a driver? It means the one who drove for him—like a chauffeur, see. Driver, see.) He said, "Bring the carriage." He brought him the carriage. He got up without saying a word, even a good-bye. He wouldn't talk to anybody.

He went down the street moaning. The further he got the more he cried, "Ah! Ah! Ah!" They passed Wad Chioua [a gully]. They passed Wad Manqa', see and got to Wad Hajar. He started screaming. They passed Wad Hjar [Thrua] to make the turn at Wad Tafkhsid—that turn-off to Madame Gilin's—Wad Tafkhsid, see? The driver turned around to look, see. He found blood flowing between his legs, see? "What's the matter, sir?" And he was lying on his side. He said, "Take me back."

He took him back to Kelibia. When he got back he didn't get down from the carriage, see. They say his anus, God forbid, you see, had come out this far [measures off distance from his wrist to the tips of his fingers] and blood was streaming from him. He said, "Bring me the dervish— from the sky or from the ground—bring him."

Two spahis went galloping off, knocked at the house and were told, "He's not here. Go look at Turi's [the liquor dealer's]." Where was Turi's? The tavern. "Go see Turi or [maybe he's] with his ancestor." They went to the tavern of Turi. They didn't find him. Immediately they went to Sidi Hmid's.

When the two spahis arrived, see, what did they find? They found the dervish embracing a lion. A lion, see. It was waving its tail this way and that and had thrown his hindleg half over the dervish, Sidi Mohamed, and his front leg on his neck and they were playing together the two of them—he and the lion. They screamed and immediately ran back.

When they got back they told him, "Sidi, we found him and a lion," see, "A lion!" He said, "How can that be?" They said, "A lion, no doubt about it, indisputably. He and it were playing, see on the threshold [of Sidi Hmid's shrine]. If it noticed us, the lion [had] seen us, ferreted us out . . ."[23]

"Let's go!" He didn't get back to Soliman. He didn't get back to Soliman and he died on the road. Loss of blood. All that on a word, see. He had chased him away. When he chased him away they asked him what did you do, Sidi Mohamed? He said to them, "He chased me away. May his anus fall out!"

There are other indications in the olive press story and the story of Farjallah of the importance of town walis and dervishes as symbols of the special status of Kelibia and Kelibians. Outside the region, alone, unprotected by traditional advantages of name and family reputation, the townsperson could be subject to abuse. Historically and even today, many townspeople have consistently been forced to seek education and employment and their "fortunes" outside the protective circle of town and region. Sidi Maouia's power to protect his own extends wherever they may travel. Notice al-Makki calls on Sidi Maouia by his right as a son.

The story of Farjallah's persecution and revenge on the wicked cadi also provides confirmation that these hikayat are told in a spirit of town solidarity and, to some extent, as a denial of factionalism within the town. In the hikayah, the sheikh's role is ignored, but according to archival records in Tunis, Farjallah actually was persecuted by the sheikh of the town (though there are implications that the cadi was in league with him).[24] In late 1905, on behalf of the townspeople, one of two men who could write French penned a letter of protest to the French secrétaire général accusing the sheikh (who was from a local family still prominent today) of "ignoble acts" and tyranny. He states that this sheikh "pendu . . . un pauvre malheureux, Hamed Farjallah, qui sans le secours de quelques personnes qui ont coupé le [sic] corde, aurait rendu le dernier soupir en plein marché en présence de quelques centaines de témoins!"[25]

The cadi did in fact appoint this sheikh in late spring of that year; so he was not entirely blameless. A petition had been sent earlier, in April 1905, to the French contrôleur civil (who had final say over the cadi's nominations) to prevent the sheikh's appointment. That petition, which accused him of incurring large debts, of bankruptcy, and of being a "pédéraste passif de premier qualité!,"[26] was dismissed on May 23. The contrôleur civil recorded that the matter had been investigated, the sheikh would pay his debts by selling some land, and "pour les renseignements touchant à sa vie privée, ils sont contradictoires."[27] According to the archives, the cadi did not die, at least not immediately, because in August of the same year townspeople sent at least two letters of petition to a Tunisian French-language newspaper warning that the cadi was in league with the ex-sheikh to have the sheikh's son or son-in-law succeed him.

The very different emphasis in the archival and hikayah accounts is significant, not only because the role of a fellow townsman as a culprit is minimized, but also for at least two other reasons. First, why does the hikayah portray justice as having been accomplished through a connection with the supernatural? One oft-repeated explanation is that people invoke the supernatural when they feel helpless to act on their own. Farjallah's situation, though, is handled very well by the townspeople themselves. Within days of their protest in August, the sheikh has been dismissed and, in fact, the new sheikh is not related to the old. So the townspeople had actual as well as symbolic control of the problem. The discrepancy between the archival records of the incident and the hikayah that subsequently emerged has less to do with symbolically defeating authority that could not be defeated otherwise than with symbolically repairing a real rift between established town families (Farjallah's and the sheikh's). In the story the central culprit is made into an outsider, and the hero becomes a descendent of a well-loved town wali. The storyteller, via the dervish, reasserts ideal town unity. In addition, of course, the account of the incident has been improved aesthetically, molded to the storytelling requirements of satisfactory and definitive ending, wonderful or miraculous incidents, and so on. Simultaneously, another rift or potential rift between community members is taken care of in this story, a generational rift. This story is a very good example of the "parenthetical" observations about Kelibia-past. The old-time administration is explained, topographical landmarks are pointed out, and fashion and means of transport described. Thus are the young made familiar and comfortable with their town and regional roots.

Today in Kelibia, one way in which regional or town reputation is enhanced is through victories in sports competitions. But it was not always so. Until the advent of the harvesting machine, a man with the strength and agility to reap quickly and well was in a position equivalent to the sports hero of today, winning an enviable reputation in harvesting competitions and thus bringing honor to his home town. In the following story, the harvester represents his town, but in addition to the harvester, the town wali as well as the living dervish descendant of the wali are present. This provides a triply reinforced signifier of the town's possibilities for power and prestige.

(19) UNCLE GACEM

And Sidi Hmid is there many many many times [when you need him]. You see, man? Lots of people have told me about [the powers of the walis], one of them, a person called 'Abd ar-Rahman Hawwas. That 'Abd ar-Rahman Hawwas would go at harvest time to Iffriqiyya. He'd go to Fahas, would go to Beja to harvest, see, man, and he was a skilled harvester.

Well over there, when they saw he was a good harvester, see what I mean, they ganged up on him because over there whoever finished first among the good harvesters, the women got up and ululated. "Re, re, re." Well! The one who receives the ululations—how does he look? He becomes like Antar ben Shadid![28]

Malek: So!

So, sir, to whom did 'Abd ar-Rahman Hawwas turn? To the owner of the crop, the cultivator. He said to him, "Divide that plot in half lengthwise and I . . . give me half of the field and them the other half on this side on the right and I on the left" (by himself, see, man) and he got ready and looked back at the cultivator, he said, "Anyone opens her mouth, I'll slit it for her." (They ululate for the winner. They ululate for the winner.) "[For] me or them. Agreed?" They said, "We're agreed."

And so, "God is my sponsor," and he started. When he'd made a dent in the harvesting what did 'Abd er-Rahman Hawwas say? He said, "Oh where are you, oh ben Hammuda, oh father of five cupolas?" (Because ben Hammuda has five cupolas [over his shrine].) "Here am I, your son and all alone."

He said, "And in the name of God, I started." He said "I didn't notice even what the harvest crop was ahead of me. I didn't know what crop was in front of me—silk or . . . until I had slashed about ten or twelve or fifteen strides into the thistles." He was harvesting thistles, see, he didn't wake up to what he was doing, see?

SW: Were his hands bleeding?

His hands were bleeding certainly he . . . not him . . . I'll tell you in a second. It wasn't *his* hands that were bleeding.

Well, among other things, when he said, "Where are you, oh ben Hammuda,"[29] see, "witness me your son and a stranger," and they were coalescing against him see, he had offered *bulgha* [shoes] to the dervish, bulgha to the dervish, you see, that dervish Mohamed who cursed Hedi Slim—made his anus fall out. [See story 18.]

When he got to harvesting the thistles, they got up to ululate. Moreover, the husband of one of those who ululated first got up, see, and hit her with the sickle, see, cut her forearm. He didn't like her ululating for him.

Anyway sir, they finished the harvest, see, and all that was necessary, see, and that was it [lit. and fell and got lost and forgotten]. He started home.

On his way he stopped off in Tunis. He went by the shoe shop to get the bulgha. He put them in his pouch, see, and continued home. How did he get home? Not in a taxi. On number eleven—on foot, you see.

That's all, he was still coming to the traffic island by city hall there [near the edge of town] and he found the dervish in front of him, see? He was waiting for him, see? He said, "You little bastard, did you bring the bulgha? You had us reaping thistles," see, "until our hands were dripping with blood. Don't ever do it again!"

He said, "I pulled out the bulgha, see." I told him, "Here are your bulgha."[30]

He said, "Good for you!" That's all, he went off . . . and, thank you all.

That 'Abd ar-Rahman Hawwas—I know him and the dervish, son of Sidi 'Alaya, I know and I love him. Shall I go on and tell you a little more about the dervish?

But, ultimately, a wali will not protect even one of his own descendants who is seriously wronging the townspeople. In the following account the guardian of the wali Sidi Hmid's tomb, a descendant of the wali, is killed because he is not hospitable to the terrified townspeople.

(20) AUNT FAFANI
When the invaders came and bombed, all the people hid in Sidi Hmid . . . That father of Mahmud ouild Sidi 'Alaya came and . . . swore at the visitors that had [overflowed] into his house. He swore at them and drove them out. He came out and a bomb fell on him. [unclear] [Sidi Hmid] said, "There! I won't forgive my son or my son's son. People were running for their lives. Let him die to know their value."

Thus, there are limits to what a wali will do for even his family when they threaten the good of the community. His family member is denying people his hospitality, that is, the hospitality of his zawiyya in time of trouble. Unlike the breaking of religious laws (drinking, cursing), laws of common humanity must not be tampered with.

Dervishes, though, are laws unto themselves. No one can be jealous or envious of them. Actions that would arouse great resentment if performed by other residents of the town quickly fall into perspective when an individual's unusual supernatural connections are recognized. In fact, people must experience a certain relief at these times, for unlike everyday life, nothing has to be manipulated, fought over or decided; the dervish will, with the approbation of God, do as he or she wishes and only good can come from association and/or noninterference. The dervishes are in control, a "higher control" that others cannot fully comprehend or judge, but only accept. Notice that, in story 16, Farjallah has in fact broken some kind of law concerning taxes. Folk justice is not sympathetic to tax collectors, anyway. The dervish, though, like the wali and dervish in story 18, reacts to the breaking of a cultural law relating to the humane and dignified treatment of community members. Everyone is subject to that control by dervishes; so no hierarchy exists to be dealt with except the division between townsperson and outsider. Dervishes, like walis, are signifiers of community uniqueness. They foster community unity not simply because they are unique, but because, by their own aberrant behavior, they illustrate the everyday commonality shared by the rest of the community members. The storytellers who recount these hikayat are themselves members of the community, as are the listeners; so the stories form a more intimate listener-raconteur bond as well.

The storytellers mediate community perspectives on walis and dervishes, though their control is limited by the (admittedly elusive) limits of dervish behavior. It does seem, however, that the dervishes' power is confined to the town region. As the story indicates, the dervish Sidi Mohamed came only to the edge of town to receive his bulgha (shoes).

But stories about walis or waliyyas do not simply effect pride in community and town cohesiveness or provide protection from harm. Neither are they, in the hands of the narrators, only a force for reconceptualizing of social structure, "tapping a power that transcends boundaries and cultural categories to generate a positive restructuring of society" (Brady 1978: 48). The anomalous quality of the local walis allows them to be absolutely central to town concerns and simultaneously peripheral to them; thus, they never belong entirely to the town, nor can the town completely control them. They are not wholly human nor wholly divine; they are dead and yet act in the world of the living; they are town members and yet originally outsiders. When this marginality to all other humans rather than their unique association with region or town is stressed, local walis become a force that draws into the community, rather than sets apart, the Muslims outside the town. Though Sidi Maouia is a regional holy man, there is no reason why outsiders should not recognize his power and legitimacy (and thus the specialness of Kelibia).

This wali role, like that of protector, is also manifested in the practice of their veneration. Visits to local shrines bring together varied groups—people, sometimes even men and women, who are associated with numerous economic, social, familial, age and occupation groups. They all have walis in common. Sidi Maouia is a gathering place for people from various rural areas and towns in the region. In these infrequent meetings, normally maintained social boundaries are suspended. The most famous walis have shrines and followers throughout the Middle East, so situated that a pious traveler can cross from Fez to Cairo and claim help from members of the brotherhood along the entire route.

These practical, extra-community ties are reflected in stories about the walis such as that involving Sidi Maouia's simultaneous presence in Meknes and Kelibia (story 9), and in stories of walis instantly traveling to far-off holy places to hear and report on a special sermon. Si Mohamed's "war" story (Chapter 1) about two people, a Moroccan boy and a Turkish woman who lived only briefly in Kelibia, is perhaps the best illustration of the supernatural as mediator among, and symbolic unifier of, various aspects of, and different areas within, the Arab world.

In that story, through the mediation of Sidi Maouia, we find western Islamdom united. In a time of trouble, normally disparate categories—male/female, living/dead, Moroccan/Tunisian/Libyan, Turk/Arab, young/old, strangers (outsiders)/townspeople, and heteroprax/orthoprax Islam—join forces.

The encounter between male and female there is particularly telling. In a time of stress a young man, for whom access to socially acceptable women, particularly unveiled women, outside his immediate family is nil, studies the face of a woman who wakes him from sleep. (Later, as resistance to colonialism mounted, barriers between unrelated men and women did fall in the face of practical need for collaboration.) Not only is this woman unveiled, she is educated, more educated than the young man. She is his teacher—a strikingly unusual, if not nonexistent, situation at the time (though, the implication is, not so unusual for a Turkish, noncolonized, woman). She had also traveled a very long distance during wartime to be reunited with her husband. The freedom, independence, competence, intelligence, loyalty of women are practical resources in the Arab world, and elsewhere, that have often remained untapped. They lie stored in stories such as Si Mohamed's, and in time of crisis they are called to full bloom.

Living/dead is a dichotomy that includes not only the encounter between a living man and a dead woman, but also that between Sidi Maouia and the Muslim community. The implication in the story is that Sidi Maouia has facilitated the meeting between the two good Muslims because they are properly respectful of him and his territory, "this area is the area of Sidi Maouia, an area of blessed people, a holy town."

It is through the offices of Sidi Maouia, representative of definitely heteroprax Islam—orthoprax Islam definitely frowning on intercessors between people and God—that the positive contact between strangers and Kelibians takes place. Just as surely though, it takes place through the medium of recitation by educated people of the Holy Koran—a mainstay of orthoprax Islam. Again, disparate categories join forces.

Walis and dervishes, then, are portrayed in the hikayat as anomalous beings, able to move through or between cultural boundaries such as the supernatural-natural-cultural, as well as to mediate or interfere with social categories such as man/woman, young/old, rich/poor, or upper/lower class. Thus, within the safe boundaries of the wali or dervish hikayah, the narrator is, at least for the duration of the narrative, able to resolve or dissolve the disparate categories. These stories give the narrator license to break down and confuse social and cultural categories, as well as the boundaries between order and chaos, the sacred and the secular, good and evil, the inside and the outside, and to contemplate alternative realities within the safety of the story framework.

Wali and dervish hikayat allow narrators and listeners to transcend the basically anomalous and unfair character of social relationships through effective use of supernatural barakah. Just as a festival may signify to individuals that normally unsocial behavior is appropriate within its bounds (Abrahams and Bauman 1978), a narrator may, with the sanction of a wali or dervish, explore normally unacceptable behavior. For aberrant behavior is, of course, one of the signs that an individual may be a dervish or wali.[31]

Hikayat about town heroes often show the hero assuming somewhat the same structural role as walis or dervishes in their hikayat. In the stories of conflict in this collection, the hero is only protecting or avenging himself, although this antagonist may be one whom other members of the town have also encountered. The heroic deeds again are achieved by transcending norms or boundaries—whether physical, social structural, or hierarchical. The hero, like the wali, is able to interact with the extra-Kelibian world, either natural or cultural, and his encounter too may be either positive or negative; he may establish rapport with it or dominate it. These stories are reminiscent of the dervish stories in that prudent actions of reasonable people are abandoned for impulsive, risky, high-gain or high-loss actions. The hero's difference from other townspeople, however, does not depend on religious distinction. Heroes are, on the contrary, "like us but more so." Often the adventures of these heroes take place outside the town. In his travels the picaresque hero may meet and master a variety of people—country folk, city folk, foreigners—within a variety of social or cultural situations. He reenters his own society after having achieved a certain status or reputation for his town. Thus, from his town, he acquires a certain power for himself. (As might be expected, none of the younger men are seen as having the grandeur of the larger-than-life earlier protagonists, rather as walis are not recognized as walis until after they die.)

The following story illustrates some of these points. Notice that Uncle Gacem not only "defeats" the hierarchically superior German and Italian outsiders, but he also learns to master nature as well, making a living on the farm until the war is over. Furthermore, his deception is certainly risky, and worth doing only to preserve his own self-respect. Unlike dervishes, however, heroes show an awareness of the consequences of failure and a willingness to plan carefully.

(21)   UNCLE GACEM

[In 1936 Uncle Gacem inherited from his father a farm he had never seen. He went out from Kelibia with his wife and children to live and work on the farm, and he would go into market at Menzel Temime to buy supplies and sell farm products—including clay pots of butter.]

Until the year '38, '39 came *la guerre*. Who came to Kelibia? The Germans and the Italians.

Sabra: The army?

And radar and . . . As usual I had six pots of butter that I took to Menzel Temime to the market area. I saw nothing but cars (Jeeps). Italians and Germans came over [to me]. "Gobble Gabble Gibble" [Germans talking]. What was this crap? [he said to himself] [An Italian] took out the pots of butter. Six pots. He gave me six hundred [francs]—a pot for one hundred francs. [I said], "Oh comrade, in Menzel Temime it's one hundred and fifty francs."

He looked at me [in Italian], "What are you saying? What are you saying?!"

I looked at him and said [in Italian], "That's fine, thank you so much." (I could speak like that a little.)

He said [in Italian], "Didn't you hear what the bey of Tunis said?"

Malek: What does that mean?

"You didn't hear what the bey of Tunis is doing now?"

I said [in Italian], "I haven't heard."

He said [in Italian], "Now the president [bey] said to eat *halfa*."[32]

I said, "Halfa?"

He said [in Italian], "After people eat halfa they can shit rope."

"By God," I told him, "good for him."

He said [in Italian], "Aren't you content?"

I said, "I'm more than happy."

Malek: He asked you if you weren't happy?

Yeah! [repeats] "Well, *arrivederci*!!"

"Gobble Gabble Gibble."

Sabra: People were afraid of them?

To them, killing a person was like killing a fly.

I rode off, my head spinning. [I was] really burned. Why? Because since I was born I don't remember myself abusing other people and they don't interfere with me. I wouldn't let anyone take advantage of me. I went on into Menzel Temime to the market—muddling in darkness.

Malek: Angry?

Angry. I got down. They were selling those plain clay pots. Pots like this [holds one up]. Simple, not . . . Mugs for ten surdi a mug. I got twenty mugs. I put them in the saddle bags and got on and rode home.

Malek: Not doing a single errand?

No tea, no sugar, no olive oil, no soap, no meat, no candy for the children. (They would usually meet me on the road, "Baba, Baba did you bring . . . ? Did you bring . . . ?" I'd normally bring them candy or give them dates or something.) [This time] I got to the house, got down, see? My wife looked at me—she knew me. "Daddy, daddy, did you bring . . . ?"

"Shhh! Quiet! Get in the house! Get in the house!" She came and unloaded the donkey. She tied it up, and put out its feed.

I had a glass of tea and a cigarette. The wife looked over and saw the twenty empty pots . . .

Time went by until it was the following Monday. I turned to the wife and said, "When you churn the milk put the butter in a separate pan." She agreed. Monday after lunch, after my kids and wife had eaten, I turned to my wife and told her, "Go to the Jemma's house."

She said, "Why? What is there to do there?"

I said, "I have guests coming from far away. Afterwards I'll call you back." She took her kids and left. And I didn't have guests, I. . . .

When she left I took a bucket and a hoe. There was a place where there was mud, mud. I went and filled up more than half of that bucket with mud. Got out the pots "slap, slap" [gestures slapping the mud into the pots].

Malek: You left a centimeter at the top of each pot?

I added, added the mud—added the mud to the pots to a centimeter from the top. I filled all twenty pots and brought out the pan of butter. It was quite a job. I had a butcher knife [gestures smoothing butter on top of each pot]. I filled the twenty pots and the pan was still . . . capable of filling forty others. I put them in the saddle bags, arranged them and all. I whistled and the wife and the kids came.

Sabra: You didn't want her to know?

I didn't want her to know. I washed up—washed the pail (I didn't want . . .) I washed the bucket and washed everything . . . all that was necessary. Why didn't I want . . . ? Maybe she would tell an Arab [country person] and he would copy me. He'd end up at the end of a rope because if they found him out by God they'd kill him there *sur place*!

Well, anyway, my wife came and said, "In the name of God! In the name of God! Praise to the Prophet! Praise to the Prophet! Praise to the Prophet! Oh son of Engliz, Sidi Ahmed al Lakhdhur visited you."

I said, "Hush, he'll doom us." [Bad luck to mention it.]

The next day, if we live,[33] in the morning I mounted [having] put the saddle bags on and we got trotting along until we got to a station where they'd put up a barricade. "Gobble Gabble Gibble."

"Oh, damn it to hell! [thinking] Who can understand you? How do I know what you're saying?" The Italian looked at me (and I know a little Italian). He said, "Do you understand what he told you?" [says the same thing in Italian this time] "Understand what he told you?"

I told him [in Italian], "No understand German, only Italian." (In Italian, "solo" means "only.")

So he said to me [in Italian], "Give" [the pots].

I told him [in Italian], "Just count them."

Sabra: What does that mean?

Malek: Yeah.

"Look and count by yourself."

Malek: In other words, you wouldn't touch them.

Yeah. . . . "Two, four, six, eight, ten, . . . sixteen, eighteen, twenty. *Bella bella* [in Italian], you're a man."

Anyway, that's it. He pulled out the money. Tekka tekka [noise of coins being handed over]. He gave me three thousand francs.

Sabra: Three thousand!

Malek: How much for each pot?

One hundred fifty. Well, you see, the other time when it was pure butter he gave me one hundred francs and when it was mud he gave me one hundred fifty francs. . .

Sabra: The same man?

Yes, that was he. There were about twenty there but those two—one German and one Italian.

I, my girl, went to Menzel Temime, stopped by the tobacco shop, got a package of cigarettes, and matches, and didn't get off the donkey and hit the road for Kelibia and turned from there and kept going and twisted and turned and twisted and went home to Menzel Brahim. Almighty God's truth I didn't go into town or return to sell butter. Hey! Hey! Good for him! Good for him! Well he, well he . . . when I go there's no need to ask my name. I have an address. I have an address by which he'd know me [i.e., the Italian could just ask for the man with one bad eye]. Certainly, he'd know me for sure. No, I didn't go back at all. I would stay in Menzel Brahim, go to Azmur, bring meat from Azmur, and olive oil and everything and tobacco, and tea and sugar from Azmur and go home. Between Azmur and Menzel Brahim there are about four kilometers.

Malek: Not too far.

No, not far.

Well, I had friends. One called Gharbi, and one called Mohamed Shkili.

Malek: 'Azazin Shkili?

'Azazin Shkili. Gharbi is dead and Mohamed Shkili, son of [unclear] Shkili, is still alive. When did I go down into town? When the Germans and Italians said "friend," and the Germans went "kaput." All of a sudden the French and the English [came back]. Well I . . . what's left for me to worry about? I'm going to go into town. I had my house in town [repeats four times], and everything.

Sabra: How many years did you stay away?

Nine years! That's all. I sought out my friends. "Come on. Where have you been? We were going to come looking for you. We were saying that one's dead or who knows." But anyway, we started getting together, sitting around. Gharbi looked over and said, "Where have you been?"

I said, "Quiet with your 'Where have you been?' As soon as the Germans and Italians left I came."

He said, "Why? What do you have to do with the damned Germans and Italians?"

I said, "Oh. Ah . . . yeah. What do I have to do with them! The truth is . . . this and that and thus and such . . ." How I fixed the butter and how I. . . . That Gharbi 'Azazin was sitting cross-legged.

Malek: On the stone bench?

In the entrance hall.

Malek: I know who he is.

He went like this [makes as if to jump up]. He said, "Mohamed Shkili." He said, "Had one pot fallen, Gacem would be dead." Mohamed Shkili leaned over and answered, "and his donkey with him."

Historically in Kelibia, prudence has dictated a patient and acquiescent attitude toward dominating powers, and hikayat such as this one clearly stand for actions many a townsman wanted to take himself or would like to think he would have taken in the same situation. In fact, the evaluative expression by Shkili, "Had one pot fallen, Gacem would be dead," has become a proverb in Kelibia, used to describe a close call by many more people than those who know the story behind it. Malek was surprised and delighted to learn that there was a narrative base for this local proverb.[34] In this collection heroes provide what supernatural characters cannot—models for townsmen—being outstanding in certain fields of endeavor (hunting, tracking, harvesting), taking chances, displaying a certain panache. And the heroes signify one way in which the town as a whole would represent its past among themselves and to the outside world—men able to master the city and the countryside without losing their own fealty and sensibility, men who could defend themselves by their wits or by physical strength. And men, as mentioned earlier, who then would marry, settle down and become the respected town elders who tell stories.

Many of the encounters, such as the following, have to do with the symbolic or actual conquering of cultural outsiders by feats of strength and coordination. In these confrontations there is none of the passionate hostility directed against the outsider as displayed in the previous story. Perhaps this difference is explained by the fact that, in both of the following hikayat, the contenders are relative social equals. In fact, though it is not stated, the Kelibian may have the social advantage here since the narrator portrays him as harvesting for the sport. Presumably, other harvesters are not in the same situation. Also, physical strength is not the only qualification needed to be a hero. In hero stories, the protagonist exhibits controlled strength, planning, and intelligence.

(22) SI HAMDAN

As for Mohamed ouild Si 'Ali, the one we all know, son of my father's maternal uncle and of my mother's paternal uncle, but I didn't know him. I still wasn't forty days old when he died. My grandfather, his brother, the father of my mother, was older than him. I remember him.

The two would go harvest and, look at the way they did it, just for pleasure! Both men were married and had children not . . . It was a hobby—not even to earn money, nothing like that. Anyway, he was well-to-do.

Malek: They were infatuated [with harvesting].

Sabra: Where did they go?

Where . . . They went to Beja.

Malek: To the area where a lot of wheat is [grown].

They went to Beja to harvest. [Mohamed] didn't smoke tobacco in front of his [older] brother. [Mohamed is showing respect (qaddir) to his older brother.]

Malek: He felt respect.

Yeah. He didn't smoke cigarettes in front of his brother. If he happened to want to smoke, he'd move off a little way. [gestures] My grandfather, God bless him, told us that he said to him while he watched him take out the tobacco, "God break your jaw. Have you no respect?"

In the afternoon [Mohamed] called the farmer over and said, "I'm going to leave, give me my earnings because I and my brother live by respect and I can't give up the addiction, therefore . . ."

"My son, I'll give . . ."

He interrupted, "Do you have other harvesters you can put me with? Don't put me with my brother. No, forget it. No use insisting."

The farmer had another area [to harvest] say from here to Tahert, so he took him there and brought another in his place. This [new] one had two wives. That harvester had two wives gleaning in his tracks. A tough guy. And my poor old grandfather, was just so-so. Just a harvester. Average. (But his brother could harvest like four [either like four hands, or four rows, or the name of a harvesting technique]—like child's play, like a game and laughing at the same time.)

Anyway . . . Until one day, that guy that they had put with [the grandfather] started changing. Not that he [the grandfather] couldn't harvest but he couldn't go into the ocean like that tough one. Yeah, real rough! Well, they started competing without the division [into who harvests which rows]. They started baiting each other, getting at each other's throats like camels, you see. He said, [the stranger] "Sir . . . ." (he insulted him), "and I called upon God [i.e., started harvesting], and where are you, Sidi Maouia? Where are you?!"

He said, "And I looked over at the team that Mohamed my brother was in." He said, "I said, [to himself] So he smokes, by damn, so what if he drinks liquor—only let him save, cover for me!" He said, "And I looked over thus [gestures with his head towards his 'partner'] [in order] to show my brother." He said, "I couldn't find an opportunity." [He didn't want to give himself away to the adversary.] He said, "And by coincidence Mohamed on one of the times he stands up, watched [the giant] tie the sheaf and go thus [throw it behind him to go on to cut the next]. He flung them over his shoulder banded as if tied by wire—as if tied by machine." He said "He tied his first sheaf and again stood up only to find another sheaf flying back."

He said, "And all I heard was running. I turned around," he said, "and found Mohamed, my brother, the scythe under his arm, and he came to me, came like an eagle." He said, "And he got here."

As soon as he arrived, he said, "Call the farmer." He told him, "Look. Divide us up. Divide us up by footsteps [pace out equal rows]."

He said, "and they started in." He said, "The other one's wives ululated in his path—the two women ululated [for their husband]." He said, "hurry, hurry, hurry." He said, "Well sir, when . . . " He said, "The other one ate up the ground. My brother was behind."

He said, "When they were halfway through the section," he said, "I don't know how—God knows it looked like the stubble trembled by itself, the harvest fell by itself." He said, "When there were only about two meters to go, his partner still had two meters to go and [Mohamed] was finished." He said, "He turned in front of him" (and it's like killing someone to come in front and harvest for him) . . . He said, "He turned in front of him and went like that!" [gestures motion of the scythe cutting] He said, "He was on the last cut—the last cut in his hand." He said, "And he reaped it for him. Out of his hand. He left him with one stub in his hand. He took the wheat stalks in his fist and harvested them. He left him only stubble in his hand. He cut below and the other cut above."

Malek: Ah! So it was the other who reaped?

No! Ouild Si 'Ali!!

Malek: Ouild Si 'Ali reaped?

Yeah! Of course. [The other] reaped thus and he harvested it from his hand. If the farmer hadn't taken his side, by God he would have killed [Mohamed]. And they went home.

The narrator, whose oldest children are now in college, remembers that he had recently married when he heard the following story:

(23)   SI HAMDAN

Aye. Until in the year that Mahmud Samoud bought the first [harvesting] machine. That Haj Mahmud. Haj Mahmud Samoud bought a harvesting machine. And he was harvesting with it in Bou Tarfa. That day he got up early to harvest Bou Tarfa, it's called.

Malek: The first harvester that came to Kelibia?

The first harvester . . . No, there was a machine [worked] by horses that Haj M'hamed Sharif had. But this that Haj Mahmud Samoud bought was the first of its kind. The first machine . . . I was married when he brought the machine. They had a piece of land called Bou Tarfa sown with wheat. That day early it was harvesting there.

Well, I got up a little late. There used to be a stone bench in front of the shop of Min Sahli. Min Sahli was a greengrocer across from the Café Slim. The little bench was there. I came around by the Hajjam's [barber's] house to find Haj 'Amor, God have mercy on him, the father of Mahmud. He was sitting on the bench. "Good morning, oh father Haj."

He said, "Good morning." He went like this [gestures him over]. "What are you doing?"

I said, "Well, I'm going to drink some coffee."

He said, "Come over by me." I came, sat down next to him. Ahmed Nubli came at that time and Ahmed Jlidi bringing me coffee.

He said, "Well, Mahmud bought a machine."

I said, "Inshallah mabruk."

He said, "And today early he harvested Bou Tarfa. Aye," he said, "By God I'd like to go watch!" He said, "That's the piece of land that . . ."

(Now, they had been friends, Haj 'Amor Samoud, they had been close friends, he and Mohamed ouild Si 'Ali—hunters and falconers.) He said, "That was the piece of land where I had outsiders harvesting." He said, "There was one . . ." (Outsiders and townsmen.) "There was one outsider who was very much a devil [at harvesting]."

He said, "Ouild Si 'Ali had given it up [by then]. He no longer wanted to harvest." (Because he harvested for pleasure, not for money. No, he harvested for pleasure.) He said, "But I decided to trick him into going out there [for a match]." He said, "I told him, 'Mohamed, tomorrow let's go hunting. We'll go to the forest and walk around.' He replied, 'Great!' I said, 'In the morning, let's meet here.' "

He said, "In the morning I put saddlebags on the donkey and filled the cartridges." He said, "And ouild Si 'Ali came on his donkey also." He said, "We mounted and immediately went out." He said, "When we arrived at Bou Tarfa . . . 'May God help you' [to the workers]. Now I had told him about him [the good harvester]. [Ouild Si 'Ali] said, 'I could eat him for breakfast, that Arab there.' "

He said, "When we got to Bou Tarfa, ouild Si 'Ali," he said, "was wearing a jebba and shamla and white clothes and didn't have a scythe." (When he used to work he had a special made-to-order scythe. He didn't like just any scythe.) He said, "Come on, here's your friend!! Come on, oh Mister ouild Si 'Ali, now you're going to get down."

He replied, "Leave me alone, oh 'Amor. Forget it, man." He said, "Let the people do their work . . . [It's a] hobby for the young. It's all over now."

He said, "By the head of Si Mohamed and the mercy of Si 'Ali, get down."

He said, "He said, 'I don't even have a scythe.' "

He said, "I went over to a worker." He said, "And I got a scythe."

He went like this to the jebba [took it off over his head] and threw it over the donkey. "Over three years I . . . ," he said, and got down.

He said, " 'Abdallah Sheikh, the overseer, that Bou Sheikh, set the divisions for them, set the divisions—each one a piece of land." He said,

"Mohamed ouild Si 'Ali stood rolling a cigarette." He said, "He looked at the group and said, 'Does he have a stroke other than that?' "

Malek: Another what?

Another stroke. Meaning, can he use any other than that one stroke. He said "And [Mohamed] got down and lit the cigarette." He said, "Still the Arab was pulling ahead. Still the Arab was making progress." He said, "Until there were only three rows left." He said, "[Then], God knows it was like Gamoudi." He said, "[Mohamed] went like that [gestures swinging the scythe] and shaved off his mustache,"[35] harvested it from his hand, as was customary. They'll tell you he had a stroke God knows and God forbid a stroke with the scythe . . . He said, "He went thus [gestures], not hurting him but . . . "

He said, "Right then [the Arab] took his children and his belongings and left. Right away."

Mohamed ouild Si 'Ali doesn't just hurl himself into the contest in either story. In the first, he attempts to regulate the contest by stopping the unstructured harvesting and calling the farmer over to divide the area to be harvested between him and his opponent. In the second case, he rolls a cigarette and smokes it calmly while evaluating the other man's harvesting techniques. Like other town heroes, he is in control aesthetically as well as practically.

Also, the man signifies a graceful combination of city and country aptitudes. He rides out to the field dressed very elegantly and all in white—like a gentleman. Yet he can defeat a country man in a country art. He even had a custom-made scythe. And he shows a cultured respect for his older brother by trying not to smoke in front of him.

The latter hikayah mediates between tradition and progress as well as city and country or nature and culture. The very last field to be harvested by Mohamed ouild Si 'Ali is the first to be harvested by the first motor-driven harvesting machine to come to Kelibia. Unlike American stories, the contest is not between person and machine. Mohamed is not even alive to see the change. His old friend is, though, and he chooses the occasion of the advent of the machine to tell a young man about his great uncle. Now as Si Hamdan tells the story to his three sons and two daughters, it has become a monument to Haj 'Amor Samoud as well.

Clearly neither the older man who relates the story to Si Hamdan nor Si Hamdan are to be "thrown" by the introduction of new technology. In this case, the mechanical harvester is not to be perceived as forced upon the farmers, though in world economic terms the farmers have little choice if they wish to remain competitive. One could, in fact, speculate that the introduction of the new machine, intrusion of a foreign "body," must be balanced by a story in which another foreign "body," the outsider harvester, is trounced. Change is not unwelcome, but must be put in its (Kelibian) place. When Hamdan meets the old man, the harvester is only briefly mentioned, the interesting story is about the past, when there were no machines, but gentlemen harvesters.

The old man, through Hamdan's eyes, is ensuring that the machine is put in proper perspective, but why does Hamdan pass the story on? The appreciation of the potential and power of the past is certainly one message, but consideration of future possibilities is also there. For Gamoudi, a Tunisian who won an Olympic gold medal in track at the 1968 Mexico City Summer Olympics, is compared to a master harvester of old. Gamoudi is not a Kelibian, but in the world context, close enough. For all of Tunisia he was the international hero they were looking for. He represented both speed and efficiency. (For Malek, of course, the analogy is particularly apt since he is a sports teacher.) Obviously, Haj 'Amor does not make the comparison of Gamoudi to the swift reaper. This is an addition by Hamdan to meet the challenges of the present day better. Like Gamoudi, Kelibians today can master the world market, and Kelibia is not perceived as a receptacle for imported teachers, hospitals, ports, police or tractors. As individuals, Kelibians, like Gamoudi, can compete and win in the wider world. Like Gamoudi, they can or should then bring their laurels home. Again, Kelibians can balance tradition and change. Overall, Hamdan is also valuing human values over machine virtuosity—historically sandwiching the harvester between Mohamed ouild Si 'Ali and Gamoudi. Again and again, simply by his loving sketches of the Kelibian landscape and human resources, Hamdan indicates one factor of these stories that is not negotiable. Kelibians must rejoin the community.

Another town hero, known for his skill in tracking, was Mohamed ben Gidara. In the following hikayah he uses his talent for tracking animals to track cattle rustlers. Mastery of natural signs is used here to thwart corrupt authority:

(24) Si Hamdan

In earlier times in Wazdra—beneath the hill on this side [is a place] we called Youssef's plot.

Sabra: Called what?

We called it Youssef's plot. It was a winter forest, a natural forest, not a cultivated one. I remember when there was still part of it left.

And the people were herders. Not like now. They owned a lot of livestock earlier. Especially, lots of cattle and the cattle were pastured out in the countryside at night. Winter to summer. In the winter in that thick forest in the warmth they could spend the night. And there were cattle rustlers.

One morning they came and found a few head of cattle were missing. And at that time a certain person was in charge (I don't know if you've heard of him) a caliph [administrator] called Nwali in Menzel Temime.

Malek: There was a caliph in Menzel Temime?

In Menzel Temime.

Malek: His name was what?

His nickname was Nwali. Well it's a family in Menzel Temime. The Nwali family. Well, that guy was involved and the group of . . . . During the day he'd keep them in jail and at night let them out to steal.

Malek: Ahhhh!

So! They started following the tracks and there's a gully, the one that had the Sidi bou Bakkir bridge. Every kilometer . . . (Is the smoke bothering you?) [Sabra: No, it doesn't matter] or less, it's known by a different name. There it is called Sidi bou Bakkir Wad. Go a little further and it becomes Lulija. After it becomes 'Ain umm Ersaf and after that it turns into 'Ain bou Driga as you keep going. The wadi is divided up. You go a certain distance and it has another name. And it's still the same wad.

So, the 'Ain umm Ersaf [lit., "rocky surface"] is a section of which you'd say the stones were cut to order. Rows of stones, thus. It goes down thus exactly so and then the stones are arranged in exact rows looking across. At that point the water gets wider. Well, as the thieves were taking the cattle, they crossed at that place. There were many of them taking the cattle. How were they caught? One of the group (they used to wear wool capes then) one of them slipped at 'Ain umm Ersaf. He was skinned here [points to his knee]. His skin was cut.

Well, as they [the trackers] were following the tracks—some on donkeys and mules, some on horses and some on foot, they got to the hill near Skalba. In view of Skalba [just before Menzel Temime] there is a big orchard—fig and olive trees. The trail died there in that orchard. They cast here, cast there. It died there.

A group stayed to keep watch and a group went down to the caliph. The caliph said, "The thieves are all in jail. I've got all the thieves of this area here in jail." That Mohamed ben Gdara looked over at him and said, "sir. . . ."

Malek: The one who could track?

Yeah, he and his brother. He was the best though. He was a little smarter than them but still, they were all clever devils. He said, "bring out the thieves, I want to see them."

He got them out and lined them up. He said, "This one did it and this one and this one." He pulled out six or seven of them. [The caliph] said, "How do you know?" He said, "That one slipped at such and such a place, skinned a place above his right knee." (Now, the cape fell to here.) [gestures below the knee] He said, "And I may add, oh Mr. Caliph, lift up his cape and if you don't find it, over his right knee let him go and put me in his place in jail." He pulled up his cape and lo and behold the place was all skinned. And he told them, "Come on, I'll take you to the place where he fell too." (Not just that he fell, but which leg, the right leg and above the knee also!)

Malek: He knew exactly!

(Because his leg—when he slipped like that—he'd find a smear of blood here [points to his right leg] above the knee.)

That was all. From there they took the spahis with them. They brought out all the cattle.

The dilemma of the countryside is like that of the city. Together with the positive aspects of the city are its dangers—loss of the town's population to sickness, permanent exile, loss of appreciation for town values to city "glitter." Together with the positive aspects of nature that a man should master—harvesting or tracking (definitely men's work in these stories)—are its dangers—the possibility that nonselective adoption of country ways may decivilize or dehumanize. The animal-like behavior in upcoming hikayah[29] is one illustration of such reversion to uncultured behavior. Rather than share with his brother the prickly pears he is eating off the cactus, a man growls at him like a dog to warn him off. Although food comes from the bounty of the countryside, it needs to be managed properly. After it is harvested or tracked, and before it is served it must be civilized; if animal, it must be killed with appropriate ceremony and, whether animal or plant, carefully cleaned, formulaically prepared, and attractively presented.

Although there is wisdom to be found in the countryside as well, a kind of folk wisdom that puts "city learning" to shame is illustrated by the following "homily" by Si Hamdan shortly after he observes that "the Bedouins know more than the children of the city":

There were two scholars traveling around in the countryside who came in early afternoon to a place where the hospitable Arabs [bedouin] were camped. (They are pleased to have guests. From the beginning of time Arabs [bedouins] have been hospitable.) They came to the place and [the bedouins] were happy to see them and took them into the tent, took them in and the woman was getting lunch. All of a sudden she was running and bringing the stack of wood inside. They looked at her and said, "What's the matter?" She said, "It is going to rain." "What?" "The rain is going to fall." They looked and saw no sign of it. She said, "The dog pissed in the *kanun* [brazier]." Rain started falling. The skies opened up—water everywhere, [one scholar] waved at his friend and said, "Come on, get up, your learning and mine just disappeared in the piss of that dog."

There are other kinds of folk knowledge now banished to the countryside as dangerous, irreligious, obsolete, or useless—culturally suspect even though their components (writing, religion, incense, medicine) in other contexts are the accoutrements of a civilized people. As can be seen in the following texts, practitioners of magic, writers of charms or spells for amulets or potions, even though these employ incense, which in other contexts has purifying properties, have gradually been literally as well as figuratively pushed to the edges of town. Now, if a young wife, for example, seeks a magician to help her control her husband or a husband his wife or in-laws, she or he must seek this magician in the countryside. This behavior, if it becomes known, is now a source of embarrassment, amusement, or alarm to other community members.

The community then is in the process of bounding out, by negotiation, these magical interactions with the supernatural, and simultaneously those people who perform them, and those who make use of their services. Some of this negotiation takes place through the manner in which these magical practices and adherents to them are portrayed in hikayat. Notice that the central characters in the following hikayat are not portrayed unsympathetically though they are not the equivalent of the heroes discussed above. They represent a different kind of town character, part clown, part bumpkin, or what Dorson would call the rogue hero.[36] Their actions are the prankish actions of younger men. The narrator is careful to point out, however, that no harm comes to the naive suppliants from their actions. In fact, one of the messages of the hikayat is obviously that all of the people with difficulties achieve their objectives without aid of the spell writer.

The existence of hikayat such as the following does not indicate that there are not townspeople who still believe, or half believe, or sometimes believe, in the existence of genies or the efficacy of spells. On the contrary, it is just their unresolved status that makes them subjects of narrative exploration:

(25) SI HAMDAN

Well now, sir, another thing. My cousin who is grown now. Look, he's got three kids. He was born the year . . . the year that . . . the day that . . . the day that Bourguiba came here and was booed. In the year thirty-eight. (He went on to Hammam Ghazaz.) Exactly that same day. He was born that year and he was called Habib.

From the time he was born in April, approximately (because it was spring), until he reached six months, until October or November, the little kid was sickly, always sick. He'd bawl or whatever. One day I was in the shop and the shop. . . . We lived in the same building. The house and the shop were like from here to the door. Close together. My uncle came home from the country. (And Slimène 'Abdellatif was our neighbor. Between his house and our house was like from here to the side of the Shaa'r house over there.)

His wife gave [my uncle] . . . What do you call it? The thing that they put on the heads of babies then—a bonnet or a hood? God, I don't know.

Malek: A bonnet? [per Salah Khoudja, a *scoufia* or protective bonnet]

Or a hood. A hood . . . They used to make a hood like the hood of a burnoose. And she gave him four eggs. She told him, "Take it to Slimène 'Abdellatif and he'll figure out [the baby's] problem. His name doesn't suit him. His name doesn't suit him." (And at the time a package of tobacco was a franc and a surdi, and four eggs were twelve surdi and . . . [That was the charge?] Yeah, that was the charge. Yeah, that was the fee.

My uncle, God bless his soul, came in and instead of going to Slimène 'Abdellatif, came to us at the shop. He said, "Do you see what your aunt . . ." This and that. "The little kid is sickly and whatever. Don't you think it's better that I should buy myself half a package of tobacco with the four eggs than give them to Slimène 'Abdellatif?"

And I at the time was studying under ben Sheikh at night. I had notebooks in my schoolbag. I said, "You know what we'll do uncle?" (The kanun was burning like it is now, like that.) I said, "Put them in the teapot and let them cook and here's a franc and surdi. You buy a package of tobacco and she, I'll get her pieces of paper ready now and we'll make the cure for her." (I was used to taking . . . Women asked me . . . [Women had sent him to consult Slimène 'Abdellatif before so he knew what his aunt would expect to receive].)

Seven nights with massaging [of the child probably with a liquid made by dissolving paper with special writing in water], and seven nights with incense [probably breathing incense burned with one of the papers with special writing]. He'd take a piece of paper like this—about two fingers wide and he'd cut it seven times but not cutting all the way through. [For] the first night one line, the second night two lines, and the third night three lines and the fourth night four lines and the seventh, seven lines. Begin with that which has one line and burn that one with incense the first night. And that which has two lines, that's for the second night, and so on. And he'd give you the amulet, a folded piece of paper. He'd tell you, "Drip a little candle wax on this and cover it with a clean piece of cloth and sew it and tie it on him and as for the massage, get some musc or a few cherry nut kernels or whatever it's called. Dissolve it in a little water and massage with it seven nights." And he'd give you a name. Whatever crossed his mind. That's the story anyway.

So anyway I came and got the paper, divided it up into pieces like that and made a line and two and three and four and five lines—-lines like when they bleed you—only with a pencil. There was nothing [written] on them and I wrote on a little piece of paper, "In the name of God, the Merciful, the Compassionate," and I folded it and said to him, "Tell her to sew this into a piece of cloth and pin it to him on his hood and what do you want to name him, uncle?"

He said, "Let's call him Hedi, maybe God will show him the way."

And now he's [Hedi's] got three kids. And here he's Hedi, his name's Hedi. He neither fell nor was pushed. [He got well completely by chance.] But his name used to be Habib.

Mohamed, teenaged son of the narrator: And what's it say on his birth certificate?

At that time no certificate or shit [laughter]. Just a name, that's all.

(26) Si Hamdan
Another one, what's his name was telling us . . . Hassine ben Hmid, God bless him, had an uncle who was a little goofy and his mother was always sickly. That is, the mother of Hassine ben Hmid. Well, they heard about some healer in Menzel Temime, a really clever healer. She gave him two francs and gave him her handkerchief and told him, "Go on to Menzel Temime, Hassine. This franc is for you and this franc give to the healer and go to Menzel Temime and get the writing."

Sabra: What was he going to write?

He'd write what she should do for her illness.

Where did he go? He went to the center of town. (This incident took place maybe seventy years ago.) [1909] He went to the center of town. He'd tell you he found a paper from a French newspaper that the wind had blown under the town wall. He grabbed it. (Normally a man going by foot to Menzel Temime would take a day to get there and back.) He sat against the wall and stayed there and started dividing it up, tearing off pieces, small pieces, and worked and folded them for her into a set of packets, packet by packet. The pieces of paper were all from that newspaper in French and he went home with it when enough time had passed for him to go and return. (In other words, he let enough time pass that he could have made a trip to Menzel Temime and back.)

And he entered as if he were tired—dead tired.

"What?"

"Well, sir, here's what, here's what he suggested."

The poor thing went and did [what he said]. She recovered and got up. Later he told her, "You stupid woman" (excuse the language) "that was a French newspaper!"

(27) SI HAMDAN

This was sometime before independence, maybe in '48 or '49. Around there. Khmais ben Hmid, God bless him, father of Habib, that shop owner in [area of Kelibia], was an older man, a son of a gun, plus [Mohamed] ben Youssef, an even bigger son of a gun. Who was it . . . a little guy from Mahdia [came to Kelibia for seasonal fishing]. He said, "I have a spell on me."

Malek: What do you mean "spell" ?

He was engaged to this girl and they put a spell on him preventing him from getting her. And he wanted to marry her.

When he got here to Kelibia and he was living at the beach they told him, "If you want to remove the spell, well, here's Slimène 'Abdellatif. Go see him." He started asking for the house of Slimène 'Abdellatif. (Now, Slimène 'Abdellatif at the time had sold the house and Khmais ben Hmid had bought it. Today, his son Haj Hamda lives there. It was still empty at the time. It had been a year since he bought it, [but] he was still at the Qarush house. It had been a year since he bought it or less.)

He ran into ben Youssef [and Khmais].

"Ahhh," [ben Youssef] said. "Here's his [Slimène's] teacher. No need to look any further. Come on father Khmais." (Now, Mohamed was [pretending to be] his apprentice.) "Come on father Khmais."

He said, "By God, shame on you. You shouldn't do that, Mohamed. You know I've stopped doing that stuff. I don't do it anymore." (And actually, he didn't know anything. He was pretending. He couldn't write for shit. He couldn't write "one" or "two," let alone his own name. He knew nothing. Even the two suras he learned so he could pray he remembered so-so. He knew nothing. Still, he wore a jebba and burnoose and the man was a camel [big, impressive guy], see, and [wore] a turban.

Malek: In other words, he was ignorant.

Yeah. He said, "I'll do it for you. Let's go to Mustafa ben Hmid, the shop owner." (The father of 'Azaiez. He was that Khmais's uncle.) "Uncle Mustafa, give me whatever it is, the things I long ago abandoned."

He brought him the credit ledger (where he listed creditors). He brought him the ledger. He brought him the inkwell. They got around in a circle. To make a long story short, he started.

He told him something like, "Go to the store that is across from the beach, buy some incense from him and buy whatever and put the thing, the talisman, under your left arm. If it's God's will, in a week your needs will be met."

"What do I owe you?"

He said, "No, no my son, I've given it up unless you want to give a little something, thanks." [But] ben Youssef stretched out his hand. What did he get? Well, God, I forget.

That's all. He worked and everything. The full moon came (well, there's nothing to do then) so he went home to his town. [Fishermen don't go out during the full moon.] As soon as he "threw out the line" she came. And all of a sudden there was no more spell. As soon as he would make a request, they were at his beck and call. When he returned, he brought [Khmais] a big fish and "thank you so much" and "whatever I can do for you Sidi Sheikh, Sidi Sheikh."

In two of the above hikayat, the subcultural practice of writing spells is balanced by an extra-cultural presence. In one it is a French newspaper; in the other it is the gullible man from Mahdia. The latter story portrays the practice, then, as something "other" people do. Use of the French newspaper in the former emphasizes not only that the writing is nonreligious, but in fact that it is not even written in Arabic. This mockery, blasphemy, of the "religious" spell writing might be expected by its adherents to have adverse effects on the deceivers or the deceived but in fact, Hassine saves money and energy, and his mother gets well. (Also, in both the first and second stories, the employment of spell writers is portrayed as the practice of uneducated, naive women.)[37] After this series of stories, discussion turned to other instances where gullible people have been duped by faith healers, to religious deceptions of various sorts. "After all," one of Si Hamdan's sons remarked, "Look at what happened at Jonestown."

Another example of the quick wit of the rogue hero is the following:

(28) Si Hamdan

Well, we had someone called Hmida ben Rjab. I knew him [when] he was a very old man—older than any of those people that I told you about. He was, God knows and God forbid, he was a riddler. And he had a brother, nothing. He knew nothing.

And they were people who worked as haulers. We didn't have trucks in those days. They would haul, for example, merchandise to the south and the Sahel and bring it back by camel. They'd stay on the road a long time. That Si Hmida ben Rjab had a place, a café, where he'd pass the evenings with people who knew him when he went south. When he got there they'd bring out their riddles. Whatever they put before him he solved. He wouldn't hesitate. Quickly, quickly he'd find the answer.

Until one journey his brother went. Now, the camels know [the way] and he told him about where the place was. He told them, "I'm the brother of so-and-so and I such-and-such."

"Do you know riddles like your brother?"

When they came, they sat, unloaded the merchandise, and prepared to spend the evening. (And here he knows maybe [four] riddles.) Whatever he gives them, they answer, until he's stumped.

He no longer has anything to tell them so he makes one up out of his head. He says, "It's about what's read and understood, and you can read it. Calculate how many prickly pears are on the cactus fences of Bani Khalad." (The cactus means the cactus fences of Bani Khalad.) How many prickly pears are on them? (In order to slow them down and rest from his dilemma.)

Malek: There is no answer?

Right! He needed a rest because whatever he said to them they answered. He left them still going around in circles.

Here, in contrast to the encounters above, the actions of this man are beginning to move him toward the area of community "character" rather than hero. Why? First, his protagonists are not uncultured but respectable outsiders, friends of his brother, and worthy riddling opponents. Second, they offer hospitality to a stranger, and in a sense he is abusing that hospitality. Third, and because of these first two points and because narrator and audience would not wish to be so unskilled in verbal artistry, though they might be amused by his actions, they would not want to emulate him. To compensate, however, he does show language skill in the fact that he made up a very acceptable-sounding riddle, though answerless. In short, the story is an amusing one to be shared privately among community members, but it is not one likely to be a source of public community pride.

In fact, community "characters" as a whole are not likely to be pointed out to outsiders with pride. Rather, their actions are sources of amusement or amazement only to town members. They are portrayed as excessively a-cultural and often their actions are related to those of animals or machines. Unlike the dervish, however, their uncontrolled actions are not modified by positive supernatural connections, but must be contained as far as possible by the townspeople themselves. Certainly mildly uncontrolled appetites and social behavior such as that evidenced in the following hikayat must have a certain appeal, especially in a community in which respect for and sharing of food is so carefully imposed:

(29) SI HAMDAN
Well, they [Hmid Birjab and his brother] would go and bring us [Hamdan and his uncle] rushes—he and his brother Maouia. They used to haul things by camel.

Malek: But Hmid was probably the stronger, right?

No, Maouia was stronger but more sensible. Maouia was more sensible. They hauled with the camel. They used to carry, that is, they would deliver [goods] for a price and if they didn't find a load to carry during the harvest [they'd haul] corn or watermelon or whatever or grains from the threshing floor to bring to town. They'd go bring in firewood to sell. Well, we took them—him and his brother—and we all went [out to the fields]—I and my uncle and those two. When we got there . . . Well, there's a rise before you get up to that bridge over Wad Qsab. On that exact rise is the house of Haj Reem. Before the rise there's a cactus patch and the prickly pears were weighted down to the ground.

He [Hmid] turned his donkey. He had a piece of a sickle that they used to chop up [cactus leaves] for the camels. He turned his donkey and his brother kept going with us. He filled one "eye" of the saddlebag with prickly pears and in the other "eye" he put his foot [to balance the load] and caught up [with us].

[In the meantime,] we [three] had laid out the rushes in bundles all ready to load them [on the camel]. We had laid out the carrier [a big net made of halfa that hooked closed at the top] and were in the process of filling it with rushes, I and my uncle and the brother. Maybe we'd filled one carrier or whatever when he arrived. When he got there he got down that saddlebag. He put it down and took up that piece of sickle [to start cutting into his prickly pears].

His brother headed towards him to eat with him and by God, he [Hmid] growled at him like a dog and almighty God he didn't let him have a bite. He growled at his brother like a dog, God forbid. By God, he didn't let him taste it. The other guy, poor thing, was nice.

(30) Si Hamdan

He [one of the Birjab brothers] said, "We [he and his two brothers] went to Dindra to bring back corn." He said, "We got there, poured in the corn, went up to the house." He said, "Mother brought us hot corn-bread and *chakchuka*."[38] He said, "We were as hungry as camels in a prickly pear patch." He said, "Mustafa said to her, 'Momma, what's this?' [holding up the cornbread]. She told him, 'Some nice hot cornbread, my son.' He said to her, 'Then, am I a pig?' and he took hold of her bread and went like this' " [gestures throwing].

He said, "He sent it all the way to the house of Haj Khmais Tanabane." He said, "Haj Khmais's wife came out. She said to mother, 'What's this bread?' 'Mustafa did such and such.' " He said, "She brought him flour bread and a plate with a couple of eggs."

He said, "We [other two] thanked God. We said, 'Thank God for the food.' We ate until we were full." He said, "We then praised God."

He said, "We're still the cornbread kind." He said, "He who didn't praise God," he said, "There he is a success."

(31) SI HAMDAN

[Hmid Birjab] is old—nearing seventy now. But to look at him he's like a camel not. . . . At the store of Saduq ben Kdous, he'd braid rope. The store near the tobacco shop belonging to Sharif—now near the Café Slim. He'd braid rope and his suit jacket was full of beans, roasted beans. He didn't toss them in his mouth one by one. No. He'd take out a handful, go like this [gestures, all in his mouth at once] and he'd shell them in his mouth like a threshing machine and blow out the husks by themselves and he'd still be braiding.

By almighty God, I didn't just hear this. Every night maybe around six or seven nights he would braid rope and we'd sit up there playing cards and he . . . and the husks piled up next to him.

Malek: Like a machine.

By God, like a machine that sorts out the straw from the grain—like that. He wouldn't even wait to peel them and eat them by the handful. No. He'd toss them in by four or four plus one.[39]

Whatever he found in his hand he'd put in, and crack open and spit out the husk and chew the rest.

Malek: And still braid?

Yeah! And all the while braiding.

The comment at the end of the second hikayah above, "We're still the cornbread kind," can easily be generalized to: "He breaks the rules and gets ahead of those of us who conform to them." Thus, as Mikhail Bakhtin points out, the fool "makes strange the world of social conventionality" (Bakhtin 1981: 172). The polite brothers pause to ponder in self-amusement, but not regret, why they conform to a system of behavior that, in material terms, gets them nowhere. Nevertheless, the cumulative message of the town character hikayat is that the a-cultural, even animalistic behavior portrayed in them is not to be emulated, for one loses some of one's status as a community member. Instead one becomes like a country person or even like an animal. Thus inappropriate community behavior is bounded out, while, by inference, the contrastive behavior exhibited by the raconteur and his audience is claimed as appropriate to the community. At the same time, what is a-cultural is being held up for possible renegotiation.

The role of the town clown is also subtly linked with that of the dervish, as opposed to that of the heroes and walis. Much of what has been written about the historical place of the fool is applicable to the roles that the dervishes (holy fools) and town clowns (secular fools) play in Kelibian narratives. Both dervishes and town clowns stand at the boundaries of town consciousness. The former occupy the juncture of the supernatural and cultural, of the known and the unknown and the latter, the boundary between culture and nature, the human and nonhuman, acceptable and unacceptable. (Both also tend to inhabit, as do children, a kind of neutral zone in which access to both men's and women's worlds is possible.) Together their stories focus the attention of the townsfolk on the unthinkable, the unthought of, the uncontrollable aspects of the above relationships and thus invite reevaluation of current attitudes and actions and force new ideas into the individual and community store. In sum, both types reaffirm the certainty of uncertainty, the dervish's actions illustrating the unpredictability and unknowability of God, and the town clown's actions illustrating the arbitrariness of people's rules for success. And finally, these two dramatis personae often effectively play the same role as town walis and heroes. As William Willeford writes,

The fool's confusion of levels of "good" and "bad" . . . and his obliteration of the distinction between the categories themselves may have some of the same effects that are achieved when the hero defeats what is bad, affirms what is good, or actively creates a conscious awareness in which these values have new functions. (Willeford 1969: 121).

Another phenomenon then is taking place in hikayat about the four community types found in Kelibia: wali, dervish, hero, and clown. Whether one is considering the positive excesses of the heroes or walis, or the problematic ones of the dervishes or town characters, contemplation of their activities in story form is visibly energizing for the event participants. As story after story unwinds, listeners and narrators become increasingly animated—the gathering becomes more intense, focused—so voices rise, laughter escalates, or, where appropriate, listeners maintain a respectful, attentive silence. Participants often draw closer, an older brother puts his arm around his younger sister. The intensified sense of community among event members when next they meet is evidenced by especially warm greetings—a hug, a compliment, a reference to the storytelling event.

Sidi Maouia and Mohamed ouild Si 'Ali are part of the shared heritage of the community. Townspeople use them in hikayat as an inspiration for their approach to contemporary life. The walis represent a spiritual and moral strength for the community—protection for members both within the community and "on the road." They, like the grandparents or great-grandparents of most Kelibians, chose Kelibia, and thus the walis signify as well the rightness of the cosmopolitan make-up of the town. This sense of place is particularly important to young men or women off studying in Tunis or France or working in Libya. Sidi Maouia has protected those working afar at olive presses or in wheat fields, and he can do likewise for workers and scholars of today. Stories of their protection during colonial occupation or during wartime have provided Kelibians with the fortitude to wait out those adversities while maintaining a culture reasonably intact. And the walis are still there to be called upon when community or personal needs arise. Just as they are contained within the story frame and storytelling event, they in turn, frame—and so define and thus help make bearable—crises in real life.

Hikayat about town heroes also remove participants temporarily from the predictable behavior of daily life, and these heroes, like walis and dervishes, are figures especially well equipped to deal with crises. Though now young Kelibians are more often artists, bankers, doctors, pharmacists, teachers, or carpenters than harvesters or hunters, stories of these past heroes set a standard. They are the best at what they do—especially measured against outsiders. Someone like Mohamed ouild Si 'Ali is a calculated risk-taker, though working within community standards and earning community approbation. Again, hikayat about past heroes like those of past walis direct listeners and storytellers to reperceive the totality of community life in all its (historical) depth and (iconic) breadth. The outside world is often used as a further foil or measuring instrument.

Even when the actual behavior of dervishes or town clowns is bounded out as inappropriate for responsible town members, contemplation of and amusement or bemusement at their antics, safely confined within the story format, enhance the quality of town life. Some dervishes are indicators of the value of cleanliness or love of nature or of children while others are examples of the need to treat kindly even the seemingly powerless, the dirty, the poor, the naive. Dervishes break social rules, religious prescriptions, and even natural laws—wrestling with lions, fearlessly approaching wild bulls—and thus create an atmosphere conducive to a community world view in which the possibility of things being other than they are is always present.

Town characters as well, though their out-of-control treatments of food or sex are rejected by Kelibians, provide within their story frameworks a pleasing, safe opportunity to contemplate the possibilities of chaos. Again, the production of accounts of chaos may lead to its bounding out, but also may be the inspiration for an act of controlled misuse of food such as that of Uncle Gacem in his "butter" sale to the Germans and Italians (21). Whatever is thinkable and then sayable, permitted, however well bounded and mediated within the verbal art of a culture, provides a reserve dynamic that keeps a community both secure and creative. Thus the community is able to incorporate successfully new circumstances and changing times.

This is not to say that change is favored or must occur. Indeed, these dramatis personae spanning a continuum from culturally responsible, controlled excess (walis, heroes) to culturally irresponsible or naive near-chaos (dervishes, characters) provide some of the dynamism necessary to effect community change, but that dynamism is counterbalanced by and contained within the structured lives of the participants in storytelling events and within traditional story frameworks and contexts. Through the stories of these out-of-proportion townspeople and the manners in which the narratives mediate past and present, insider and outsider, the "normal" and the unexpected, present and future "norms" of town life are reprocessed, reexamined, but not necessarily changed. As I have shown, hikayat can be conduits for the rejection of magical practices or for the reinterpretation of traditions concerning genies. However, belief in the value and efficacy of local walis is reconsidered and reconfirmed in several stories, and in snippets of conversation as well. My point is, though, that, as much as traditional art forms may be a resource for celebrating community or for conserving traditional values, they may be a useful medium through which to conceive of and negotiate changes in community world view. Furthermore, as we have seen, the hikayat are a useful Kelibian resource for reflecting on the process by which community members in a crossroads community like Kelibia can deal with changes more or less imposed from without. It is quite clear that one of the reasons younger people are interested in the doings of older community members during times of war, occupation and invasion of new technology is that all around them these similar sorts of invasions are going on. A whole community of Swedes come in with Tunisian consultants to build a fishing port and a maternity hospital. The police, by government decree, are all from elsewhere. French school teachers, often fulfilling military service, come in to teach French in the local schools. Of course all of these people think their place of origin better than Kelibia and, in some cases, say so. "Lucky French," said the then fourteen-year-old Leila to me once as we were sneaking into the back door of a new beach hotel to use their showers. "My French teacher says that in France people can take a bath with 'sweet' [not salty, sea] water every day."

How do Kelibians cope? First, they cope by knowing, "reading," and mastering their town and countryside better than anyone else—its landmarks and its people, its practical and aesthetic features. Even when heroes are not pitted against outsiders, as the trackers were in story 24, or as Uncle Gacem was in story 21, their stories help emphasize town values. Second, there is the religious edge provided by the regional and town walis. Again, aesthetically and practically these walis and their descendants provide a slight edge for a Kelibian finding her or himself at a disadvantage. There is a strong tradition in Kelibia of defending the culturally defenseless—like dervishes, adolescent girls, and so on. If Kelibians find themselves culturally at a disadvantage, they too will be protected.

This is not to say that Kelibians are not to help themselves. As I argued earlier, in most stories where a wali is given credit for the success of a masterful deed, the Kelibian harvester or olive oil processor, for example, might have succeeded on his own. Even the young Hmida might have found his lost hawk. He was in the right neighborhood, having tracked the hawk just as he had learned from the older men. So, third, Kelibians are expected to be calculatedly and gracefully audacious in dealing with outsiders (or fathers who promise and do not deliver). And in their very form and content, they demonstrate to individual Kelibians the reward of non-passivity—either in the face of external cultural restrictions, or in the face of the future, or before a good storyteller. Protagonists take control of events, and storytellers and audience together control stories.

These hikayat, with their juxtaposition of the dramatic and everyday, are but one vehicle for the creation and maintenance of a communal world-view, and for the challenging both of that communal world-view and of the world without through time. They are powerful, however, in their ability to evoke and manipulate other representations—other stories, other verbal art forms, iconic indicators from cornbread to cadis to certain centuries-old appreciations of the town and its people as desirable, as vulnerable, as enduring despite the devaluation of its resources and the hegemonic impulses of outsiders.

Notes

1. Actually at the level of abstraction presented here I daresay men and women are not much at odds about what they want for their community. Given the number of hikayat or accounts by women, five, versus men, twenty-eight, it would seem that the male point of view is very over-represented. Yet I was steeped in the women's world. Most of my time was passed with women and children. I found that ambitions for daughters of the town, for example, varied as much among women as among men.

2. This may be true as well for individual stories since they were inspired by questions about the community past.

3. I did hear a story about a woman waliyya, Lella Khadhra (told by a woman), and also about two women dervishes still living (told by young males). Unfortunately these were told in social contexts where it would have been inappropriate to race for notebook or recorder. Still, it is clear that the doings of the holy people of both sexes are of interest to both men and women.

4. In 1884 Louis Rinn, chef du bataillon d'infanterie hors cadres, chef du service central des affaires indigènes au gouvernement général, vice-président de la Société historique algérienne, tried to distinguish among the various Islamic religious figures found in Algeria. He distinguished among Muslim clergy, local marabouts, and brotherhoods (al-Ikhouane). He then mentioned various subsets of what he sometimes refers to as "marabouts" (a term coined by the French from the Arabic) or "saints."

As for the wali [ولي], it is the friend of God, the saint of all religions, the most privileged being of all and having the gift of miracles; the Arabic word signifies properly: he who is near to God [from ولي , oula, to be very near]. . . . This ولي wali qualification, can only be applied to a dead person; no one living can take it: it is the veneration of the faithful which realizes/confers the honor posthumously.

It is estimated that in the early 1970s there were six thousand wali tombs in Tunisia, compared to 1,645 mosques. (lecture, Lacoste-Dujardin 1983)

5. This discussion invites exploration of "themes and variation in circum-Mediterranean popular religion" as Margaret Mills points out (personal communication). I have received several comments concerning the surface similarity between, say, patron saints of cities and towns as portrayed in southern Italy and Kelibian walis, as well as comparisons of Tunisian folk religion (as portrayed in these hikayat) with Greek, Spanish, and especially Sicilian folk religion, but this subject still needs to be investigated. The setting up of overseas shrines for walis, something Mills asked about, would seem antithetical to Islamic practice, but again, this would need to be investigated. There is some evidence of such shrines in France. Certainly, the setting up of zawiyyas for Sufi orders could occur anywhere.

6. In Kelibia, these walis are sometimes identified as coming from farther west. Evans-Pritchard notes also in *The Sanusi of Cyrenaica* that ancestors of sacred tribes "are almost invariably believed to have come from the west" (Evans-Pritchard 1949: 52). Ernest Gellner (1970), on the other hand, mentions that in the High Atlas range of Morocco, holy men descended from Sidi Saïd Ahansal became too numerous for their community and some of them migrated. Could this be an explanation for the origins of these Kelibian walis? The holy men and women, perhaps drifting toward Mecca, were also in search of a "congregation."

7. According to Emile Dermenghem (1954) miraculous appearances of dual or even plural tombs are not uncommon in North Africa or among Christian saints or the heroes of ancient Greece. More often, however, the tombs are not in the same place. It is believed that the body can be in more than one tomb at a time and that a wali's barakah can be disseminated. To add to this story, Khalti Jamila told me that, when Sidi Maouia died, he left his wife pregnant. The children were twins, born not from her but from the foot of each tomb.

8. For a brief comparison of men's and women's narratives in Kelibia see Webber (1985).

9. The actual word was, " مهبول ," "crazy," but the implication seems to be that a little splashed water is not important enough to bother a wali or waliyya. It is almost as if Sidi Maouia "doesn't know his own strength."

10. Thus, it is not unusual for a people to claim that their wali was, say, the barber of the Prophet, or some other close associate of Mohamed. Tunisian scholar Mohamed-Salah Omri confirms that dervishes at their deaths can be elevated to wali status, shrine and all. Gradually, people may then create cemeteries near their zawiyyas—another possible sign of well-respected walis. This phenomenon is still occurring (Mohamed-Salah Omri, personal communication). No one except Khalti Fafani claimed prophetic descent for a particular wali. Her claim for Sidi Maouia was rather offhand, almost an aside. Descendants and their behavior seem a more interesting topic. Almost fifteen years ago, Eickelman noted that "the hierarchical assumptions implicit in much of popular Islam are largely unrecorded and poorly understood" (Eickelman 1976: 11). This is still an important, neglected area of research.

11. An island off the east coast of Tunisia.

12. Sousse is and was a center of olive oil production in Tunisia. The newer olive presses have a grindstone turned by electricity. After the first oil is extracted from the crushed olives, the pulp is placed in straw baskets one upon the other and compressed again. Finally, hot water is added to the pulp in big pans to extract even more oil. It is the fire to heat the water that is referred to in this story. (For an account of a Tunisian olive-growing village see Abu Zahra 1982.)

13. "Kill two birds with one stone."

14. At the same time, there is a "school" of thought (including Islamic thought) that abjures foregrounding of the self by fancy dress, rich living, high achievement, or acts of daring or audacity. In Islamic practice this means dress and lifestyle should be modest, and special intellectual or physical strengths should be counted gifts from God, barakah. Hubris-like pride will go before a fall, either through the envy of others (sometimes explained as the evil eye) or God's chastisement. Of course in Kelibia some people feel this more than others, or apply it only to certain cultural domains. Also, there is the traditional Arab value of al-hishmuh for men and women, a value placed on modest, quiet behavior that also is a factor for some in the desire not to aggrandize oneself in story. Still, in a story told by a man about another man the teller would not have these reasons to emphasize a wali's help. Emphasis on the wali is one way, however, to convert a story for family and close friends into a community story.

15. Unlike Sidi Maouia's zawiyya, Sidi Hmid's (Ahmed) is in the middle of a very dense and old section of town on a small knoll. One enters a large yard, to the left of which is the shrine. Directly ahead is the home of the elderly woman caretaker and her husband and daughter. On Tuesday, December 19, 1978, I went to Sidi Hmid to join in a celebration for the successful recovery of the husband of a family member from an auto accident. In the yard, children were cavorting among grave markers (including that of Sidi S'eed). Inside the shrine, I found more than a hundred women and girls sitting in two rows on straw mats and sheepskins. One row of women ringed and leaned against the walls; the other sat facing them. Beside a niche in one wall women were reheating food brought from the hostess's home. In succession we were served tea and peanuts, soft drinks and cookies, and, finally, a lamb cous-cous. As is usual on religious occasions, lumps of sugar and colored candies decorated the semolina of the cous-cous. Behind us, in a screened alcove, was the tomb of Sidi Hmid. Every so often, for a small tip, the guardian of the tomb would open the padlocked screen, and a guest would discreetly enter to say a fatiha, ask help of Sidi Hmid, make a promise, or perhaps leave a gift. The tomb was covered with brilliant multicolored and gold-embroidered cloths that visitors had donated to the wali. Harcous, an inky, black, clove-scented liquid cosmetic used to decorate the hands and feet, especially of brides, was applied to our little fingers if we wished. One young wife whispered laughingly that she was going to put her finger next to her husband's nose that night. Thus, a powerful wali, controlled sexuality, and abundant, artistically prepared food—all the traditional resources of women—were combined in the celebration. Despite my account here of a women's visit, notice that neither in Khali Gacem's statement nor elsewhere is

there indication that walis are "women's business." Remember too that it is Malek who undertakes at the birth of his daughter, Myriam, to promise Sidi Maouia a sheep if she lives. I wonder if this gesture might not be more powerful coming from a man since fathers traditionally are supposed to want boys. As I recall, Si Mohamed, Malek's father, is said to have paid the midwife twice as much at the birth of his daughter Leila as he did for either of his first two sons.

16. I was told that properly in classical Arabic Sidi Hmid should be Sidi Ahmed. Lella Nesria in playing with her granddaughter would use a baby talk version of Hmid, so that he would become Sidi Mhid (accent on the second syllable).

17. These dervishes may be part of what Michael Meeker refers to as "little lineages." ". . . they were seen as descendants of a saint, and in this respect they were usually closely associated with a particular tomb" (Meeker 1979: 211). He goes on to say that their ethnography is exceedingly scant but that they are not considered walis (saints) and may have often been tomb caretakers (Meeker 1979: 212).

18. More literally, "shit under him," "نحتو" "اخري." Swearing is a very creative art form in Kelibia in terms of both what is said and the context chosen. Men and women have some different sorts of swearing routines, though they also share expressions. Contrary to what might be expected, a good cursing routine may evoke laughter, appreciation, or admiration rather than anger. Thus, a townsmember might be able simultaneously to vent his or her spleen and receive approval (although it is not dignified to lose control). Curses can also be made jokingly. This folk art form would profit from more attention.

19. Possibly a variation on the following (see pages 129 and 160 also):

S'eed El-Khadir, c'est le prophète Élie qui, comme le prophète Idris (Henoch), a bu à la source de vie et a été exempté de la mort. Sa personnalité est dédoublée: Elias erre sur la terre, El-Khadir vit au fond de la mer. Un jour par an, ils se rencontrent pour se concerter: El-Khadir est alors l'intermédiaire ordinaire entre Dieu et les hommes, il leur dévoile l'avenir et, surtout, leur confère les dons de Baraka (1) et de Tessarouf (2), c'est-à-dire le pouvoir de faire des miracles et d'être exaucés dans tout ce qu'ils demandent, pour eux ou pour les autres.

(1) La Baraka "est la bénédiction," mais ici avec le sens "d'abondance," de profusion, de surabondance de biens. Le sens primitif de barek برك est s'accroupir, s'agenouiller, mais d'abord, s'accroupir écrasé sous le poids de la charge.

(2) Le Tessarouf تصرف de صرف est le don d'être dispensateur, et de disposer des forces de la création, dans l'administration du monde. (Rinn 1884: 59–60)

S'eed El-Khadir is the prophet Elijah who, like the prophet Idris (Henoch), drank from the springs of life and was made exempt from death. His personality was divided in two: Elias roams the earth, El-Khadir lives at the bottom of the sea. One day out of the year, they meet to consult one another: At that point, El-Khadir is the everyday intermediary between God and mankind, he reveals to them the future and, most importantly, gives them their gifts from barakah (1) and from tessarouf (2), that is, the power to do miracles and to be granted everything they request whether for themselves or for others.

(1) Barakah is "the benediction," but here with the meaning of abundance or

Figure 6. (1) Nejoua in 1979 before her wedding, feet and hands decorated by Khalti Jamila with henna and harcous, an inky, black, clove-scented liquid cosmetic used to decorate the hands and feet, especially of brides.

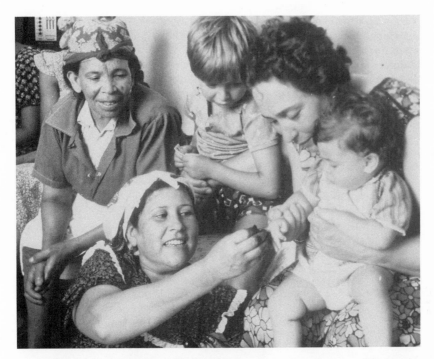

(2) The day the bride is adorned with harcous, guests may also have small designs applied. Khalti Jamila is decorating Myriam. Lella Nesria is holding Myriam and Mohamed, her nephew, younger son of Lella Fatma and Si Mahmoud (Si Mohamed's younger brother).

profusion, of overabundance of wealth. In its original sense, barak (برك) means to crouch or to kneel down, usually under the crushing weight of some burden.

(2) Tessarouf تصرف from صرف is the gift of being a dispensator and of having at one's disposal the forces of creation in the managing of the world.

The embodiment of profusion, superabundance, and nature's bounty, his name, from the same root as "green" (Kh-D-R), indicates fertility and multiplication.

20. Notice the personification of Ramadhan. Something abstract and universal is made personal and local. "Ramadhan" becomes a respected member of the community.

21. From the dervish point of view, it seems to me there is no conscious recognition that conventions or laws of nature are being broken. The fascination with dervish behavior for the townspeople lies both in the flaunting of the "rules" and in the particular ways in which they are flaunted (hence, the hikayat about them).

22. 'Assida is a special thick porridge served to women who have just given birth. For the dervish to have eaten it at the cadi's birth would mean that he was

older, a close friend of the family, and thus able to take certain liberties. It is made from tiny black seeds ground to a fine powder and cooked with flour, water, and sugar. The resulting dark brown pudding is covered with a vanilla pudding. On the birthday of the Prophet in Kelibia, 'assida is sprinkled with powdered almonds and decorated with a variety of nuts and candies. The custom of serving it to women who have just given birth dates at least from the First World War. One older woman remembers making 'assida from flour that washed ashore from a sunken supply ship.

23. The special relationship between walis and lions is well known. "Chevaucher les lions est un privilège des saints . . ." (see Marçais and Guîga 1925: 209–210 and 229). Notice also the wali-lion transformation in story 4.

24. General Archives, Series A-120-9, A-168-13, A-168-23.

25. "Hung a poor wretch, Hamed Farjallah, who, without the help of some people who cut the cord, would have drawn his last breath right in the middle of the marketplace in the presence of hundreds of witnesses!"

26. "A first-rate passive pederast!"

Figure 7. On the birthday of the Prophet in Kelibia, large and small bowls of 'assida are sprinkled with powdered almonds and decorated with a variety of nuts and candies. Lella Nesria and Leila with a dish of 'assida on the morning of the Mouled, early 1970s.

27. "As for the intelligence information regarding his private life, it is contradictory."

28. A nice literary allusion that effects alliance with the Arab past, with nomads and settled people and, perhaps, diverse races as well, since Antar was half black. Antar was an early Arabian hero of legend.

29. 'Alaya ben Hammuda Sidi Hmid.

30. Probably Hawwas would have gone to Sidi Hmid's ('Alaya ben Hammuda's) zawiyya to leave the bulgha at his tomb, but, as we have seen in other stories, dervish descendants can claim cows or bulgha meant for their ancestors. Knowing about the future or happenings far away is part of the "dervish-ness" of dervishes. I expect that the dervish, though, is especially attuned to events that are crises and that concern his ancestor.

31. This brief sketch of the position of the wali (or waliyya) in a present-day Tunisian town raises myriad comparative questions concerning the role of walis in the past, as well as in other areas of North Africa and the Middle East. It also introduces or reintroduces the necessity to study carefully specific local distinctions among sheikhs, marabouts, zawiyyas, walis, dervishes, Sufis, and so on. (See Crapanzano 1985/1980: 16–17 for a discussion of the supernatural spectrum in Morocco.) In keeping with the flexible nature of folk or vernacular Islam, answers to these questions are time- and area- and probably even class-specific. Many contradictory accounts exist. In this particular account, I use community terminology as devised from hikayat and conversation. In Kelibia at least, walis are indicators of higher reality. They control a range of "facts" outside the range of the sensory perceptions of town members. They are geographically, culturally, or spiritually set apart. The wali provides a personal link through which the greater world of Islam and the figure of the Prophet can be comprehended. In many ways walis present a challenge to orthoprax Islam, despite or perhaps because the religion is, on paper, so democratic and nonhierarchical. They continue to offer a useful resource to draw upon, or a balance against a central authority that may not have the interests of a particular region or town at heart, or even a balance against a town member who betrays town members (see hikayah 20). Finally, since walis can be women (waliyyas), problems of a larger segment of society may be felt to be addressed. While genealogical descendants of walis are known (some, not many, are dervishes), little interest is displayed in the ancestry of the walis. Claims of Prophetic descent are not often made. Although mention of living walis is made for other regions of the Maghrib, people in Kelibia say that the special wali status, despite witnessing of miracles, is not communally realized or recognized until after death.

32. Grass used to make rope.

33. Predicting what we will do tomorrow is tempting fate. Thus, some people qualify any statement about plans for the future with "if we live."

34. These narrative-based proverbs would reward more study in terms of how much meaning is tied to the narrative base as opposed to immediate context, and just how many proverbs have narrative bases, and what sorts. They can come from khurafat as well as hikayat. For example, Lella Nesria had been trying to convince

Malek of something and he was not attending. "Oh," she said, exasperated, "One hundred ants just went through that hole." She then proceeded to tell me a story about a man who felt his young boy needed a serious talking to. The man waxed eloquent and was pleased to see his son, head down, apparently drinking it all in. After he finished talking he waited for his son's response. After a pause the youngster looked up and said, "Oh Baba, one hundred ants just crawled through that hole in the wall!"

35. In other words, cut so close to him with the scythe that he could have shaved off his mustache (with the additional meaning of emasculating him).

36. Although hikayat often have a rather anti-establishment or heteroprax flavor, they also frequently develop the possibility of fakes and exploiters.

37. For one reason or another, most Kelibians, male *and* female, now consider these practices "un-Kelibian." Either the practices are felt to be ineffective, scams perpetrated on ignorant people by charletans, or they are seen as a kind of black magic—effective, but irreligious, uncultured, and dangerous. Vows to town holy figures or shrine celebrations are not in the same category. Although vows are made more by women than by men, and celebrations at shrines are practiced more by women, they often occur on behalf of men. I have not met even a young man who dared scoff at the practice. Celebrations take place at a woman's expense, if she is holding the celebration, and represent an unusual public display of affection and regard for a son or spouse.

38. An egg dish mixed with vegetables, olive oil, and tomato sauce.

39. Reluctance among traditionalists to say, "five," because of its association with the evil eye.

Chapter 4

In Defense of (Maghribi) Folklore

> . . . the resolution of the problem of communication between
> rival paradigms lies largely in the domain of history.
>
> (Bob Scholte)

> [Hayden] White's scheme is of interest to us here precisely be-
> cause it translates the problem of historical (and anthropologi-
> cal) explanation, most often conceived as a clash of theoretical
> paradigms, into the writer's problem of representation.
>
> (George Marcus and Michael Fischer)

> If the professional applies himself to the task of listening to what
> he can see and read, he discovers before him interlocutors, who,
> even if they are not specialists, are themselves subject-producers
> of histories and partners in a shared discourse.
>
> (Michel de Certeau)

In Egypt in the summer of 1987 I was introduced by a French anthropologist friend and colleague to two young French ethnographers. "She is a
folklorist," he explained, "but not," he hastened to reassure them, "in the
usual sense." In the last two chapters I have addressed the Kelibian contexts
of place and time upon which hikayah tellers draw creatively in order to
endow their hikayat with a rich depth and breadth of meaning. In this
penultimate chapter I want to step back to address directly the fourth
chronotopic situation mentioned in Chapter 2—that of me, the writer-
ethnographer, and you, the reader-scholar—as that situation defines and
affects a western study of a Maghribi folklore genre. In doing so I will be
unpacking from the simple phrase "folklore in the usual sense," a complex
of contradictory notions that have accrued to the terms "folk" and "lore"
and the study of folklore over at least the last century and a half.

As we have seen, Kelibians are very aware of their exposure to diverse
cultural models and influences through time and evaluate them in terms of

their possible effects on themselves and on the community. The study of such a cross-culturally aware people has taught me that this anthropological folklore study also needs to be situated in its time and place. It needs especially to come to grips with two conflicting scholarly (partly folk) paradigms (world-view touchstones) concerning the folk, folklore, and North Africa and the ways each of these paradigms have fashioned and are fashioned by our representational strategies and traditions.[1] Just as Kelibian units of world-view are formed by as well as form hikayat, so western paradigms of folklore can both project certain acceptable ranges of cultural representation and be challanged by representations too spirited to remain within "acceptable" boundaries. Opening up dialogue among paradigms will help ensure the negotiability of boundaries, provide a spectrum of perspectives, and broaden discourse.

Only by understanding something about this process of communication (cultural and cross-cultural) in our own academic subculture, about how we arrived at our own time and place vis-à-vis the study of folklore and culture (folklore "in the usual sense," for one), can we come full circle, back to the teller(s) and the tale(s) and to a more complete understanding of that dialogue about culture-in-process that Kelibia carries on continuously with its citizens and with the outside world. For, in making explicit what Marcus and Fischer refer to as "the underdeveloped, relatively implicit side of ethnographic description focused on a cultural other . . . the reference it makes to the presumed, mutually familiar world shared by the writer and his readers" (Marcus and Fischer 1986), we also illuminate one of the worlds, the colonial or neocolonial world, in which Kelibians operate and to which they must formulate understandings and responses (Marcus and Fischer 1986: 29), including those embedded in the narratives found in the last two chapters.

For purposes of reconceptualizing the anthropological and ethnographic process as level with, and not superior to, Kelibian community process, I suggest we acknowledge that the "work" of formation and dissemination of the basic premises (the paradigm) of a particular school of social scientists is accomplished to a greater degree than is usually taken into account, through negotiation carried out informally in small (folk) groups before those premises become all-pervasive as disciplinary doctrine. Scholarly paradigms of folklore are fashioned through a process very similar to the process through which a Kelibian world view is put together. Thomas Kuhn's research into the formation of scientific paradigms, despite his ambiguous use of the term "paradigm," is still a powerful tool for looking at the scientific community precisely because it provides insight into this folk history behind rival paradigms, including the "central role played by personality and passion," and thus provides the opportunity to reperceive and rethink aspects of those paradigms. "[Kuhn] maintains that the practice of science is monitered by 'local' traditions of thought" (King 1980: 104). Viewpoints on scientific, including social scientific, authority rest on certain "unstated premises which underlie the thought and action of a given group of people, . . . the building blocks of . . . world view. . . ." (Dundes 1971: 905–996), what Braudel would call a group's *mentalité*. These (folk) ideas result in a certain (folk) ethos, including aesthetic evaluations that in turn help formulate folk ideas. These are developed and negotiated in much the same way that a Kelibian world-view is constructed. In the scientific world too, traditions are negotiated toward possible change, and "changing patterns of consensus are formed and reformed" (King 1980: 106).

In the fashioning of this narrative of place and time, I am looking at the convergence of four contexts: that of French folklore scholarship in the Maghrib (folklore in "the usual sense") during the colonial period, that of the folk/folklore component of post- or neo-colonial research in the Maghrib, that of my own folklore scholarship about Tunisia as it has emerged both from certain North American folklore practices and theoretical touchstones (anthropological and literary) and from the Maghribi research of other scholars, and that of Kelibian culture itself as I was taught to understand it—my own fieldwork. Loosely speaking, the first two contexts result in one paradigm or tradition about folklore and the latter two the opposing paradigm. As will become clear, approaches to, theories about, or uses for folklore are, in all these cases, subsumed within much broader cultural discourses. Here, I find and foreground the effect of these broader concerns on folklore and folklore studies (and vice versa). This retracing and juxtaposing of the development of two basic sets of powerful but opposing ideas about the significance of folklore for a culture group makes explicit some of the ideas that have been implicit, and thus not heretofore subject to much needed scrutiny.

To trace here just how the intellectual history of folklore scholarship in the Maghrib and of my grappling with it affects and is affected by the hikayat of Si Hamdan, of Bidwi, and of each storyteller, is to confront more directly than I have done thus far the unavoidable complexities to be faced in the anthropological study of verbal art and just how much cultural baggage both the student of a culture, the studier, and the teacher, the studied, bring to the casual tea-drinking, storytelling sessions discussed in the previous chapters.

Colonial Folklore Studies and Ethnographic Representation

The most important historical fact for the current problematic state of folklore research in the Maghrib is that France colonized the area. The effect of that colonization was, and is, felt in three interrelated ways. First, the French were facilitators for the imposition or privileging of a good many, especially southern, European societies—primarily Spanish, Italian, and French—with their special traditions and culture theories, including that asserting the superiority of the West. Second, French scholarship past and present dominates western scholarship on the region (and much Maghribian scholarship, for that matter). Third, this very fact of colonization with the trauma of subsequent separation and the guilt and thus rejection of colonial scholarship (including folklore scholarship) resulted in a postcolonial "escape into theory" from the pain and awkwardness of their new, raw, and more vulnerable relationship with these proximal ex-colonies.

The French entered Algiers in 1830 under the pretext of protecting the honor of the French consul whom the bey (ruler) had swatted with a fly swatter during a financial dispute. They gradually extended their occupation to include all of Algeria and, around the turn of the century, Morocco and Tunisia as well. There they remained until the second half of the twentieth century.

French colonialists described their presence in the Maghrib as a continuation of the Roman "civilizing mission" aborted more than a millennium earlier. The hardships encountered during this new *mission civilisatrice* were made tolerable in part by the inspiration drawn from archeological and literary evidences of the ancient Roman accomplishments in the region. In his study, *Le Cap Bon*, Joseph Weyland paid tribute: "aux pionniers de la première heure, [qui] sans doute, quelques-uns se sont-ils rappelés la prospérité qui y renaît à l'époque ancienne et ont-ils trouvé dans se [sic] souvenir un encouragement" (Weyland 1926: i).[3]

Folklore was appropriated to support this colonial vision. Colonialist interpretations of the indigenous folklore had to be consistent with other representations of a people in need of civilizing. After all, "the colonized's devaluation . . . [extended] to everything that [concerned] him . . ." (Memmi 1965: 67). Items of, especially, Berber folklore—certain rituals, tales, and even material culture and folk medicine practices—were selectively appropriated by some French scholars to give proof of the prior Roman occupation (the Arabs would not arrive until the seventh century C.E.), and thus lend legitimacy to their own occupation as heirs to the Romans. "Civilized" attributes of Arabo-Berber society discovered by the French were ascribed for the most part to the Roman, Greek, or Carthaginian legacy. Since Arabs and Berbers themselves were considered to be groups still at a cultural level between savage and civilized (Desparmet 1932), they were lower on the evolutionary scale than the colonialists, and thus the colonialists, having been civilized themselves by ancient Rome and Greece, felt they had an historical mandate to relight the old lamp of civilization in North Africa.

At the same time, some folkways were perceived, quite rightly, I would argue, as powerful forms of resistance to colonial rule. One example is the study of folk or popular religion in practice by Louis Rinn, a military officer fluent in Arabic who was attached to the *Service des affaires indigènes*. He warned in his text on Muslim brotherhoods in Algeria that France had an interest in looking into those orders because, by emphasizing pan-islamism, they were a danger to European interests in Africa and Asia and interfered with attempts by the West to draw the Orient into the current of modern civilization. He wrote:

Sous prétexte d'apostolat, de charité, de pélerinages et de discipline monacale, les innombrables agents de ces congrégations parcourent ce monde de l'Islam, qui n'a ni frontières ni patrie, et ils mettent en relations permanentes La Mecque, Djerboub, Stamboul or Bar'dad avec Fez, Tinbouktou, Alger, Le Caire, Khartoum, Zanzibar, Calcutta ou Java. Protées aux mille formes, tour à tour négoçiants, prédicateurs, étudiants, médecins, ouvriers, mendiants, charmeurs, saltimbanques, fous simulés ou illuminés inconscients de leur mission, ces voyageurs sont, toujours et partout, bien accueillis par les Fidèles et efficacement protégés, par eux, contre les investigations soupçonneuses des gouvernements réguliers. (Rinn 1884: vi).[4]

E. Michaux-Bellaire, head of the Mission Scientifique in Morocco from 1906 until his death in 1930, also justified study of the Moroccan brotherhoods as almost that of an intelligence mission to discover the implications for political resistance to the French of their ties with the greater Muslim world. After the Moroccan uprisings of 1907–8, 1911, and 1912 against colonialist rule, he wrote a history of Moroccan brotherhoods claiming that the Derqaouï [Darqawi] brotherhood, for example, was organized solely to group together all elements of resistance to foreign penetration (Michaux-Bellaire 1921).

Joseph Desparmet, a French colonial scholar, interpreted the folk poetry of the colonized as grass-roots resistance to the colonizers. In a series of articles in *Revue Africaine, Bulletin de la Société de Géographie d'Alger,* and *l'Afrique Française,* he linked oral epics, ogre stories that "almost unconsciously" equated ogres with the French, and the formal Arabic-language Reformist Movement by demonstrating that all three represented linguistic resistance to the French conquest (Colonna 1976a; Lucas and Vatin 1975).

Other lore was perceived as benign, amusing, or useful for paving the way to smoother daily interaction between masters and subjects. Collectors simply collected and presented folklore texts, for example, riddle or proverb collections, items of embroidery, or samples of bread or pottery appreciatively, or with an eye to ensuring that these charming folk practices were preserved even as they regrettably, but necessarily, were lost from everyday practice as Maghribians became more "civilized."[5] Sometimes markets for indigenous goods were found among Europeans. Hikayat of the Kelibian sort were not studied, perhaps because of their semi private nature and perhaps also because their regional and individual specificity made it difficult for scholars to fit them into the universalistic mold expected of folk expressive culture like myths, riddles, or proverbs.

An assumption widely held about folklore in the late nineteenth and early twentieth centuries makes even such seemingly benign attempts to appreciate and preserve folklore suspect today; most researchers assumed that folklore would fade away when a culture became truly civilized. European collectors, for example, talked about folklore "survivals" found in out-of-the-way rural and lower class areas of Europe. Thus, signs that the Maghrib was a folklore-ridden culture implied that it had a long way to go on the road to social evolvement.[6] So those who studied these folk phenomena in the Maghrib today stand convicted of fussing with details, ignoring the essentials for the peripherals, and trying to freeze the culture into their own romantic image of it (Lucas and Vatin 1975). Rather than perceiving folklore as barbaric or rebellious, some colonialists sterilized and then popularized the lore of the colonized, rendering it trivial. Jean-Claude Vatin and Philippe Lucas point out in *L'Algérie des anthropologues* that Algerian-Muslim culture was reduced through its popularized folklore to a decor (Lucas and Vatin 1975: 12). North Africanist Fanny Colonna disdains colonial ethnography because it was "folkloristic" and degraded Algeria "to the status of a rather exotic province." Although she admires the work of the folklorist Desparmet, she sees most folklore studies in Algeria, at least during the twentieth century, as having contributed to making Algerian culture appear simplistic (Colonna 1976b).

Unfortunately, most scholars of the late nineteenth and early twentieth centuries agreed that a folk for whom this folklore represented a collective world-view and who belonged, unlike the fieldworker, to closed, traditional, or lower class culture groups were little differentiated and had little individual control of their worlds. "Thus the living speech of human beings in their specific social relationships in the world was theoretically reduced to instances and examples of a system which lay beyond them" (Williams 1977: 27). Speech was converted to texts, and texts given priority over "what were described as 'utterances' (later as 'performance')" (Williams 1977: 27). The colonial observer

was observing (of course scientifically) within a differential mode of contact with alien material: in the texts, the records of a past history; in speech the activity of an alien people in subordinate (colonialist) relations to the whole activity of the dominant people within which the observer gained his privilege. This defining situation inevitably reduced any sense of language as actively and presently constitutive. (Williams 1977: 26)

A further unfortunate effect was that "the 'language habits' studied, over a range from the speech of conquered and dominated peoples to the 'dialects' of outlying or socially inferior groups, theoretically matched against the observer's 'standard', were regarded as at most 'behavior' rather than independent, creative, self-directing life" (Williams 1977: 27). Thus, for example, Basset described "Moorish" speech as "incorrect language" of "coarse rhythm" (René Basset 1901: iv). The Kelibian storytellers spent their youths and, for some, much of their adult lives in this oppressive atmosphere, where they were treated as objects or subjects, but never actors (Lucas and Vatin 1975: 50). Their language (and therefore its artistic products like hikayat) was considered a "given" system that lay beyond the control of the speaker, rather than an instrument that the speaker could use creatively.

In sum, as throughout the colonial world, scholarship was harnessed to the colonizers' ends. Folklore data were "used" by colonialists to portray North African Arabo-Berber culture as picturesque, shallow, barbaric, or rebellious, inferior to western culture and in need of civilizing by the culturally superior French. By pointing to "survivals" of Roman, Greek, or Carthaginian folk culture, the colonialists also skewed folklore in order to prove the rightness of the colonialist presence.

Compounding this complicated picture of colonial perfidity-in-folklore is the fact that often material was acquired under duress. E. Laoust in his introduction to *Mots et choses berbères* indicates that he got some of his best data from political prisoners (Laoust 1919). Obviously (almost) no one is comfortable doing research "on" occupied peoples. The political manipulation of cultural materials and the resort to the cultural hierarchies that justified the colonialist enterprises have become anathema to modern scholars. Folklore studies produced during the colonial period are now understood by a new generation of French, among others, to be perniciously tainted by colonialism. Research done during the colonial period was inextricably linked, whether the researcher wished it or not, to political struggles for domination. The control of folklore became part of the colonizer's booty.

Given this legacy of dubious practices, it is understandable that many social scientists studying the Maghrib today are suspicious of research centering on traditional lore and only use the term "folklore" or "myth" as a perjorative. The *mythe kabyle*, for example, is used to mean the incorrect and self-serving manner in which the colonialists chose to interpret Kabyle (mountain-area Berbers in Algeria) history and culture (Ageron 1976). Edmund Burke III labels late French colonialism a "producer of irrelevant folklore" (Burke 1980).

Certainly postcolonial scholars are not incorrect to criticize these phenomena, but the devaluation of the word "folklore," along with its scholars and its folk, has spilled over into folklore studies and has inhibited the study of Maghribian traditional expressive culture. Thus we lack the opportunity to hear what North Africans themselves have to say in their most widely accessible media about their colonial past and their future plans. Some reputable scholars do not want their names associated with either folklorists or folklore "in the usual sense" (Jacques Berque, personal communication).

Cognitive Remnants and Anachronistic Social Mechanisms

But the implicating of folklore field studies in the colonialist enterprise, and the subsequent delegitimizing of the word and the field, is not the entire story. Folklore studies are not simply tainted by unfortunate associations with colonialist practices. Unfortunately, ideas about the nature of traditional expressive culture are not much different now from the colonialist assumptions Williams discusses above. American folklorist Richard Bauman, writing in 1986, noted that perspectives on verbal art forms,

> strongly colored by ethnocentric and elitist biases that privilege the classics of western written literature over oral and vernacular literature and by nineteenth-century conceptions of 'folk' society, have established an image of oral literature as simple, formless, lacking in artistic quality and complexity, the collective expression of unsophisticated peasants and primitives constrained by tradition and the weight of social norms against individual creativity of expression. (Bauman 1986: 7)

Everywhere there are fieldworkers, whether anthropologists, sociologists, linguists, or folklorists, who continue to define folklore and the folk very much as the collectors of the late nineteenth and early twentieth centuries did. That is, folklore is regarded as the collective world-view of a people (a folk) who belong, unlike the visiting fieldworker, to closed, traditional, or lower-class culture groups. From this point of view derives the rejection of colonial folklore studies as attempts to preserve and romanticize the "quaint" ways of a "backward," *tradition-bound* people, an attempt that prevents them—by design or by misplaced enthusiasm—from participating in struggles for social, political, and economic parity with the "First World," to render them more vulnerable to exploitation and control by the world system. Folklore, from this perspective, is always disabling, a set of social mechanisms perhaps viable in simpler times, but anachronistic for dealing in the world system, another snare for those living on what western scholars perceive as temporal or geographical peripheries.

For this reason, scholars working in the Maghrib since the colonial period often interpret folk traditions as phenomena that separate and isolate the "folk" from mainstream culture.[7] They have found folklore, even as private group dialogue, repressive, controlling, mystifying, and falsifying. In his utopian sociological study of a southern Tunisian village, *Change at Shebika*, French scholar Jean Duvignaud finds both folklore and folk language inadequate to provide its people with an effective modern-day discourse. For him, Shebika's inhabitants are guided by a cultural myth that actually hinders their facing and dealing with current circumstances. Living in the "mythic" past, getting poorer and poorer, the Shebikans wait passively on the edge of the desert for the Tunisian government to make good the promises it has made them via Radio Tunis. According to Duvignaud's interpretation, Shebikans do not manipulate their folklore and language; rather, they are manipulated, isolated, and held back by their lore. They need dialogue with outsiders to help them reperceive the unproductive "myth" in which they are living.

French anthropologist Pierre Bourdieu, in his study of Berber Algerians of the Kabyle mountains (again, an "isolated" group), found the proverbs, magical practices, and tales of the Kabyles gentle forms of mystification through which the potential negotiability of economic and political situations was masked. All of expressive culture in homogenous, isolated societies such as Kabylia (as Bourdieu perceives it) reinforces the status quo and serves to hide economic and political inequities. A person's actions within this symbolic sphere "are the product of a modus operandi of which he is not the producer and has no conscious mastery" (Bourdieu 1977: 79). Culture members are homogeneous, according to Bourdieu, and therefore every aspect of the community from religious and agricultural practices to the interior design of the home to language tends to reinforce one circular, unchanging, doxa. The possibility of self-reevaluation of the culture is not possible:

When the conditions of existence of which members of a group are the product are very little differentiated, the dispositions which each of them exercises in his practice are confirmed and hence reinforced both by the practice of other members of the group (one function of symbolic exchanges such as feasts and ceremonies being to favour the circular reinforcement which is the foundation of *collective belief*) and also by institutions which constitute collective thought as much as they express it, such as language, myth and art. (Bourdieu 1977: 167)

For Bourdieu, performance of traditional expressive culture (myth, art, festival, ritual), like other community practice, constitutes and expresses collective thought and maintains an institutionalized status quo harmful to the community. Even in capitalist societies, he says, "The denial of economy and of economic interest . . . finds its favourite refuge in the domain of art and culture " (Bourdieu 1977: 197), the aesthetic realm again.

Any possible role folklore might play in cultural innovation is overlooked or ignored for yet another reason. There is a long time scholarly and popular fascination with the "timeless" components of folk phenomena—the persistence of a folktale, an epic, a ballad, a certain design of plow or boat, or an irrigation technique. Concommitantly there is the persistent notion that oldest is best, that bits of lore become adulterated over time through folk contact with outsiders or with "modernity." Thus, Fanny Colonna considers the verbal art of the proletariat not worth studying precisely because it has become sullied by modernity and contact with other ways of life. She observes that the proletariat has neither culture nor history, but only a badly integrated mélange of the knowledge of the upper class and its own class of origin (Colonna 1976a; see also Dundes 1969). One again gets an image of folklore as the province of the noble peasant— pure but isolated from the mainstream of society, and not in cultural control. Again, because the folk are defined as "not us," as the other, as peasant, folklore is relegated to the preindustrial world. It cannot and should not endure in a modern age.

As for Bauman's second point, as long as literary criticism derived for written literature sets the artistic standards for analysis of verbal art forms, oral literature naturally will be found a flawed imitation of written. In such studies, the folk genre under consideration will tend not to be considered within a spectrum of verbal and nonverbal artistic communication, and crucial situational, social, historical, and cultural context is overlooked. When verbal art (not to mention material culture) is approached as merely an inferior or incomplete form of communication—doing what texts do, but not as well—rather than responded to on its own terms and in its special contexts using the range of folklore theory available for looking at traditional expressive culture, the conviction that folklore is not seriously viable as artistic commentary in a modern global context is reinforced. Again, this accords well with colonialist perspectives on the language and verbal art of the colonized, perspectives that overlooked the fact that speech activity is presently constitutive.

The usable sign . . . is a product of . . . continuing speech-activity between real individuals who are in some continuing social relationship. The 'sign' is in this sense their product, but not simply their past product, as in the reified accounts of an 'always given' language system. The real communicative 'products' which are usable signs are, on the contrary, living evidence of a continuing social process, into which individuals are born and within which they are shaped, but to which they then also actively contribute, in a continuing process. (Williams 1977: 37).

Although Williams does not mention verbal art as a specific instance of speech activity, it is clear that his observations on the defects of colonialist language study can be applied not only to colonial researchers but to those scholars today who assume that interesting verbal art, like interesting dialects, belong to the people on what they consider the peripheries—dominated and socially inferior—and that speech activity is something over which these people have no control, by which they are controlled, in fact.[8]

In sum, folklore is perceived still today by nonfolklorists as an artistically inferior mystifier that not only indicates a less developed culture or subculture (isolated, unchanging, homogeneous), but reifies those very traits that inhibit a culture from improving its status in the world arena, from moving from "traditional" to "modern." Of course, this perspective of folklore as preindustrial and repressive rather than enabling has serious implications for the study of Maghribian language, and thus its verbal art. Folklore, thus situated, is denied its artistic place as one medium through which change, either imposed or invited, is confronted and through which new cultural configurations may emerge.[9]

In this first paradigm, as I have "recovered" it here from a set of ideas embedded in colonial and postcolonial scholarship, folk cultures and lore like hikayat have become stigmatized to the extent that they are considered not viable within the current world system. The very doing of folklore qua folklore arouses suspicions that the folklorist possesses a repressive colonialist mentality or is hopelessly politically naive or is being intellectually irrelevant.

That recent ethnographic studies continue to see the culture or culture members they study as isolated in time or space [10] accords well with and helps reinforce the interpretation of folklore as cognitive remnant or anachronistic social mechanism. When a culture or culture member is perceived as trapped in time-past or in timelessness, its, or his or her, traditional expressive culture (myths, legends, folk religion) can be portrayed as partly to blame for an inability to adjust to a modern world that has outgrown such coping mechanisms. When the culture in question is isolated in space, scholars can perceive this isolation as ensuring both the continuity of folklore and the inability of culture members to imagine alternative ways of life.

But what happens to the perception of folklore as anachronistic remnant if we acknowledge that non-western culture groups are not isolated either in time or in space and are not homogeneous? Recently, some anthropologists have come to agree that most of the "isolated" groups we are fond of studying are not isolated after all. Addressing cultures as if they were isolated in space or time has been a convenient literary conceit arising more, perhaps, from geographical naiveté than from expediency. The most perfunctory perusal of Kelibian hikayat shows that individuals are very much differentiated, that the community is not timeless and is, in fact, very historically aware, and that the Kelibians are not and have not been isolated.

And, in the Maghribian context, it is not only in Kelibia that the folk demonstrate an immense awareness of cultural difference across time and space. It is evident, for example, simply from reading *Shebika* itself that Shebikans, like Kelibians, were not living in a vacuum before the advent of the French and Tunisian scholars. They had traveled, soldiered, married out or outsiders, owned distant plots of land, had visitors, and so on.

Bourdieu's *Outline* makes no reference to the rich Kabyle and extra-Kabyle exchanges of verbal art and material culture that occurred over centuries of religious, scholarly, occupational, or military cross-cultural contact.[11] Although Mouloud Mammeri, the Algerian Berber poet and intellectual, tells Bourdieu that even before the advent of the French there was a good deal of movement in and out of Kabylia by "les colporteurs, les poètes, les femmes, les imusnawen, les marabouts, les simples gens" (Mammeri and Bourdieu 1978: 53), this movement is not taken into account in *Outline*. Since Bourdieu is addressing in his study a circular, curiously static sort of Kabyle time, cupped within a very bounded mountain space, cross-cultural movement holds no place in his theory of Kabyle practice.

Ignoring this cross-cultural movement of diverse sorts of people, including women, gives an erroneous impression of Kabyle culture as static and isolated, unaware of historic process, untouched by the outside world. We know from other sources that the success of the Algerian independence movement depended very much on the effort from Kabylia. At the very time Bourdieu was conducting fieldwork among the Kabyles, they were struggling, along with other Algerians, for their freedom. As a "periphery," they were vital to the "center" of the struggle, Algiers (or Paris, if you will), and Kabyles were not "innocent" of their strategic significance nor of their historical "situation." If this situation had been addressed in Bourdieu's study, the "uses" of tradition in changing times might have come to light. Simply knowing as one reads the book that the Kabyles were in the midst of their struggle for freedom makes it difficult to think of them as a people who are isolated or stagnant or whose folk traditions mask from them the fact that they are economically exploited.

Is it not we anthropologists, some scholars are now asking, who have tended to play down cross-cultural communication and historical process in the groups we study because of the difficulty of incorporating such *variable* variables neatly within an anthropological model? Today cross-cultural contact surely is only a question of kind and degree. Is it imposed or sought after, frequent or infrequent, with similar or very dissimilar groups? And what is the degree of cultural or political control the culture group has vis-à-vis these outsiders? Not incidentally, these are the sorts of questions Kelibian hikayat often address as well.

That cultural change or cultural reevaluation is likely to be stimulated by cross-cultural contact is also evident. Surely change depends most anywhere on a pool of local and extra-local processes.

Anthropologists are also rejecting now the ethnographic "faceless natives," the portrayal of culture groups as if members were more or less interchangeable with others of similar age and sex—the "peasant," the "worker," the "woman"[12]—and fundamentally different in their responses to their natural and social environs from the researcher and her or his culture—separate but equal. Such representations arise from western folk ideas about the nature of Third World villagers or of tribal groups, as well as from difficulties in "penetrating" close-knit communities, getting to know well a number of group members, and then writing about their differences in addition to their similarities. In these times of the global community, the "savage mind" becomes increasingly elusive. "We are all natives now, and everybody else not immediately one of us is an exotic. What looked once to be a matter of finding out whether savages could distinguish fact from fancy now looks to be a matter of finding out how others, across the sea or down the corridor, organize their significative world" (Geertz 1983: 151). This perspective has resulted in a leveling of difference between us and the other, broadening and personalizing our range of subjects. North American anthropologists and folklorists now see the value of "studying up," and anthropologists now more frequently study those like North Africans and southern Europeans who are geographically and historically close. Studies of people geographically and historically close render representational conceits of isolation useless, and they leave us vulnerable to the responses and evaluations of our subjects, who can no longer be an unnamed mass from which the ethnographer draws to support a theory or construct a model. This experience in turn is teaching us that all culture groups must be approached in a spirit of reciprocity. The studied are also the students. No longer can we confine our research to people we assume are unable to respond. No longer can we interpret for them as if they have not the resources to speak for themselves.

In much of North American traditional anthropological and folklore theory I feel there is a tendency to look for the familiar, oneself, in the strange, another culture, as well as to look for the strange in the familiar,[13] to learn about one's own community by studying another.[14] This tendency provides another touchstone through which to construct a new paradigm for folklore, for it implies not only the basic "alikeness" of folk but, further, an interest in what we can learn from the historically or geographically removed other that we cannot learn at home. This idea of "traveling" among strangers to look for alternative, adoptable strategies for conceptualizing the world is very "American." I will quote Robert Pirsig:

By going very far away in space or very far away in time, we may find our usual rules entirely overturned, and these grand overturnings enable us the better to see the little changes that may happen nearer to us. But what we ought to aim at is less the ascertainment of resemblances and differences than the recognition of likenesses hidden under apparent divergences. Particular rules seem at first discordant, but looking more closely we see in general that they resemble each other; different as to matter, they are alike as to form, as to the order of their parts." (Pirsig 1974: 259)

And James Boon says,

Our own streetcorners are perhaps microsocieties, and our own quadrangles enclose semantic universes; but studying them alone cannot reveal the ultimate culture that they contrastively represent. Hence anthropology's apparent inefficiency, its worldwide circumlocution, and its most distinctive fetish. (Boon 1985: 4)

Similarly, anthropologist Stephen Tyler writes, "For it is not for us to know the meaning for them unless it is already known to us both, and thus needs no translation, but only a kind of reminding" (Tyler 1986: 138).[15] All that is lacking in these quotations in order to legitimize cross-cultural dialogue is acknowledgment that the other can knowingly participate in this process—also teaching, learning, adopting, and adapting within the arena of common humanity.[16] We "tend to allow our senses to penetrate the other's world rather than letting our senses be penetrated by the world of the other " (Stoller 1984: 93)

Each of these quotes addresses the break with the "savage mind" in which "natives" are thought to have a completely different way of thinking about their natural and social environs—separate but equal. The move back from this perspective is a delicate one, liable to accusations of a return to the old, culturally relativistic, nonevaluative anthropology of the first half of the twentieth century, but a move that is particularly important when studying a people like Kelibians who are a part of the same circum-Mediterranean tradition out of which much of western culture is formed. Kelibians are so close to us culturally that we may miss the differences or we may emphasize the differences to *make* a difference. What sets Kelibians off from us culturally is not a "savage mind" but small surprises about communicative techniques and aesthetic standards, and larger variations from at least what most of us are used to in social structure, and very large differences in historical baggage.

It is from this leveling process wherein we are "all natives now," and the other has something to teach us, that an important basis is established for a shift in emphasis within the field of cultural anthropology to a folklore paradigm with productive potential for the representational challenges in the doing of ethnography that we will face in the twenty-first century. It is only a small step from the jettisoning of the savage mind to the realization that folklore is not the product of a special kind of mind, whether savage, rural, or preindustrial.[17] At a certain level of abstraction we have, at least potentially, access to similar, mutually comprehensible ways of dealing with the world-in-process. We all share the potential of drawing upon diverse rhetorical media, some folk and some not, depending on specific historical, social, and cultural situations in which we (as individuals or members of folk or nonfolk groups) find ourselves.

There are several potentially powerful ideas floating around now in the mainstreams of anthropology and folklore that when pulled together form a paradigm of folklore useful, perhaps even essential, as one component for meeting the demands of the "new" ethnography. Among the several fronts on which folklore theory and anthropological theory are reaching basic points of accord that would allow for this more profitable role for folklore within the arena of cultural representation, the most important is this leveling of basic barriers among culture groups. For many North American folklorists the similar leveling premise in folklore to "we are all natives now" is "we are all folk now" too. Reference to North American folklore studies in the *Journal of American Folklore* indicates that, in fact, folklore—from lullabies to foodways to jokes, proverbs, riddles, and stories—is found in all strata and spectra of society. Most of us are members of several folk groups—familial, academic, religious, regional, linguistic—some with more powerful performative resources than others. It is this concept of common folkness[18] in addition to my involvement in the worlds of Kelibia and academia that enables me to see that the two perspectives on folklore presented in this chapter are formed in very much the same way Kelibians form their community "paradigm"—often starting with face-to-face inter-action in congenial small groups sharing very particular historical and cultural (including, in this case, scholarly) contexts. In turn, these folk ideas about folklore, embedded and sometimes hidden in larger scholarly or social discourses, inform two different kinds of social-scholarly rhetoric about how folklore appears (or does not) in ethnographies.

American folklorists' long tradition of studying folklore not as the province of a specific class or social setting, but as a vital component of our common humanity (one of the touchstones of the second paradigm) derives from a cultural and intellectual history very different from that described in the first half of this chapter. Under the influence of the American populist tradition and Thoreauian celebration of the rural, folklorists neither confine lore to the peasantry nor use the term "peasant" to describe rural farm folk. Américo Paredes points out that most folklorists in the United States cannot use the term "peasant" without feeling they are being insulting and elitist, or undemocratic. Since many American folklore studies are reflexive rather than directed at the other, it is not surprising that the definition of "the folk" has gradually expanded so that "the folk" in its broadest sense is *"any group of people whatsoever* who share at least one common factor" (Dundes 1965: 2). We are all, then, members of several folk groups—I, no less than the Kelibians. Besides the folklore of those who traditionally have been studied as folk groups (the rustic, isolated, homogeneous, unsophisticated), the lore of groups such as college professors, students, Wall Street brokers, pilots, and the patrons of singles bars and fast-food restaurants must be taken into account.[19]

A second point of accord that mainstream anthropologists and folklorists as well as other scholars are beginning to reach is that folk communication is not an inferior form of communication. Folklore can be as powerful a cultural tool for change or aggrandizement in cross-cultural or intra-cultural dialogue as any other artistic medium. On the one hand, this is evident when looking at the folk forms of Emersonian civil disobedience with their accompanying folksongs, folk poetry, folk heroes. In this context we realize the power of our folkness and folklore to use tradition artistically in the cause of change as much as to resist change. Since 1888, when folklore was established as a discipline in America, folklore has been perceived as emergent. Scholars have watched as traditions have been adapted to unique personalities and new lifestyles, Old World to New World, country to city to suburb, cornfield to oil field. Those folk most visible were those ethnic, occupational, or age groups militating through song and story for social change, or those involved in physical, dirty, and dangerous occupations. Thus, the rhetorical dimension of folklore as significant in the fashioning of emergent culture was very evident. In addition, as the lore of the lumberjack, for example, was adopted and adapted by the oil-field roughneck, and the protest songs of the dust bowl 1930s were evoked in the anti-war 1960s, the adaptability of traditional forms to new expressive needs was demonstrated.[20] Even when the lore of the folk was romanticized, and distinctions made between folk and nonfolk, American folklorists seem always to have felt that the "folk" were our teachers, that we needed to listen and learn from them. Many folklorists emphasized and were proud of their own "folkness."

"Activist" folk traditions in the United States from sit-ins (lunch-counters, all men's clubs, university presidents' offices) to marches (integration, women's rights, anti-Vietnam war, gay rights, abortion rights) to burnings (books, flags, bras, draftcards) are recycled with similar structures but new content. As cities expanded, scholars began to appreciate the power and vitality of the lore of city folk. Little wonder, then, that the lore of the people (all of us) came to be perceived not as mystifying or static but, complexly, as ammunition on a cultural battlefield—a source of strength for any community, even a Mediterranean town or a Kabylia or a Shebika to draw on, no matter how lacking in financial or formal institutional strength.

At the same time, we now are realizing that despite the potential for powerful insight that literary criticism brings to an analysis of folkloric forms, be they verbal, material, or textual, the impulse in our culture (and, even more, in the Arab world) to privilege institutional or establishment literature and art is one factor that can lead us to overlook in less overt folkloric performances, especially of the other, artistically and rhetorically powerful strategies, especially *strategies of intimacy*, that are not possible (or not possible in the same way) in so called high culture forms. From the examples of the hikayat, however, we can see that oral folk performance is far more than a text, and even that performance itself exists in a dialogue both about and with tradition and the past, with insiders and outsiders, with the present and the future. We need to respond to orality (or traditional material culture or any folk form) on its own terms and in its special contexts, whether we draw upon analytical techniques such as narratology, new criticism, formalism, or structuralism or not.

To understand and participate in the potential richness of folk dialogue, scholars are now paying close attention to logical connections among the corpus, its situational context, and its cultural matrix as well as to the structure and processual unfolding of specific performance events. Only thus can one discover the unique qualities that "performer" and audience together bring in the details of a specific performance (the social context in which society and folklore merge) to a traditional folkloric item—be it poem, riddle, game, or artifact—qualities that potentially allow for transformation of the social structure.[21] As has been shown, the "message" of a hikayah, for example, is not contained simply within the narrative itself, but is a product of relationships among narrator, narrative, audience, and their cultural and personal past, present, and (projected) future histories.

In this way we are continuously reminded that it is as impossible to exhaust the multivocalic range of a particularly good piece of folk literature performed over time as it is to "complete" an analysis of Hamlet, for example. A study like this one of the meshing of the aesthetic and the social in Kelibian hikayat can touch only some of the most significant and surprising messages or meta-messages realized by the interplay of the texts and contexts I participated in.

Anthropologists today are rejecting old methodologies and ideologies and casting about for methods of ethnographic representation that are dialogic,[22] that include the voice of the other, that include both affective and objective components of a society, and that seek to describe groups as they are situated in space and time. If we accept our common "nativeness," our common "folkness," and attend to folklore as a powerful artistic and rhetorical resource for subversion or celebration, then the interpretive potential of folklore and folkloristics to speak to these issues is evident. It is through folklore that we can look into social groups more thoroughly, to find displayed, to have described to us, and to discuss with members of another folk group the centripetal forces that bolster them. And we can look outward with them to understand better, to have explained from their centered point of view, their micro-place in the macro-scheme of things.

When one turns to study traditional anthropological communities in their neglected historical and cross-cultural contexts, community resources available for handling that outside contact seem pitifully inadequate when gauged by western standards. At first glance, Kelibia, Shebika, and Kabylia would seem vulnerable to the impositions of outsiders. They are all members of former colonies peripheral from a western perspective in the global scheme. They are also all peripheral, geographically and culturally, to the centers of power within their own countries. What resources would such groups have through which to maintain a sense of cultural control or pride? I am convinced that, as in the case of Kelibians, Shebikians, and Kabyles, more attention to the affective (including folkloric), in conjunction with the objective, dimensions of other cultures, including those beloved of ethnographers, will reveal that these communities too are neither isolated from awareness of historical process and from the outside world nor helpless before them.

Once we acknowledge our common folkness and the right to privilege other artistic media than the written, it is clear that Kelibians could not, any more than we in similar circumstances could not, be ignorant of the nature of the colonizer discourse on the colonized. In a very real sense, the hikayah-telling events presented in the last two chapters are a response by the narrators to outsiders in positions of power who would devalue their way of life and their very means of communicating. They are a part of this larger dialogue whether I choose to recognize that or not. What we have begun to see is that colonizers and "culturally superior" outsiders of yesterday and today are an unseen presence to which the male storytellers are responding across genres, across channels (written-oral), across time, and across cultures even while, and also because, they are engaging in conversation with the young men and children of Kelibia. If outsiders would assert that Kelibians lack control of their lives, their past and future, their individuality, their very speech, hikayat are a forum for revealing various configurations of folk power. Their aggrandizement of Kelibia and Kelibians vis-à-vis the outside world is necessary precisely because of the devaluation of their culture and is, I argue, one thing that makes the old stories so attractive to the young—part of what gives them, both men and women, their remarkable self-confidence and success in the face of political, linguistic, and economic devaluation and difficulty.

A look at one Kelibian folk form has revealed that Kelibians are aware of their vulnerability vis-à-vis the outside world and of the devaluation of their folk culture as homogeneous, isolated, nonviable, inferior, and so on by that world. Kelibians know at least some of the ways in which they are stereotyped by outsiders, and (as is their custom) they couch an oblique and embedded reply to me, to the outside world, in hikayah-telling events as one level of their multivocalic communication. Are Kelibians homogeneous, passive, "constrained by tradition and the weight of social norms"? Are they insular, unchanging, unlettered, "peripheral" culturally and geographically? As we have seen, every narrative event moves Kelibia center stage. Cultural standards are set by the narrator in collaboration with his or her audience and their shared communal and cultural context. We see individual cultural "deviance" or defiance or change valued along with conformity or continuity. In two different sequences we witness the negotiation of beliefs about magic practices and about genies—examples of community change both influenced by and influencing hikayah-telling. We find cosmopolitan Kelibians listening to war news on the radio and following battle progress on a map. Insularity is belied as well, in the person of the narrator and audience, many of whom have traveled and have distant connections. And, of course, community coherence itself has been forged around the fact that every family traveled to Kelibia in the not too distant past. We see Kelibian respecters of knowledge arranging for their children to study at night because they are needed to work during the day. We hear stories where Kelibians get the best of improperly behaving (by community standards) Germans, Italians, French, Tunisians, Ottomans. We see cultured Kelibians harvesting, hunting and tracking better than migratory country folk, and traveling Kelibians besting those they encounter on the road. One day the young men in the group will tell similar stories. In sum, the stories demonstrate control, rather than passive fatalism. They signal, "Do not understimate us—the richness of our dialect, the resourcefulness of our people, our love for and understanding of our community."

Listening when Kelibians tell me about their strengths through their hikayah-telling events forces a kind of response. Taken together these storytelling events are at one level of abstraction an answer to any non-Kelibians who would marginalize or underestimate the affective and practical power of the community and its individual members. Kelibians have powerful national and international connections never mentioned in these stories—doctors, politicians, scientists, artists, media personalities, lawyers. But these people too need to prove themselves by Kelibian standards of family and community loyalty, including weekly returns, participation as "one of the boys" in the evening sahrah, as "one of the girls" in the drama of motherhood and in the serious talk and banter involved in the lengthy communal preparation for an extended family meal, a wedding, or a holiday celebration.

Most of the stories I heard had to do with notable community members of the recent (twentieth-century) past—heroes, tricksters, walis, or dervishes. Most were told by older members of the community to younger. It quickly became obvious that the stories were not just accounts of the past, but prescriptions for the future—prescriptions that consistently emphasized certain values, including both the importance of community ties and the desirability of travel, adventure, and extra-community contacts. Further, it became clear that community reality too was being negotiated. Had a certain man or woman led an exemplary life or was he or she a rascal? How should our community members relate to the outside world—city or countryside? How are certain situations dealt with ethically? Do we or do we not believe in individual encounters with jnoun (spirits)?[23] A host of significant community concerns are juggled, using a medium that communally celebrates the experiences of individual town members. Observed in this way, Kelibia emerges not as a helpless, isolated, homogeneous, unchanging community needing external attention to "teach" it how to keep up in the twentieth century, but one that (in the opinion of a group of its older families, at least) through its folklore and the uniqueness of its community members is able itself to give social meaning to alien events. The various sets of both synchronic and diachronic relations among myriad actors (insiders and outsiders, taletellers and protagonists, taletellers and audience) contain the tensions and contradictions that may lead to change and new structures or may simply provide community members with the means to cope as gracefully as possible with inevitable changes.

What happens if we turn to look at the Kabyles, or Shebikans, or an individual, Tuhami, with this alternative set of analytical touchstones? Vincent Crapanzano wrote in *Tuhami*, his sociopsychological study of one Moroccan individual, "Where . . . there is no longer any relevance in the cultural code to the 'on going social process,' there can be no adjustment. The gap is too great. The individual is destined either to lead his life in terms of the frozen symbols of the now irrelevant cultural code . . . or to be cast adrift in the flux of meaningless social activity" (Crapanzano 1985/1980: 83). Certain communities, like Shebika, founder as well. But need small communities always be helpless in the face of changes imposed by the world system? I think that we have seen that they need not. Has not the privileging of persistence over change in the study of folk or traditional culture, and the school of thought that perceives lore as "anachronistic" or "remnant," obscured the alternative notion that the very "stuff" of folklore is a tool for which people, including ourselves, find new applications over time and in response to varying circumstances, even cataclysmic circumstances like invasion and upheavals in the world market? Could not Tuhami's problems be the result not of frozen traditions, but of a loss (for him personally, at least) of the very traditions that can be a resource for navigating the shoals of change? Cannot culture codes and their "symbols" embedded in traditional expressive culture, as well as elsewhere, be made to be relevant by the people and communities who use them? Perhaps it is those lost souls like Tuhami, family-less misfits who cannot master their own Moroccan culture code well enough to lead successful lives, who suffer. Could not one argue that such significance as life holds for Tuhami comes precisely from certain folkloric options open to (but not only to) misfits in Morocco—storytelling, magic, and possession?

Even the people of Shebika, after spending time with Duvignaud's research team, showed signs finally of effectively reuniting symbol and practice toward practical results: "They no longer regarded themselves as objects of outsiders' curiosity: they began to question and think things out on their own account" (Duvignaud 1970: 229). But, on the one hand, might not this process have occurred even without the unsettling, *thought*-provoking presence of the research team from France and Tunis? When they went on strike to resist the plans that the central government had for them, I, at least, got the impression that the Shebikans were resisting in ways that emerged from the encounter between Tunisois's (the city folk's) views of what was best for them, and the Shebikans' own set of traditional values and expectations. Waiting, perhaps more patiently than many of us can imagine, for a propitious moment and a small victory is, after all, as we have seen from the Kelibian narratives, something that colonized people have learned to do. It would not be surprising if Shebikans had sized up and used the advent of the research team to their own benefit.

And finally, Mouloud Mammeri observes of his own folk tradition that the Kabyle poet is "capable non seulement de mettre en pratique le code admis, mais de l'adapter, de le modifier, voire de le 'révolutionner' "[24] (Mammeri and Bourdieu 1978: 64). Later he adds, "Le rapport public-poète est tel qu'une performance poétique peut être véritablement une espèce de pièce jouée à deux, le poète et son public. Le poète n'est pas seul à créer "[25] (Mammeri and Bourdieu 1978: 65)

I would not argue that Kelibia is Kabylia, of course, or that Kelibia is Shebika, for that matter. Kelibia is bigger; it is on the Mediterranean periphery rather than in the mountains or on the desert periphery. Kabyles are of Berber origin. Ethnographic or ethnography-of-speaking studies of each of these three places would look very different, for these and many other reasons. The people of Shebika or Tuhami's fellow Moroccans do not necessarily count change as such a central part of their tradition as Kelibians must. I do maintain, however, that for change to be addressed gracefully and effectively anyplace, tradition must be the conduit and the inspiration and that an approximation of the lively engagement of tradition and change found in Kelibia can be found in the other two places as well. The cultural strength that Kelibia or Shebika or the Moroccans maintained during the colonial period must stem from a powerful counterhegemonic discourse that can in some circumstances as much be appropriated by subgroups within the culture as be directed towards outsiders.

And folklore, particularly the hikayah, relies on its intimate nature not only for its rhetorical and artistic power but for its noncapturability. It is debatable whether the lore itself could be effectively appropriated or damaged.[26] The dynamic intra-cultural communication that takes place when a verbal art form or an item of material culture is shared is elusive, not easily harnessed except most superficially by outsiders for their own purposes—be they scholarly or political (Keesing 1974: 88). Colonial scholars often seemed to feel that some essence was constantly eluding them, that they could never quite get behind the cultural "veil." This failure may be the very reason that present-day scholars like Jean-Claude Vatin, Philippe Lucas, Kenneth Burke, and others find these old studies somewhat vapid.

In my study of Kelibian hikayat, I have found folklore to be not a fetter, but a potential weapon to be used by people against repression or domination by cultural outsiders. The ambiguity, the multivocal nature of aesthetic communication, so central a concern to many American folklorists and anthropologists working with traditional expressive culture today, should be especially useful in studying a postcolonial or minority group where traditionally what one wanted to say to one's own group often was precisely what one wanted to avoid saying to the dominator. Rather than finding that a folk are stultified by, or open to manipulation through, their lore, I have found in my research that at least one community of folk take control of the communicative and shaping potential of their lore.

Much of Kelibian folklore, not simply the hikayah, works to enlarge the realm of the possible for the culture group or subgroup presenting the lore in the face of various sorts of pressures and repressions—not simply those of the colonial or western world, but the governmental, the "professional," the natural worlds, and even the domination of men over women or of learned speech over colloquial, of age over youth.

The consequences of ignoring the folk component of any culture become clearer as well. It is not in our own best interests to limit discourse by insisting that it be carried on in one medium only, the textual medium of western "high" culture. Failure to attend to traditional expressive culture as powerful and viable means that certain culture groups, most certainly a majority in the world, are thus denied the right to carry on a philosophical defense of their own culture using the media that most of them have best mastered, and the only ones to which those we most need to hear have access, folk media. (Those we do hear often are those who consent to speak to us in western modes of discourse and using western theory and, to some extent, perspective.) As in the case of Kelibian hikayat, this fact may be more to our detriment, as scholars of the workings of cultures than to theirs, for until we find a way to understand the affective strengths of cultures perceived through western eyes as peripheral, we will not comprehend the centripetal forces that hold these cultures (and our own) together to one degree or another despite their economic and political vulnerability before more global forces.[27]

Furthermore, if folklore (or attention to it) is blamed for the nonviable aspects of a Third World person or traditional community, practically speaking, that attribution diverts attention from more likely culprits (imperialist, postcolonialist, anti-Islamic or Islamic, anti-Arab, government, even of urban folk ideas of certain scholars about the non-western and the nonscholarly in general)—many of which are dealt with via the structure and content of hikayah-telling sessions themselves.

In sum, we do these cultures and ourselves no good if we refuse to listen to them in their most culturally evocative media. More attention is needed to folk idioms, both theirs and ours. In my Kelibian studies I have shown that it is precisely a genre of folklore that assists Kelibians as we have seen in coping with this "modern age." Nevertheless, when I posit an enabling role for folk expressive culture and study it as an agent of effective cultural process and as part of the Kelibian dialogue with the outside world, I am not, to borrow Michel Foucault's term, "dans le vrai" for a large segment of the scholarly community (Foucault 1972: 224).

Finally, there are a number of scholars who would not privilege western classics over folk art,[28] in one sense, that is, that both are judged equally liable to be tainted through cooptation by the status quo. This is the school of western thought that argues that we are all trapped by culture or the world system (and especially trapped by language) but that Third World people, except, perhaps, for some intellectuals in large cities, are more trapped, because unaware of their plight. "As in the utopianism of the eighteenth century, the other is the means of the author's alienation from his own sick culture, but the savage [or the North African] of the twentieth century is sick, too, neutered, like the rest of us, by the dark forces of the 'world system,' IT has lost the healing art" (Tyler 1986: 128). It is accepted today that we are channeled into certain ways of thinking and acting, but as I have suggested in previous chapters, folklore like all aesthetic culture and like cross-cultural and historical study (not necessarily or even primarily that performed by "scholars") is not a cultural trap but a resource potentially useful for reconceptualizing and enlarging the cultural discourse. This brings us back to Kuhn and the observation that "traditions [including scientific traditions] are not passive entities helplessly battered about by circumstance, capable only of adapting to a concrete, externally defined given" (Hollinger 1980: 201).

In sum, if we avoid perceiving folklore (including traditional practice) as only the province of the other and as inferior art forms that evolved in more "advanced" circles into "high" culture (the value of which is pronounced upon by a cultural elite of intellectuals, experts, and scholars), we then can escape seeing it as the cause of unenviable positions in the world system. We can acknowledge a commonality with the other that will enable us to listen for dialogue rather than find (or impose) structure. This leveling leads to discourse where the folklore of the other can be taken seriously at its community value. Only then can we hear Kelibians, for example, telling us what their situation is in the media they feel are most compelling.

Notes

1. In the last few years social scientists have been particularly concerned with the effect on their research directions and perspectives of the historico-philosophical

climate in which they live and work. Personal or national backgrounds of researchers have been evoked to account for theoretical differences as well as discrepancies in data. There is danger, Bob Scholte points out, in thinking all scholarly differences are factual. (My thanks to Alan Dundes for first drawing my attention to this line of inquiry.) Rather, they derive from culture-specific learning about ways of thinking and perceiving. Thus, in his article "Epistemic Paradigms," Scholte accounts for the often very different French and American approaches to anthropology by taking into consideration implicit historico-philosophical as well as explicit socio-anthropological differences. "I believe," he writes, "that the resolution of the problem of productive communication between rival paradigms lies largely in the domain of history" (Scholte 1966: 1192).

More specifically, Edmund Burke maintains that to understand the discrepancies between French and American scholarship in North Africa we must look as much at the observers as at the observed. Two sets of traditions—those of French and American scholars, the observers—inescapably influence how we perceive and interpret the traditions of an observed third—those of the Maghribian other, the observed. As Burke notes, because of our own political and intellectual backgrounds we begin our studies with certain "inherited" assumptions about society in general and North African society in particular (Burke 1980).

I cannot divide attitudes about tradition, traditional expressive culture, and folklore theory by national schools of thought (French versus American), or even by discipline. These concerns are, in fact, rather peripheral to the main foci of many of the scholars I mention, especially those considered in the first half of this chapter. Scholte's and Burke's insistence on making explicit the historico-philosophical, political-intellectual forces implicit in theoretical differences among scholars is, however, basic to the discussion in this chapter. The "rival paradigms" concerning folk and folk tradition between which I am trying to "establish communication" are those of certain folklorists, anthropologists, literary theorists, sociolinguists, and historians of a populist bent versus those French *sociologues* and others, including Americans, closely associated with them who are of a more traditional western Marxist intellectual inclination and who, unlike most in the first group, have worked in the Maghrib and suffered the legacy of colonialism. I find that the two groups of scholars do not fall into two camps but rather along a continuum. Thus I quote Williams in *Marxism and Literature* to support my "populist" understanding of the power of verbal art. Sometimes their earlier works seem to be mediated on this subject by their later. The populists' paradigms are often informed by western Marxist social science theory as well, but this theory is diluted for them in interesting ways by an overlay of populism that empowers individuals and small groups or the underdog in ways not attended to by the former. To the question "can groups—ethnic, national, village, neighborhood—still make a difference, manage to maintain an effective sense of identity," the former populists would be more likely to make the positive answer, the idealistic choice. (See Clifford 1980b for a short discussion of the usefulness of "culture" as an organizing principle.) (For a more general discussion of some implications of western Marxist theory for folklore studies see José Limón 1983: 34–52.)

2. Much of my research on the subject of French folklore scholarship in the Maghrib during the colonial period was done with the help of a National Endowment for the Humanities fellowship. If my interpretation or chosen examples seem to some social science scholars who are devoted to this region and time period to be a bit skewed, I ask them to keep in mind that my central focus was and is fieldwork done on traditional expressive culture: verbal art forms (riddles, jokes, myths, proverbs); visual presentation of self (tattooing, hair design, clothing, body decorations); folk religion; rituals, festivals, and carnivals; material culture (handicrafts, folk architecture, boat building); or folk medicine. Thus I may seem to slight at times the more well-known scholars of the day for the relatively obscure.

The study in progress on French folklore scholarship in the Maghrib from which I have drawn much of the material for Chapter 4, is designed with two objectives. The first is to describe the development of French colonial folkloristics in the Maghrib in the context of late nineteenth- and early twentieth-century western scientific thought. What shared scientific and historico-philosophical background led French sociologists, ethnographers, and linguists to make so many folklore studies in the Maghrib? Which traditional aesthetic structures did they choose to concentrate on? What did they expect to find?

The second objective is to analyze the best early French works in light of the very different theoretical tools and fieldwork methodology of current trends in American folkloristics and anthropology. This analysis will be used to answer two questions: How can contemporary folklore theory be employed to give new perspectives on early materials and on the colonial context in which the materials were gathered? And how can those older and colonially tainted texts (which are often ignored and attacked today) be drawn on to enhance the work of contemporary social scientists?

3. "to the pioneers of the first hour, some of whom no doubt remember the prosperity that the ancient era revived there and find encouragement in this memory."

4. Under the pretext of apostleship, of charity, of pilgrimages, and of monachal discipline, numerous representatives of these bodies of worshipers travel throughout the Islamic world, which has neither borders nor country, and they put in permanent contact Mecca, Djbouti, Istanbul, or Baghdad with Fez, Timbuctu, Algiers, Cairo, Khartoum, Zanzibar, Calcutta, or Java. Taking a thousand forms one after the other, these merchants, preachers, students, doctors, workers, beggars, charm-makers, showmen, fools deliberately shamming others, or visionaries unaware of their mission are, often and everywhere, well received by the faithful and effectively protected by them from the underground investigations of governments.

5. See, for example, Jean Besancenot's short work on Moroccan clothing or S. Biarney's ambitious ethnographic and linguistic study of North Africa.

6. This perspective fits in with the psychology of the day. C. G. Jung traveled to Tunisia in 1920 and observed a festival for a "marabout" down in Nefta: "This scene taught me something: these people . . . are moved and have their being in

emotion. . . . the ego has almost no autonomy" (Jung 242). In his widely known *The Philosophy of History*, G.W.F Hegel observes:

We now leave Africa never to mention it again. For it is not a historical continent, it shows neither change nor development, and whatever may have happened there [that is in Africa] belongs to the world of Asia and of Europe.(Hegel 1900: 99)

7. Please notice that I am not directing myself necessarily to folklorists, but to scholars who work with or comment upon folkloric material (verbal art, folk architecture, ritual, festival) in their field studies in the Maghrib. Also, I am not considering those scholars, either French or American, who confine themselves to literary, textual analyses of verbal art forms.

8. The oral-written division is as effective in its own way as the folk-nonfolk dichotomy in inhibiting the development of a dialogic anthropology. See, for example, Finnegan (1973) for a careful look at how our assumptions about literature affect our attitudes toward nonliterate groups.

9. In the study of folkloric events as in the study of any sign system:

'Sign' itself . . . has to be revalued to emphasize its variability and internally active elements, indicating not only an internal structure but an internal dynamic. Similarly, 'system' has to be revalued to emphasize social process rather than fixed 'sociality' . . . . Here, as a matter of absolute priority, men relate and continue to relate before any system which is their product can as a matter of practical rather than abstract consciousness be grasped or exercise its determination. (Williams 1977: 42)

10. Eickelman notes that ". . . until the last three decades the main thrust of anthropology has not been in the study of complex societies or civilizational traditions. As late as the 1950s most anthropological studies of the Middle East concentrated upon villages and pastoral nomads" (Eickelman 1984: 282). Or, as Elizabeth and Robert Fernea observe, ". . . until recently much anthropological research has assumed that the group being studied exists in a kind of isolation, a never-never land of self-containment . . ." (Fernea and Fernea 1985: 315). Also see Rosaldo (1980: 24–28) and Marcus and Fischer (1986: n.1) for useful discussions.

I am very much taken by the similarities between critiques of orientalist approaches to the study of the Third World and critiques of the study by some folklore scholars of women in American culture. Debora Kodish writes of two women folksingers, "Both women are described [by the folklorist researcher] as . . . awakened to the new worth of their heritage, tranformed by the folklorist's visit" (Kodish 1987: 574). She continues:

We have descriptions of silent folk waiting for discovery by outsiders. Taking these accounts at face value, some scholars have debated the marginal status of expressive and creative individuals within folk society. While opportunities for creative expression may vary within small-scale rural communities (especially for women), it is still true that the depiction of such encounters has the power of a convention, functioning as symbol rather than fact. However marginal, individuals have voices and identities within their communities. (Kodish 1987: 575)

"Folklore Theory," she concludes, "[no less than literary theory, writing, or ethnography] is constrained by powerful and patriarchal subtexts. [The studied] are our guides in deconstructing standard or canonical texts " (Kodish 1987: 577).

11. What seem impassable to us, Kabyle mountains, the Sahara, the Mediterranean, get us "stuck" in geographical and thence cultural clichés.

12. This definition limiting "the folk" to peasants is shared by Latin American folklorists. Thus folklorists should properly study only peasant culture. "To the [Latin American] folklorist belongs the peasant, and he must be careful not to step out of bounds into the other social groups" (Paredes 1969: 31).

13. See also Roy Wagner, "Whether [the anthropologist] knows it or not, . . . his 'safe' act of making the strange familiar [by calling the situation he or she is studying 'culture'] always makes the familiar a little bit strange. And the more familiar the strange becomes, the more and more strange the familiar will appear" (Wagner 1978: 11). In other words, self-knowledge is drawn "from the understanding of others, and vice-versa" (Wagner, 16).

14. Dundes (1971: 101).

15. Eickelman writes, "Anthropologists are particularly concerned with eliciting the taken-for-granted, shared meanings that underlie conduct in given societies and are so familiar a part of routine that they are taken to be 'natural' " (Eickelman 1989: 21). When David Schneider writes about American kinship or Erving Goffman gave a lecture on "The [Academic] Lecture" or Mary Douglas writes about British working class eating patterns or Danielle Roemer writes about her college students' visual riddles, then certain "ways we go about things" that seemed natural suddenly do not. Surely other societies have culture members who reconceptualize for everyone what has been going on under their very noses, and outsiders, like anthropologists, might, as outsiders, be very good at this. This is something members of social groups, *sans rancune*, can do for themselves and each other. But it is for community members themselves to acknowledge or deny that crucial "flash of recognition" that comes from an astute insight, well presented.

16. Jane Bachnik writes, for example,

process, reflexivity, and understanding are increasingly acknowledged in the social reality of the ethnographer, but they have not been similarly acknowledged for the native in the cultures we depict ethnographically. This oversight creates a gap between ethnographic texts (which are increasingly self-conscious, multi-leveled, and dialogic) and their depictions of social life that are markedly devoid of the same characteristics. (Bachnik 1986: 76)

And Wagner adds, "every time we make others part of a 'reality' that we alone invent, denying their creativity by usurping the right to create, we *use* those people and their way of life and make them subservient to ourselves" (Wagner 1978: 16).

17. See Linda Dégh (1988) for a concise summary of this "new folkloristics," which, as she indicates, is no longer very new.

18. This perspective is not that of all mainstream American folklorists. It is one I acquired from the scholarship of Alan Dundes, from Richard Bauman's early penchant for looking for folklore "in all the wrong places" (among Quakers and at the La Have Island General Store, for example), from Ellen Steckert's emphasis on

"subtle" folk singing performance styles, and from my own already formed inclinations and interests. Patrick Mullen points out that national culture scholars (e.g., Henry Glassie, John Vlach) tend at times to idealize the folk as other (than the scholar), being "lower-class, communal, and sharing" rather than "middle-class, hierarchical, and acquisitive" (Mullen, personal communication). Obviously some of the exploited also exploit or would if they could. As Mullen also points out, many American scholars of urban legend, like Jan Brunvand, at times slip into "debunking," thus implying a certain contrastive lack of sophistication and subtlety for the legend tellers.

19. It should be emphasized that a folkloric study of these groups would focus on their expressive culture (verbal art, material culture, visual presentation of self) as communication. In this text, a restricted range of storytelling phenomena is being treated ethnographically: so, only certain, albeit highly significant, aspects of Kelibian culture are being attended to.

Although one study of culture-in-general cannot "speak for" all members of a culture—men and women, rich and poor, young and old—I do feel that my observations on the communal aspects of the hikayat are valid and central to their interpretation. While making some general observations about the Kelibian world view, my particular emphasis is on the implications of the hikayat for a group of older and younger men from some of the older, more established families in town. Class is very fluid right now because of the opportunities, educational and otherwise, opened up since the end of colonialism. Even the richest of the old families have poor members and vice versa. On the other hand, some of the wealthiest families in town (the wine merchant's and that of a man who is a member of the secret service, for example) are not considered quite respectable. One claim to high status in the town, however, is membership in one of the older, respectable town families, including but by no means limited to those of Ottoman descent. All of the people, rich or poor, men or women, who contributed stories share this long-time resident status.

20. See as well Bruner in Turner and Bruner (1986) for an illuminating account of how ethnographic "stories" change from acculturation stories to resistance stories.

21. For further discussion of the viability of this perspective see Bauman (1977b) and Keesing (1974: 92–94). Pierre Bourdieu cautions against the "occasionalist illusion which consists in directly relating practices to properties inscribed in the situation," but although "the truth of the interaction is never entirely contained in the interaction" the seeds of change, or strategic responses (imposed or possible) to change are sown in those settings (where else?) and so some truths can never be arrived at without attention to specific occasions. See Bourdieu (1977: 81).

22. See Dwyer (1982), Crapanzano (1985/1980), Lacoste-Dujardin (1985) for self-conscious examples of other attempts to right the dialogic balance.

23. For more discussion of the social phenomenon of "agreeing to agree" or the necessity of negotiating reality consult Berger and Luckmann (1966) or Blount's

"Introduction" (Blount 1975b: 1–10) and "Agreeing to Agree on Genealogy: A Luo Sociology of Knowledge " (Blount 1975a: 117–136).

24. "capable not only of putting into practice the accepted code, but of adapting it, modifying it, even 'revolutionizing' it " (Mammeri and Bourdieu 1978: 64).

25. "The public-poet relationship is such that a poetic performance actually can be a kind of play for two actors, the poet and his public. The poet is not the only one who creates" (Mammeri and Bourdieu 1978: 65).

26. Lore can be lost (see also story 23): Musical, artisanal, foodways traditions, and so on can be jettisoned even by a group itself in favor of something that seems to speak more appropriately to the moment or is more convienient—listening to music rather than making it, harvesting by machine rather than by hand, buying food or pots rather than making them, or making another kind of pot, music, or food. These phenomena are inherently neither good nor bad though to folklorists the more or less wholesale adoption of outsiders' productions would seem culturally impoverishing. This is how a person (or group) might lose the "healing art" to which Tyler refers.

27. Perhaps for this reason, Gans sees the economic and military superiority of western civilization as grounded in "a superiour ethic":

If Mohammed and Marx are understood, as they should be, as heirs of the Judeo-Christian tradition, there is virtually no nation in the world today in whose reigning ideology this tradition is not dominant, however much it may be tempered with or colored by a particular regional heritage. Those countries that are the least successful are precisely those that have found the assimilation of western culture most difficult. (Gans 1985: ix–x)

28. In the sense that is, western bourgeois "aesthetic responses," perhaps even more than "folk" art, lead "almost inevitably to new kinds of privileged instrumentality and specialized commodity":

Yet it is clear, historically, that the definition of 'aesthetic' response is an affirmation, directly comparable with the definition and affirmation of 'creative imagination', of certain human meanings and values which a dominant social system reduced and even tried to exclude. Its history is in large part a protest against the forcing of all experience into instrumentality ('utility'), and of all things into commodities. (Williams 1977: 151)

Final Remarks

> In the tale, in the telling, we are all one blood. Take the tale in
> your teeth, then, and bite it till the blood runs, hoping it's not
> poison; and we will all come to the end together, and even to
> the beginning; living as we do, in the middle.
>
> (Ursula K. Le Guin)

The Kelibian hikayah-telling events in this study define and redefine the
town and situate it vis-à-vis the outside world by means of accounts of its
past inhabitants and their concerns. They do this both for Kelibians and
for the outside world too, if we choose to pay attention. They represent
themselves to themselves, and to us, but they also overtly, obliquely, or by
implication represent us. Nevertheless, it would be a mistake to think that
the kind of "resistance" that Kelibians mount to outside hegemony is always or even usually reactive. The most powerful "resistance" is to have a
community that demonstrably works. The community coheres because it
effectively fulfills its own value criteria—close-knit families, hospitable
neighbors, opportunities for education, a decent living for most, a certain
cosmopolitan outlook in a beautiful and healthy setting—none of which,
as we have seen, comes without effort.

Despite the increasing pervasiveness of the modern, technologically
adept nation-state, a significant number of the world's population still live
within towns that until recently were walled and that still retain a sense of
cultural distance from both city and surrounding countryside. These communities have been the largest organized social systems that could provide
some security and continuity to most individuals and groups, and that
could provide a reputation and identity for a person traveling in the world
outside them. As Richard Bauman points out, there have been few folklore
studies oriented toward the community level of organization. "The community, representing the social matrix within which much of folklore is
learned, used, and passed on, has been largely overlooked" (Bauman 1982:
8). Thus we miss an opportunity to understand more fully by means of

community members' own traditional expressive culture spectrum the process of vital change in communities—how some of them can keep their
footing and sense of identity in a world where decisions that affect them
and their populations are often made thousands of miles away. For Kelibians this balancing act is nothing new—though intensified.

I have touched upon the role of Kelibians as mediators between, and
peripheral to, both city and rural life. Like Mohamed ouild Si 'Ali, or Gacem Lengliz, if we can "do" both city and rural while remaining centered,
at least attitudinally, in the town, we have a certain amount of quiet power.
This network power is quite apparent if one looks closely. Go to Tunis. In
the dark coffee shop where artists gather, receive telephone calls, exchange
news, there is a Kelibian. The world of sports? Secret service? Doctors?
Customs officers? Academia? Politics—left, right, center? Kelibians can
find Kelibians. Go to Paris, for that matter. Kelibians do not necessarily
spend time with other Kelibians, the tie need not be cultivated, though
young, homesick Kelibians away from home for the first time will seek out
a familiar, more established face. Network or migration studies could
profit from a look at narratives people living outside of, but in touch with,
their community have to tell about the place. What people, places, events
have taken on significance, and thus narrative potency? How do these narratives then comment on and deal with city life, life in the new environ-
ment? What do they tell us about a Kelibian's sense of obligation to the
community and about what the community can do for her or him? When
are Kelibians no longer Kelibian, but Tunisois, or French, or American?

Listening to narratives about events in their community from Kelibians,
we see that one rural town, at least, does not fit the image of these rural
settlements as stagnant, homogeneous, and so burdened by their own out-
moded traditions that any significant change must be initiated from outside. Scholars of theoretical perspectives ranging from Marxist to
functionalist to structuralist clearly must, if my analysis of Kelibian hikayat
is correct, take another look at life in rural villages and towns and at the
dynamic possibilities of the discourse(s) of traditional expressive culture in
enabling such communities to negotiate controllable change and to deal
with imposed change.

Of course, change anywhere is stimulated by outside contact, and I think
researchers would be hard pressed to find even a much more isolated community than Kelibia that has been devoid of members with important contacts—religious, kin, occupational, educational—to primary cities in their

own region and beyond. Reciprocally, travelers pass through—pilgrims, soldiers, entertainers, nomadic groups, merchants, poets, adventurers. But as these hikayah-tellings show, it is community members themselves who are uniquely qualified to mediate between outside stimuli and the traditional town customs and values. Even unwelcome changes imposed upon a community by a changing or invading world can be managed by drawing upon analogous situations from the community's past and showing how they were dealt with. And some of these mediators have impact far beyond their own communities. Out of the villages and towns of the Middle East come some of the region's greatest revolutionaries, scholars, and leaders. So we see communities effecting changes on the outside world as well.

Hikayah-telling is one means by which this particular community of Kelibia, drawing upon internal and external resources, initiates changes that are (or that are claimed to be) consistent with grass-roots and historical trends and values and inhibits those felt to be inconsistent with those trends and values. At the individual level, of course, taletellers work to persuade an audience toward, or away from, certain changes precisely by drawing parallels, or demonstrating discord with, these same agreed-upon values. Hikayat are examples of one artistic medium through which new information and unusual or unexpected events can be accommodated. By "obscuring, hedging, confusing, exploring or questioning what went on, that is, by keeping the coherence or comprehensibility of narrated events open to question" (Bauman 1986) narrators through narratives not only negotiate and renegotiate a shared vision of the past but thereby fashion and refashion a vision of the future. The shared past is creatively drawn upon by narrators to analyze and evaluate the implications or possibilities of new knowledge or unusual events that touch the town. In differences, similarities are sought—one of the similarities being that change and disharmony have occurred and been successfully dealt with (incorporated, modified, rejected) in the past. Richard Bauman writes, "If change is conceived of in opposition to the conventionality of the community at large, then it is only appropriate that the agents of that change be placed away from the center of that conventionality, on the margins of society" (Bauman 1977b: 45). In Kelibia, change cannot be conceived of like this. It is as central a *concept* as tradition. Change *is* a tradition. *Both* must be negotiated. So, whereas the subjects of the hikayat are often other in the community, and the protagonists so central as to be peripheral, the hikayah-tellers—as keepers, interpreters, manipulators, changers of tradition, and moderators of emergent social practice—are, like tradition and change, *central* in the community.

Of course the hikayat are not the only vehicles for town definition. Kelibia's location(s) in the mental and physical spaces of her various townspeople depend(s) on a pool of synchronic and diachronic indicators that storytellers can usefully draw upon or omit. Their incorporation into a hikayah strengthens it by drawing on their known relevances as town signifiers. Reciprocally, this signifying power of the person or family or landmark mentioned is enhanced for townspeople who happen to recall the appearance of that indicator within one or more of the stories. A certain set of buildings and other landmarks (older and newer) represent Kelibia's physical-spatial parameters and march through time, whereas certain sets of people, past and present, represent (and define) its cultural limits and possibilities. Since, after all, orientation is cultural *and* physical (each with a physical dimension), people and stories about them, like buildings and stories about them, are good "landmarks."

Robert Smith points out that artifacts on display are iconic representations of a story. The relationship between icon and story becomes more complicated, however, when, as in Kelibia, a certain building, like the tomb of a wali, itself takes on a new historical depth because a town member has acquired a story about it. I, for one, cannot walk past the zawiyya of Sidi 'Ali Qsibi without seeing the shadowy figure of a hot, dusty boy distraught over the loss of a falcon. Here we have the important juncture among people, stories, and landmarks—each category drawing significance from its association with the others. The same is true of natural landmarks—a particular hill, field, or wadi.[1]

And then, what about people? Earlier I said that a simple roadside encounter with a townsperson could evoke a story from my companion(s) about that man, woman, or child, or a member of his or her family. Introductions and chance meetings are likely to inspire reminiscences as well.

This process goes yet further. Descendants of town members also acquire a historical aura or depth after one knows a story or set of stories about one of her or his other ancestors. When two people meet, there is a mutual awareness of each person's background—parents, grandparents, neighborhood, occupation. Many times I have heard Lella Nesria call from the veranda to a child playing or passing by: "Oh, child, come here. Whose child are you?" [Child answers.] "Take this money and run to the store and get me some sugar." In a small sense the child's family's honor is put at risk.

The child knows and Lella Nesria knows that the dutiful completion of the task comments favorably on his or her family. The child always comes back and never refuses the errand. So movement within and around the community every day also has both a synchronic and diachronic character. Everywhere one turns in the community, past and present co-exist, and co-exist, as we see here, very practically. The fact that there is a story about the immigration of the very earth upon which the community is built ensures through story that the iconic representation of the land is consonant with the history of people-as-icons. As the land was appropriated by Arabs, so the renaming of the town Clypea-Qalibiya takes control away from the Phoenician, Roman, and Greek occupants of the distant past.

The "icons" are not only powerful metonymic representations of a story or stories. The very presence of descendants, tombs, and numerous other made and natural landmarks in the town also serve to ensure that stories are retold. They trigger the retelling. People and places in the town are at once encapsulated in stories and come to encapsulate them. This latter phenomenon explains, as Robert Smith points out, "the difference in meaningfulness of a landscape to people who live in an area and to those who are only passing through" (Smith 1975). Collapsing together of the diachronic and synchronic in verbal and material icons makes them a powerful affective resource. The selective, artistically organized slice of the past of a local legend within its spectrum of contexts represents a tremendous compression of information, insights and emotions. But this layering of chronotopes is more than "good to think." A community self is being constantly reconstructed, renegotiated through shared linguistic reflection on the past and present. For examples: Why have, do, should young people leave town? What have been our experiences (and the town's over two thousand years) with "foreigners" and what can we learn from this? As an individual constructs a personal saga using past experience and reflection, so town members construct a town story through a weaving together of stories about community members. One criterion of a good Kelibian hikayah is that other people know it and tell it. It has become or is becoming communized. In 1986, Si Hamdan again, without prompting, told Malek the story of al-Makki, Sidi Maouia, and the olive press (story 12). "Wonderful," said Malek, "word for word as he told it to us last time!"[2]

Pinning down, negotiating the truths of the past through stories, confirms them, emphatically does pin them down, at least for a time. Thus do the verbal icons complement the physical icons. Paradoxically the storying process also tacitly acknowledges that, due to their affective components, they are *made* truths. As illustrated by the genie stories (3 and 9) or by the spell-writing stories (25, 26, 27), storytelling sessions are a kind of brainstorming for meaning—an ongoing dialogue about the participants' mutual situation and its triumphs and dilemmas. And again a kind of two-way motion can be observed. People of the present define those of the past and in turn are defined by them. Past deeds in story form make up a town history mutually constructed in such a manner that it becomes a measure for current events and future possibilities—the challenge of the dead to the living (Glassie 1982).

How does one avoid an ambiguous analysis of these complex local legends? B. H. Smith observes, ". . . in seeking to identify the *functions* of storytelling for the individual narrator or his community, a recognition of the variety of possible narrative transactions and the range of interests that they may thereby serve should encourage us to acknowledge and explore the *multiplicity* of functions that may be performed . . . by any narrative in particular" (Smith 1980: 235). The narratives are obviously multivocal and open-ended.[3] Their intent also changes, at least to some extent, not only with every narrator but with every telling by the same narrator. One static, explicit interpretation will always be inadequate to cope with what is by definition ambiguous and in flux. What I have provided then are various contexts and theoretical tools for *approaching* interpretation of the narratives. (Others, such as a review of Arab literary criticism, would also have been appropriate.)

But interpretation can only be "a kind of reminding," as Tyler said. If we insist on imposing an interpretation on the other—whether a class or group within our own or another social or culture group—over their denial of the "truth" of that intepretation, then we attempt a powerful and destructive psychological domination. If what I say about Kelibia and hikayat does not resonate, hit home in some way, for at least some Tunisians and especially Kelibians, I cannot then decide that my "truth" is simply too subtle and sophisticated for them to comprehend, or too "threatening" to be consciously admitted.[4]

Study of hikayah-telling events gives us the opportunity to focus on one way internal change can come about in a culture. "Art" often carries an expectation of challenge to existing cultural boundaries. It seeks to enlarge the field of choice—not only aesthetic choice but a whole range of ethical, practical, imaginative possibilities; hence, a portion of its attraction, its power, and its threat. One characteristic of these stories' dramatis personae is their ability to shake up the community. Because these protagonists are larger than life (being either natural or supernatural heroes or deviants) they serve as conceptual blockbusters through their potential to inspire or energize community members. At the same time, they unite those members in a common regard for, or amusement at, their exaggerated figures. (This unity, of course, provides one foundation for negotiated change.) The characters and their situations make everyday life unfamiliar, in the Russian formalist sense, "strange." Everyday life is defamiliarized just enough for the narrator and her or his audience to reperceive or reappreciate that life. These stories are not typical turning points in an individual's life (birth, coming of age, marriage, death), perhaps because there are rites of passage in place to take care of these expected events. No, these stories deal with surprises that occur in the midst of everyday life—while churning butter, harvesting, going to market. Legend can be used as a gauge to measure the uncommon stresses of the present, making them more common and thus solvable and endurable, or by relating them to stresses of the past.

Certain paradigms of the past are latched onto as particularly versatile for artistically reperceiving present events and future possibilities, and these are the representatives of the past chosen to endure within the storytelling framework. (Here then, I have been exploring not only "why some part only of experience becomes tradition" [Davis, 1977: 250] but also why some part only of experience becomes part of a particular traditional expressive culture genre, the hikayah.) Sometimes, in the case of walis, and often in the case of heroes, their descendants also represent the continuing vitality of the community—one bond across time and community factions. It is the unusual town figures who clearly also are core symbols for hikayah-tellers and their audiences. They absorb and disseminate meaning for the community. In fact, without them, community meaning is not complete.

As Roger Abrahams (1980) suggests, this same shaking-up of a community that sparks the rethinking of community folkways and mores can also come from the "stranger in our midst." Stories tend to cluster around these two sets of figures. After all, heroes, clowns, walis, and dervishes are as unpredictable in their own way, and as inviting of a story format, as the strangers encountered at home or abroad. Furthermore, the potency of many stories is increased by the incorporation of an opposition between foreign and domestic energy—in miniature, the creative surge that so often occurs with cross-cultural encounters. (And added to this potency of the story characters was my presence—at least part stranger as well.)

Many of the stories consider the *geographical* peripheries of the community. The antagonists in the stories are frequently forces, natural or cultural, symbolic or actual, that are outside the community. The meeting between these forces and the community is not necessarily unfriendly (see story 1), but an encounter between them and the community provides a yet greater spark, gives community members newer and richer material against which to measure themselves, to think about, and to work into the traditional story format, reaching toward nontraditional conclusions and possible change. How can (or should) the strange be incorporated into community life?

Certainly, the activities (or the stories about the activities) of aberrant community members with or without interaction with "strangers" cannot be studied except with reference to their effect on the larger group. As Abrahams and Bauman note:

We have not yet begun to take adequate account of expressions of disorder and license as persistent elements in cultures, either ignoring them completely or writing them off as deviance. There is no denying the existence of ideal normative systems on the part of community members, but we must also attend systematically to the *licensed* and *expected* contraventions of such systems in society and culture. (Abrahams and Bauman 1978: 196, my emphasis)

If art is expected to challenge the limits of cultural discourse, the Kelibian local legend is no *Ulysses* or *Déjeuner sur l'herbe*. Neither does it challenge Kelibian discourse or the boundaries of the possible as assertively as do other forms of verbal art in Tunisia, like jokes or khurafat. As folk narrative, it invites and requires a degree of community acceptance. As history, its affective component is subordinated to its narrative so as to nudge gently at the edges of town identity, reaffirming as often as it renegotiates. This observation is reenforced in a narrative such as number 7, in which the raconteur is included as a young figure juxtaposed with his older, changed, storytelling self—an embodiment of the need for both continuity and change in a community.

The stories emerge because they are good to be thought of in conjunction with puzzling, powerful, unusual, or dangerous acts or events that need to be controlled by linking them to an acceptable story patter. A drill breaking, a man's anus falling out, or a person suddenly displaying superhuman strength or incredible luck can be explained by the interference of "comfortable" hometown walis or dervishes. If the explanation is acceptable to enough people, we find the gradual unfolding of a new town story, a new shared understanding of an incident. The fresh insights contained within the story are incorporated into the ongoing dialogue about "our" situation, the continuous creation of a community self.

Victor Turner quotes Hayden White's description of contextualism as picking out "the threads that link the event to be explained to different areas of context. The threads are identified and traced outward, into the circumambient natural and social space within which the event occurred, and both backward . . . and forward in time" (Turner 1981: 140). Tellers of community local legends do this for us, and in the process they link for a moment the wills, feelings, desires, thoughts of specific individuals to a history and destiny of the community as a whole. Furthermore, at the same time that the entrenched world-view of a given society influences "both the course of conduct in observable social events and the scenarios of its genres of cultural preference" (Turner 1981: 138), so can the scenarios of a particular genre not simply reveal but influence the deep structural configurations of its own culture. Implicit in any historical narrative, including our own, is the idea that (for better or worse) "things are not as they once were." It is only a small mental step to (for better or worse) "thus, things do not have to be as they are."

Notes

1. See Charles Briggs (1988: 248) and Keith Basso (1983) for similar observations about the culture and geographical "aliveness" of certain landscape features and the fashion in which narratives can embue sites with meaning and vice versa.

2. I wish I had been present to record this second version of the same story for, of course, as Malek confirmed when I questioned him further, the two versions were not completely word for word. Probably the point of the story, told seven years later after one of Si Hamdan's sons had married and another had been tragically killed in a traffic accident, was modified. My observation here though is that from a Kelibian perspective there is value in telling a good story more than once. Malek will now refer to the story and his evaluation of it some night while playing cards in a café, or sitting at a family dinner, as we were when he mentioned the retelling. The stories belong to a certain narrator, but community significance cannot be achieved for those stories until they are distributed around town by

appreciative listeners. (For a study that includes more than one version of several narratives, see Bauman 1986.)

3. This is one problem in using literary analysis intended for institutional or establishment texts to talk about folklore texts. Whether written or spoken, folk texts denote not simply "a kind of context but . . . the circumstances of performance" (Errington 1979: 243). To continue, "form cannot be located in a [musical] score or a text; . . . it is not a content but an arrangement and performance; . . . its end does not grow out of its beginning" (Errington 1979: 244). The folk-literate know that a written record is neither "necessary nor sufficient." On the other hand, besides the danger that folklore works will be perceived, treated and measured as institutional literature and come up lacking in very basic ways, there is also the danger that folk literature will be analyzed in light of just those textual features it does not share with establishment literature. For example, institutional literati talk about the patternedness of folk literature—its formulaic dimensions. This discussion is important in the sense that it illuminates an essential aspect of the process of performance of oral literature, but the essence of folk literature as far as its structural complexity and information richness (and thus its possibilities for multivocality and emergent meaning), I would argue, does not lie in its patternedness or formulaic repetition of certain phrases or sequences but precisely in unexpected deviation from what an audience expects in the way of pattern and repetition. These innovative introductions are, of course, what is foregrounded for a folk literate audience—meaning emerges from the contrastive interplay between the expected and unexpected (Webber, n.d.b). Even referring to hikayat as a genre means something very different from calling the short story, for example, a genre.

4. In spring 1989, I wanted to find a Tunisian who would read my manuscript—not so much to find out if it resonated as to check that I was not going to say anything about the people named in the manuscript that they would consider insensitive. I heard about a young man, formerly a graduate student in English literature at the University of Tunis and now a graduate student in comparative literature living in Missouri. Mohamed-Salah Omri eventually wrote a rather detailed commentary and a list of suggestions, many of which I have incorporated into the book. He suggested, for example, that the history chapter needed more reference to the forthcoming stories, he confirmed some speculations about the relationship between dervishes and walis, he commented minutely on certain aspects of the stories, including subtle points of "translation," and he developed enthusiastically on the relationship between hikayat and community icons.

Many Tunisians are suspicious of Western scholars, and I had not met Omri before I gave him the manuscript to read that spring; so I did my best at our initial meeting to show that I did not want to be fitted into the slot of plundering anthropologist or, worse, folklorist. Later he wrote that indeed on his way to meet me, he had been "on his guard." Memories of archeologists, anthropologists, sociologists, and foreign teachers "filled his mind," he told me. He also recalled "the feelings of loss and defeat" he had experienced upon visiting the Louvre and the British Museum to see ruins from Carthage, Sufeitula, and Dougga. He thought about

French anthropologists who "befriended" hospitable tribespeople and villagers "only to report to the French authorities evidences of opposition and resistance among those very people. Anthropology was colonialism continued with other means."

"I remembered," he continued, "that when I was in fourth year secondary school my classmates and I . . . used to think of every foreigner as a spy." Just prior to meeting me he had listened to an NPR interview with David Pryce-Jones, author of *The Closed Circle*. Pryce-Jones was defending his book's thesis that Arabs are a closed society incapable of innovation or progress.

So, for him, with all of this cross-cultural baggage, a reading of my manuscript turned out to be first of all a reading and a judgment of me. I think these observations of his in a way can "stand for" a good bit of what I have said in the last four chapters about historical relations with the other (at least the North African other), about ethnographic "representation" of the other, about academic involvement in the colonial enterprise, and about the ambiguous feelings of Tunisians toward the West and western culture. One is tempted to say in reference to the Pryce-Jones book, "Oh yes, *that* again." But of course, it is not that *again* if you are listening with your half-American little girl—an observation that, of course, brings us back to the community structures of feeling that are the antidote for, if not the vaccination against, such incidents.

After Pryce-Jones and his "closed society," my discussion of process had a good chance of being well received by Omri and he did like the book. He wrote that "the heroes of hikayat as well as narrators and audience are portrayed in their human faces. . . . Anyone from a similar background would identify with them. I do."

Since he is a young man "traveling" like Malek and the other young men of Kelibia, to me his most poignant comment was, "Sixteen months ago I left Tunisia, my town Kasserine, and the warmth of my friends and family. [Your] Kelibian scenes revived the feeling of loss I've endured. Detailed and somehow passionate, the book made me feel nostalgic, almost homesick."

Appendix: Transliterated Dialogues

Tunisian Arabic Transliteration System for the following Hikayat

CONSONANTS

/b/   - voiced bilabial stop, as in box
/m/ - voiced bilabial nasal, as in men
/f/   - voiceless labio-dental fricative, as in fresh
/th/ - voiceless interdental fricative, as in think
/dh/ - voiced interdental fricative, as in those
/t/   - voiceless alveolar stop, as in tape
/d/   - voiced alveolar stop, as in den
/s/   - voiceless alveolar fricative, as in sin
/z/   - voiced alveolar fricative, as in zinc
/n/   - voiced alveolar nasal, as in north
/r/   - alveolar tap, as in Spanish pero
/l/   - alveolar lateral, as in light or pull
/sh/ - voiceless palato-alveolar fricative, as in sheep
/zh/ - voiced palato-alveolar fricative as in American garage
/k/   - voiceless velar stop, as in Christ
/g/   - voiced velar stop, as in gauge
/kh/ - voiceless uvular fricative, as in German hoch
/gh/ - voiced uvular fricative, as in French reine
/h/   - voiceless glottal fricative, as in hat
/ḏẖ/ - voiced interdental emphatic fricative
/ṭ/   - voiceless alveolar emphatic stop
/ṣ/   - voiceless alveolar emphatic fricative
/ʕ/   - voiced pharyngeal fricative
/ḥ/   - voiceless pharyngeal fricative
/q/   - voiceless uvular stop
/y/   - palatal glide
/w/ - labio-velar glide

VOWELS

/a/ - low vowel (pronounced front or back depending on
       environment) as in f<u>a</u>t or f<u>a</u>ther /ā/ as well as the "not high" vowel
       as in b<u>e</u>t or b<u>u</u>t /a/
/i/ - high front vowel, as in f<u>ee</u>t (tense) /ī/ or in f<u>i</u>t (lax) /i/
/u/ - high back rounded vowel, as in French t<u>ou</u>t /ū/ or as in p<u>u</u>t /ū/
/e/ - mid-front vowel, as in French <u>été</u>

Any of the preceding vowels may be long; lengthening is indicated by a
macron over the vowel as in the examples above. Diphthongs are represented by a long vowel immediately followed by its corresponding glide.

In the following transcriptions I have tried to represent what was actually
said. If certain vowels or consonants are not realized, they are not transliterated (restored). For example, Si Hamdan sometimes uses "g" and sometimes "q" and I have not tried to regularize such pronunciation. Unstressed
vowels vary in representation because they tend to fall together and thus
are not easily distinguishable and also because there is indeed much variation in their pronunciation from person to person. Initial or final l,m,n,
and r are often transliterated as if they were syllabics as there is no clear
vowel.

I. SĪ ḤAMDĀN

kan   l-gēyd   hadhāya   'andū   mkhāznīya   'a-l-khīl,
Was   the-Cadī   that one   he had   cavalry   on-the-horses,

zhā   hadhāya . . . sismu   u-kānit   famm   'qīda
He came   that one . . . what's his name   And-it was   there   a custom

illī   yuṣul   l-ḥram   l-zāwya   min-z-zwīy
he who   enters   the-sanctuary   the-zawiyya   among-zawiyyas

kī mā   sīdī ḥmid   wla   sīdī m'awīya   wla   ḥāzha   kī mā
such as   Sīdī Ḥmid   or   Sidi Maouia   or   a thing   such as

hekk . . .   yuṣul l-ḥram . . .   m'ā . . .   u . . .   haṣṣl
that   He enters the-sanctuary . . .   with . . .   and . . .   beat out

l-ḥsana,   mā   'ādshi   ymssūh,   hūwa   hrab   li-sīdī   ḥmid,
the horses,   not   be   he touch him.   He   ran   to-Sīdī   Ḥmid.

hūwa . . .   'mal . . .   shkūn   y'rif   'lī,   matlūb
He   did . . .   who   he knows   on him,   dunned

fī māl,   <u>dh</u>riba mta' l-ḥākim   wla ḥā<u>zh</u>a mu<u>sh</u>
for money,   taxes of   the-government or   a thing not

'andū qātl ruḥ   wla ḥā<u>zh</u>a r-rā<u>zh</u>l hadhāy illī
he has killed someone or   a thing, the-man that   that

hrab, u-hūwa <u>zh</u>āya bi<u>sh</u> iḥzū t'īynlū
ran. And he was coming going to take him, instructed to him

min <u>gh</u>ādi, <u>zh</u>ay bi<u>sh</u> iḥazū hadhāy mu<u>sh</u>
from over there. He came going to take him. That not

wṣul li-lḥram,   lā, ṭabb li-z-zāwya w-sakkr
entered the-sanctuary [yard] no, went in to-the-Zawiya and-shut

'alā ruḥ l-bāb, [d<u>kh</u>al l-d-dā<u>kh</u>l?] ay,
on himself the-door. [M. went in to-the-inside?] Yeah,

sīdī ḥmid, w-ṣal<u>h</u> l-bāb 'la rūḥu, hadhāya <u>zh</u>īy,
Sīdī Ḥmid, and-sealed the door on himself, That one came,

sīdī, w-itakka 'ala l-bāb u <u>dh</u>rab l-bāb ba-r<u>zh</u>lu,
Sīdī, and-he leans on the-door and-hit the-door with-his foot.

[bi<u>sh</u> ikassru?] bi<u>sh</u> ikassr l-bāb u-bi<u>sh</u> id<u>kh</u>ul, qāllak
[M. to break it?] to break the-door and-to enter. He told you

dūb <u>dh</u>rab l-bāb bi-r<u>zh</u>lu rabbi y'arf... <u>dh</u>bah,
soon he hit the-door with-his foot God knows... he howled

ṣah, t-ri<u>zh</u>lu ana n'arifha mufaqsa hekk,
he yelled. t-his leg I know it crooked thus.

That Cadī had cavalry. That [Khenīsī] came. . . . Well, it used to be the custom that anyone who entered a zawiyya sanctuary like Sīdī Ḥmid or Sīdī Maouia or such . . . [was immune from arrest]. [One particular man] entered the sanctuary beating out the horses so they had no right to touch him. He ran to Sīdī Ḥmid. Who knows what he did—owed money, government taxes or something. He hadn't killed someone or anything, that man who was running.

[Khenīsī] was coming to take him on instructions from over there. [gestures to the government offices] He came to take him. The [fugitive] not only entered the sanctuary [yard], he went right into the zawiyya and closed the door on himself.

Malek: Went inside?

Yeah, Sīdī Ḥmid. And shut the door on himself.

That one [Khenīsī] came, sir, and leaned against the door and hit the door with his foot.

M: To break it?

To break the door and to enter. They'll tell you that as soon as he hit the door with his foot, God knows . . . he howled, he yelled. I know he walked crooked thus.

II. Aunt Fafani

khālik   muṣṭaf-z-zmarlī   kān   mahbūl,
Your maternal uncle   Mustafa Zmarli   was   crazy.

ṣ-ṣbāḥ . . .   ānā   narbuṭ   l-'abāyir,   kunna
The morning . . .   I   am tying   the-little container,   we were

nomkhudh,   u-khālī   muṣṭafa   izhī   (nmidlu
churning,   and-my maternal uncle   Mustafa   he comes.   (I give him

kīf   yiskharnī   rabbī   hak   itshaysha   rāyīb,   walā
when   he makes me good   God   thus   a little   yogurt,   or

hak   shwaya   hlīb,   wlaka   shwaya   lban   qadīm,)   nhār,
thus   a little   milk,   or such   a little   buttermilk   old.)   Day,

ānā   tāyritlī   min   khālik   mahmūd,   maris
I   he made me fly   from   your (maternal uncle)   Mahmūd.   March

kīf   tāwwā,   u-qālī,   sbāh-l-khīr,   u-qutlū,
like   now.   And-he said,   morning-the-better,   and-I told him

yiṣabbhak   bi-l-khīr   illī   mārāsh   wazh-hak
he morning you   with-the-better   he that   doesn't see   your face

khīr   u-ānā   numkhudh   fam,   ānā   numkhudh
better   and-I   am churning   there.   I   am churning

wa-l-kānūn   fi-zhanbī,   zhī   qa'd,   u-qāl,   w-allah
and-the-kanum   on-my side.   He came   sat   and-said   by-God

hadha   'īb   w-allahi,   'īb   'alayk,   wash-bīk
that   shameful   by-God,   shame   on you,   and what-with you

mitghashsha,　w-allahi　'ib,　　w-allahi　'alīya　　b-illah'i
angry.　　　By-God　shame.　By-God　elevated　by-God

l-'abār,　　　taqsam　fī-ithnīn,　'alīya　　b-illah,　fī-ithnīn,
the-container　broke　in-two,　elevated　by-God,　in-two,

fī-ithnīn,　l-'abār　　qalī,　　　hawānu　tkassir,　nizhri,
in-two　the container.　He told me,　here it　breaks.　I run,

nqūm,　　nshid　hak-l-'abār　　hakkaka,　nkhallīyh,　ntakīh
I get up,　I grab　that-the-container　thus,　　I leave it.　I lean it

nzhīb,　　'andī stal,　zawazti-s-stal,　　ighsaltu,
I bring,　I have pail,　I brought in the-pail,　I washed it,

u-sabbit fīh,　　qutlu,　　bara　'ād　ishrīlī　'abār,
and-I poured in it.　I told him,　go　then　buy me　a container.

u-qālī,　　　　w-inti　'lāsh　mitghashsha　'līya　'lāsh
And-he told me,　and-you　why　angry　　　at me　why

mitghashsha　'lī　　inti,　il-tawwa　kissā'at-ha　mufīda
angry　　　at me　you.　To-now　that hour-it　Mufīda

binti　　　tadhhak,　　tadhhak　　mufīda,　bintī
my daughter,　she laughs,　she laughs　Mufīda,　my daughter

tathbit　　'lāha　'ād　hadrat-l-　'abār,　　ahh　hslha
she recalls　on it　then　talk-the-　container.　Ahh　consequence it

d-drāwish　hadhuma, . . .
the dervishes　those

[Soft voice] This Uncle Mustafa Zmarli was crazy [dervish].

Malek: Um huh.

The morning . . . I was tying cloth over the churn (we were churning) and Uncle Mustafa comes in. (If God moved me I'd sometimes give him a little yogurt or milk or old buttermilk.)

[Louder] That day, I was angry at that Uncle Mahmud [her husband]. It was March like now, [laughter] So, he said, "Good-morning!" and I replied, "Good-*morning*? If I weren't seeing your face, it would be a *better morning*!!" [laughter] And I kept on churning, the kanun by my side.

He came and sat [by the Kanun] and said, [deep, slow man's voice] "By God that's shameful, By God, shame on you. Why are you angry?"

Just then, by God, the churn broke in two [exclamations], by God on high in two, the churn! He said, [deep, slow monotone] "There now, it broke." [laughter]

[Speaking quickly] I ran. . . . I jumped up, grabbed the churn thus [holding the crack together so the liquid wouldn't spill out], and left it leaning [against the wall]. I brought in a pail, washed it, and poured [the liquid] in. I ordered him, "Well, go on then and buy me a churn!" And he repeated, [deep monotone] "And why are you angry at me? [loud normal voice] Why are you angry!?"

To this day my daughter Mufida laughs about it. My daughter Mufida remembers the churn story.

[Low voice] Ahh . . . those dervishes are . . .

Malek: Frightening.

III. SĪ ḤAMDĀN

fammā,	maw	qutlak	ekhuwa	huwa	u-bū	umī
There's,	well	I told you	brothers	he	and-father	my mother

'nd-hum	fī	sīdī	'amor	qat'a	maqsūma
have-they	in	Sīdī	'mor	a plot	divided

bīnāt-hum,	qad qad,	maqsūma	bi-l-limīn,	qsma
between-them,	exactly,	divided	by-the-trust,	division

ekhuwa,	wa-shsh'īr	aw'ar	min	l-qamḥ
brothers.	And-the-barley	harder	than	the-wheat

fi-l-ḥsad,	myimshīsh,	l-qat'a	fīha	yizhī
in-the-harvesting.	It doesn't go.	The-plot	in it	it comes

murzha'īn	wa-nuṣf,	wa-wīnu	wīnu	r-rāzhl	illī
two merjas	and half.	And-where he	where he	the-man	that

inazhm	marzha'	sh'īr	fi-nhār,	qlīl	yāssir,	bābā
he can	a merja	barley	in-a day.	Few	very.	Father

wa-'ammī	u-khālhum	hadhāya	khū
and-my paternal uncle	and-their maternal uncle	that one	brother

slīmān,   thlatha,   hṣdu   kharzhtīn   ma'   lqsīr,   qsīr
Slimène,   three,   they harvested two strips   with   the short,   short

mush twīl, u-qā'dīn   yuklū   fī   gidma   khobz,   ftūr
not   long, and-sitting eating in   piece   bread,   food

ṣ-ṣbāh,   wa-huwwa   izhī   rākib   'a-l-bhīm,   nhārkum
the-morning,   and-he   comes   riding   on-the-donkey.   Your day

tayyib,   nhārkum   sa'īd,   qāl,   ga'miz   m'ā na,   klēy
ripe,   your day   happy. He said, he squatted   with us,   ate

gidma,   qāl   khzar   l-khūh,   qāl   (ya'ayit
a piece,   he said he looked to-his brother, he said (he calls

l-khūh   sī,   mush sīdī)   qāl   qālū   ya
to-his brother   Sī,   not Sīdī)   he said he said to him   oh

sī slīmān   (hadhāya   yihaddith   fīnā   bābā   'ād)
Si Slimène (that one   he tells   to us   my father   then)

qālū,   ya   sī slīmān   hāyyā   nṭabbis   m'ākum,
he said to him, oh   Si Slimène come on I go in   with you,

nkamlū   mtā'k   u-nirzha'u   li-mtā'ī,   esh   qālū
we finish yours   and-we return   to mine.   What   he told him

khūh,   qālū,   (l-b'īda), ikassir   hnākik,   ahna
his brother, he told him,   (the-far), he breaks your jaw. We

thlatha   w-hṣadna   kharzhtīn   w-inti   rāqid   fi-l-bled,
three   and-we harvested two strips   and-you sleeping in the town.

tāwwā   tizhī   ṭhebb   tkammal   m'āna
Now   you come   you want   you finish   with us

bash-n kamlūlak   zirēy'ak, (dim.) barra   imshī   tilqashī,
we will finish for you your harvest.   Go   go   do you find. . . .

qāl   u-dhhak,   qāl   l-behīm   sārih
He said and laughed. He said, the donkey   he grazed

fi-sh-sh'īr,   qāl   l-zhibba   hakka   u-rmayha
in-the-barley. He said the-djebba thus   and-threw it

fōq   zanbīl,   qāl   u-ṭabb   (mush   iquṣṣ
on   a saddlebag. He said and-entered   (not   he cuts

fi-sh-shāfa),   qāl   ahna   fī-l-kharzha l-ikhara māzelna
in-the-edge). He said we   in-the-strip the-last still

kī-bdīnāha,   qāl   wa-huwwa tabbis   'ala hamla
like-we began it. He said and-he   bent over on   armful

sh'īr   'lfa li-l-bhīm,   irmayha fi-z-   zanbīl,
barley food to-the-donkey, throws it on-the- saddlebag.

qāl   w-irmi   zhibtu   'ala qitfu   u-dab   'lī,
He said, and threw his djebba on his shoulder and-started on.

zhī   fōq l-bhīm,   hāyā   qāl   rabbi y'āinkum,
He came on the-donkey, Come on he said God He helps you.

[M. kammal]   kammal u-rawwā   fihimtnī
[He finished?] He finished and-went home you understood me?

There's. . . . Well, I told you he [Mohamed ouild Si 'Ali] and my mother's father were brothers. They shared a plot of land in Sīdī 'Amor, an exact split made by verbal agreement.

And barley is harder to harvest than wheat. It doesn't flow. The plot was two and a half merjas. Where is the man who can take out a merja of barley in a day? Very few.

My father and uncle and their uncle, his [Mohamed ouild Si 'Ali's] brother, Slimène, those three, had harvested two widths, widths not lengths, and were sitting eating some bread for breakfast and he came riding up on the donkey.

"Good-morning."

"Good-morning."

He said. "He squatted down with us, ate a piece of bread," he said, "he looked at his brother, and said" (he addressed his brother as "Sī" not "Sīdī"). "He said, 'Oh Si Slimène, come on . . .'" (Well, this is my father telling us this.) "I'll go in with you, we'll finish up your [plot] and then do mine."

What did his brother tell him? He said, God forbid, "May God break your jaw. We three have harvested two strips while you were sleeping in town. Now you come and want to finish with us so we'll do your harvest for you.

God see if you can find . . . [for example, . . . a mule and take off its shoes."
This expression has obscene endings as well but they wouldn't be used
between brothers.]

He said, "He laughed." He said, "The donkey was grazing on the barley.
He went like this to the jebba [gestures pulling the jebba over his head]
and threw it on the saddlebag." He said, "And he went in" (he never cut
from the edge) "to his crop and started cutting."

He said, "We were still beginning the last strip," he said, "and he was bend-
ing over to get an armful of barley, fodder for the donkey, threw it in the
saddlebag," he said, "and threw his djebba over his shoulder and got on
the donkey. 'Well,' he said, 'God be with you.' "

Malek: He'd finished?

Finished and left. Understand?

IV. SĪ ḤAMDĀN

qāl	imshīyna	li-dindra	nzhībū	l-qtānya,	qāl
He said,	he went	to-Dindara	we bring	the corn,	he said,

khlaṭna,	ṣabbīna	l-qṭanya,	khlaṭna	l-d-dār,	qāl,
we went	we poured	the corn.	We went	to-the-house,	he said,

ummī	zhābit-lina	khobz	qṭanya	skhūn	u-shkshūka,
my mother	brought-to us	bread	corn	hot	and-chakchuka

qāl	aḥna	zhwā'a	kī-zhmal	ṭaḥ	fī-ḍ-ḍlif,	qāl
He said	we	hungry	like-the-camel	fell	in-the-cactus.	He said

muṣṭafa,	qāl	qālha	y-ummī,	shnūwa	haḏhī,
Mustafa,	he said	he said to her,	oh my mother,	what	this,

shad	khobza	qtānya	qālha,	y-ummī	shnūwa
He took	a loaf	corn	He said to her,	oh my mother	what

haḏhī,	gitlu,	khobz	qtānya	skhūn	bāhī	wildī,
this,	she told him,	bread	corn	hot	good	my son,

qālha,	ekh-ānā	ḥllūf,	u-qāl,	shad	l-khobza,
he told her,	then-I	a pig.	And-he said.	He took	the-loaf,

qālha	hakka.	qāl,	zhābha	ḥattā	dār	l-ḥāzh
he told her	thus,	he said,	he brought her	until	house	the-Haj

khmāyis   tanabān,   qāl   ṭl'at   mart   l-ḥazh   khmāyis
Khmais   Tanabane.   He said,   came out   wife   the-Haj   Khmais

qālat-l-ummī,   shnīya   hadhīa   l-khobza,   muṣṭafa   rahu
she said-to-my mother,   what   this   the loaf.   Mustafa   see he

heka u-heka,   qāl,   zhābatlu   khobza   farīna   wa-ṣhan
this and-this.   He said, she brought him a loaf   flour   and-plate

fīh   ka'btīn   'dham,   qāl   ahna   hmādna   rabbī,   qulna,
in it two cubes eggs.   He said we   we praised   God,   we said,

l-ḥamdu   li-llah   ya-rabbī,   klīna   ḥatā   shba'na,
the praise to the God oh-God.   We ate   until   we were full.

qāl   ahna   'ad   hmadna   rabbī,   qāl   q'adna   li-l-tāwwā
He said   we   then   we praised   God.   He said   we sat   to-now

khobz   qṭanya,   qāl   huwwa   kī   ma-ḥmiddish   rabbī,
bread   corn.   He said he   that   he didn't praise God,

qāl   hawānu   lābās   'alī,
he said, there he is well   to him.

(Story 29)

Come now, what masques, what dances shall we have
To wear away this long age of three hours
Between our after-supper and bedtime?
Where is our usual manager of mirth?
What revels are in hand? Is there no play
To ease the anguish of a torturing hour?

A Midsummer Night's Dream V: i, 32–37

References

Aarne, Antti and Stith Thompson
  1961   *The Types of the Folktale: A Classification and Bibliography.*
  [1928]   Second revised edition. Folklore Fellows Communications, volume 75, no. 184. Helsinki: Suomalainen Tiedeakatemia.
Abrahams, Roger D.
  1968a   "Introductory Remarks Toward a Rhetorical Theory of Folklore." *Journal of American Folklore* 81:143–158.
  1968b   "A Rhetoric of Everyday Life: Traditional Conversational Genres." *Southern Folklore Quarterly* 32:44–59.
  1969   "The Complex Relations of Simple Forms." *Genre* 2:104–128.
  1977   "Toward an Enactment-Centered Theory of Folklore." In *Frontiers of Folklore*. Edited by William R. Bascom. Boulder, CO: Westview Press.
  1980   Address at the Annual Meetings of the American Folklore Society. [my notes]
  n.d.   "The Play of Worlds in Story and Storytelling." Manuscript. Austin: University of Texas Folklore Files.
Abrahams, Roger D. and Richard Bauman
  1978   "Ranges of Festival Behavior." In Babcock 1978.
Abu-Lughod, Lila
  1986   *Veiled Sentiments: Honor and Poetry in a Bedouin Society.* Berkeley: University of California Press.
Abun-Nasr, Jamil M.
  1975   *A History of the Maghrib.* Second edition. New York: Cambridge University Press. First edition 1971.
Abu-Zahra, Nadia
  1982   *Sidi Ameur: A Tunisian Village.* London: Ithaca Press.
  1988   "The Rain Rituals as Rites of Spiritual Passage." *International Journal of Middle East Studies* 20:507–529.
Ageron, Charles-Robert
  1976   "Du mythe kabyle aux politiques berbères." In *Le Mal de voir.* Cahiers Jussieu 2. Université de Paris VII. Paris: Coll. 10/18.

Al-Azmeh, Aziz
  1986   "L'Historiographie Arabe," *Annales ESC* 2:411–431.
Altoma, Salih J.
  1969   *The Problem of Diglossia in Arabic: A Comparative Study of Classical and Iraqi Arabic.* Cambridge, MA: Harvard University Press.
Ammar, Hamed
  1973   *Growing Up in an Egyptian Village.* New York: Octagon Books
  [1954]
Anderson, Jon W.
  1985   "Sentimental Ambivalence and the Exegesis of 'Self' in Afghanistan." *Anthropological Quarterly* 58: 203–211.
Anderson, Lisa
  1986   *The State and Social Transformation in Tunisia and Libya, 1830–1980.* Princeton, NJ: Princeton University Press.
Archives Générales du Gouvernement Tunisien, Dar el Bey: Series
       A. Tunis: Ministry of Foreign Affairs.
Armstrong, Robert Plant
  1971   *The Affecting Presence: An Essay in Humanistic Anthropology.* Urbana: University of Illinois Press.
Asad, Talal, editor
  1973   *Anthropology and the Colonial Encounter.* Atlantic Highlands, NJ: Humanities Press.
Attar, Farid al-Din (1119–1230 C.E.)
  1966   *Muslim Saints and Mystics: Episodes from the Tadhkirat al-auliya'.* Translated by A. J. Arberry. Chicago: University of Chicago Press.
Babcock, Barbara A.
  1977   "The Story in the Story: Metanarration in Folk Narrative." In Bauman 1977b.
Babcock, Barbara A., editor
  1978   *The Reversible World: Symbolic Inversion in Art and Society.* Ithaca, NY: Cornell University Press.
Bachnik, Jane M.
  1986   "Native Perspectives of Distance and Anthropological Perspectives of Culture." *Anthropological Quarterly* 59(2):75–86.

Bakhtin, Mikhail M.
  1968   *Rabelais and His World*. Translated by Helene Iswolsky. Cambridge, MA: MIT Press.
  1981   *The Dialogic Imagination: Four Essays*. Edited by Michael Holquist. Translated by Caryl Emerson and Michael Holquist. Austin: University of Texas Press.
Bardin, Pierre
  1965   *La vie d'un douar*. Paris: Mouton.
Barnes, J. A.
  1951   "History in a Changing Society." *Rhodes-Livingstone Journal* 11:1–9.
Barthes, Roland
  1970   "Historical Discourse." In *Introduction to Structuralism*. Edited by Michael Lane. New York: Basic Books.
Basgoz, Ilhan
  1970   "Turkish Hikaya-Telling Tradition in Azerbaijan, Iran." *Journal of American Folklore* 83: 391–405.
Basset, René
  1901   *Moorish Literature*. London: The Colonial Press.
Basso, Keith H.
  1984   " 'Stalking with Stories': Names, Places, and Moral Narratives among the Apache." In Bruner 1984.
Basso, Keith H. and Henry A. Selby, editors
  1976   *Meaning in Anthropology*. Albuquerque: University of New Mexico Press.
Bauman, Richard
  1971a   "Differential Identity and the Social Base of Folklore." In *Toward New Perspectives in Folklore*. Edited by Américo Paredes and Richard Bauman. Austin: University of Texas Press.
  1971b   *For the Reputation of Truth: Politics, Religion, and Conflict Among the Pennsylvania Quakers, 1750–1800*. Baltimore: Johns Hopkins University Press.
  1972   "The La Have Island General Store: Sociability and Verbal Art in a Nova Scotia Community." *Journal of American Folklore* 85:330–343.
  1977a   "Settlement Patterns on the Frontiers of Folklore." In *Frontiers of Folklore*. Edited by William R. Bascom. Boulder, CO: Westview Press.

1977b   (editor). *Verbal Art as Performance.* Rowley, MA: Newbury House.

1982   "Conceptions of Folklore in the Development of Literary Semiotics." *Semiotica* 39(1–2): 1–20.

1983a   "The Field Study of Folklore in Context." In *Handbook of American Folklore.* Edited by Richard M. Dorson. Bloomington: Indiana University Press.

1983b   *Let Your Words Be Few: Symbolism of Speaking and Silence Among Seventeenth-Century Quakers.* Cambridge: Cambridge University Press.

1986   *Story, Performance, and Event: Contextual Studies of Oral Narrative.* Cambridge: Cambridge University Press.

Bauman, Richard, Roger D. Abrahams, and Susan Kalčik

1976   "American Folklore and American Studies." *American Quarterly* 28:3.

Bauman, Richard and Joel Sherzer

1975   "The Ethnography of Speaking." In *Annual Review of Anthropology.* Volume 4. Edited by Bernard J. Siegel. Palo Alto, CA: Annual Reviews.

Beaussier, Marcelin

1958   *Dictionnaire pratique arabe-français contenant tous les mots employés dans l'arabe parlé en Algérie et en Tunisie.* New edition by Mohamed ben Cheneb. Alger: Maison des livres.

Beeman, William O.

1986   *Language, Status, and Power in Iran.* Bloomington: Indiana University Press.

Bel, A.

1938   *La religion musulmane en Berberie.* Volume 1. Paris: Librairie orientaliste Paul Geuthner.

Belhalfaoui, Mohamed

1973   *La poésie arabe maghrébine d'expression populaire: défense et illustration d'une poésie classique d'expression 'dialectale.'* Paris: François Maspero.

Bellah, Robert

1970   *Beyond Belief: Essays on Religion in a Post-Traditional World.* New York: Harper and Row.

Benachenhou, A.
1960   *Contes et récits du Maroc*. Rabat: Omnia.

Ben-Amos, Dan
1974   "The Memorate and the Proto-Memorate." *Journal of American Folklore* 87:225–239.
1976   "The Concepts of Genre in Folklore." In *Folk Narrative Research*. Edited by Juha Pentikäinen and Tuula Juurikka. Studia Fennica 20. Helsinki: Finnish Literary Society.

Benjamin, Walter
1969   *Illuminations*. New York: Schocken Books.

Berger, Peter L. and Thomas Luckmann
1966   *The Social Construction of Reality: A Treatise in the Sociology of Knowledge*. Garden City, NY: Doubleday.

Bernard, Augustin
1924   *Enquête sur l'habitation rurale des indigènes de la Tunisie*. Tunis: J. Barlier.

Berque, Jacques
1954   *Les Seksawa: Recherches sur les structures sociales du Haut-Atlas occidental*. Paris: Presses Universitaires de France.
1957a   *Histoire sociale d'un village Egyptien au XXème siècle*. The Hague: Mouton.
1957b   "Quelques problèmes de l'Islam maghrébin." *Archives du sociologie des religions* 14(2):3–20.
1967   *French North Africa: The Maghrib Between Two World Wars*. New York: Frederick A. Praeger.
1978   *Cultural Expression in Arab Society Today*. Austin: University of Texas Press.

Berreman, Gerald D.
1972   " 'Bringing It All Back Home': Malaise in Anthropology." In *Reinventing Anthropology*. Edited by Dell Hymes. New York: Random House.

Besancenot, Jean
1940   *Costumes et types du Maroc*. Paris: Éditions des Horizons de France.

Bloch, Marc
1953   *The Historian's Craft*. New York: Random House.

Bloch, Maurice

1977   "The Past and the Present in the Present." *Man* 12(2):278–292.

Blount, Ben G.

1975a   "Agreeing to Agree on Genealogy: A Luo Sociology of Knowledge." In *Sociocultural Dimensions of Language Use*. Edited by Mary Sanchez and Ben G. Blount. London: Academic Press.

1975b   "Introduction." In *Sociocultural Dimensions of Language Use*. Edited by Mary Sanchez and Ben G. Blount. London: Academic Press.

Boon, James A.

1977   *The Anthropological Romance of Bali, 1597-1972*. Cambridge: Cambridge University Press.

1982   *Other Tribes, Other Scribes*. Cambridge: Cambridge University Press.

Boratav, Pertev Naili

1978   "The Tale and the Epico-Novelistic Narrative (1961)." In Dégh 1978.

Borofsky, Robert

1987   *Making History: Pukapukam and anthropological constructions of knowledge*. Cambridge: Cambridge University Press.

Boulares, H. and Jean Duvignaud

1978   *Nous partons pour la Tunisie*. Vendôme: Presses Universitaires de France.

Bourdieu, Pierre

1977   *Outline of a Theory of Practice*. Translated by Richard Nice. Studies in Social Anthropology no 16. Cambridge: Cambridge University Press.

Brady, Margaret K.

1978   "Navaho Children's Narratives: Symbolic Forms in a Changing Culture." Ph.D. dissertation. University of Texas, Austin.

1984   *"Some Kind of Power": Navajo Children's Skinwalker Narratives*. Salt Lake City: University of Utah Press.

Braudel, Fernand

1980   *On History*. Chicago: University of Chicago Press.
[1969]

Brenneis, Donald Lawrence and Fred R. Myers, editors

1984   *Dangerous Words: Language and Politics in the Pacific*. New York: New York University Press.

Brett, Michel, editor

1973   *Northern Africa: Islam and Modernization*. London: Frank Cass.

Briggs, Charles L.

1988   *Competence in Performance: The Creativity of Tradition in Mexicano Verbal Art*. Philadelphia: University of Pennsylvania Press.

Brown, Kenneth L.

1976   *People of Salé: Tradition and Change in a Moroccan City, 1830–1930*. Manchester: Manchester University Press.

n.d.   "Discrediting of a Sufi Movement in Tunisia." In *Religion and Religious Movements in the Mediterranean*. Edited by Eric R. Wolf and Ernest Gellner. Berkeley: University of California Press.

Bruner, Edward M., editor

1984   *Text, Play, and Story: The Construction and Reconstruction of Self and Society*. Washington, DC: American Ethnological Society.

Bruner, Edward M. and Victor W. Turner, editors

1986   *The Anthropology of Experience*. Urbana: University of Illinois Press.

Burke, Edmund, III

1976   *Prelude to Protectorate in Morocco: Precolonial Protest and Resistance, 1860–1912*. Chicago: University of Chicago Press.

1980   "The Sociology of Islam: The French Tradition." In *Islamic Studies: A Tradition and Its Problems*. Edited by Malcom H. Kerr. Malibu, CA: Udena Publications.

Burke, Kenneth

1969   *A Grammar of Motives*. Berkeley: University of California Press.
[1945]

Chelhod, Joseph

1964   *Les structures du sacre chez les Arabs*. Paris: G.P. Maisonneuve et Larose.

Chock, Phyllis Pease and June R. Wyman

1986   *Discourse and the Social Life of Meaning*. Washington, DC: Smithsonian Institution.

Clifford, James

1977   "The Writing of Ethnography." *Dialectical Anthropology* 2:69–73.

1980   "Fieldwork, Reciprocity, and the Making of Ethnographic Texts: The Example of Maurice Leenhardt." *Man* 15(3):518–532.

1983   "On Ethnographic Authority." *Representations* 1(2):118–146.

Clifford, James and George E. Marcus, editors

1986   *Writing Culture: The Poetics and Politics of Ethnography*. Berkeley: University of California Press.

Colonna, Fanny

1972   "Une fonction coloniale de l'ethnologie dans l'Algérie de l'entre-deux guerres: la programmation des élites moyennes." *Libyca* 20:259–268.

1976a   "Questions à propos de la littérature arabe comme savoir." *Revue de l'Occident Musulman et de la Méditerranée* 22:17–26.

1976b   "Production scientifique et position dans le champ intellectuel et politique. Deux cas: Augustin Berque et Joseph Desparmet." In *Le Mal de voir*. Paris: Université de Paris VII. Union générale d'éditions, Coll. 10/18.

Comaroff, Jean

1985   *Body of Power, Spirit of Resistance: The Culture and History of a South African People*. Chicago: The University of Chicago Press.

Connelly, Bridget

1986   *Arab Folk Epic and Identity*. Berkeley: University of California Press.

Cothran, Kay L.

1972   "Women's Tall Tales: A Problem in the Social Structure of Fantasy." *St. Andrews Review* 2: 21–27.

1974   "Talking Trash in the Okefenokee Swamp Rim, Georgia." *Journal of American Folklore* 87:340–356.

Cox, Harvey

1969   *The Feast of Fools: A Theological Essay on Festivity and Fantasy*. Cambridge, MA: Harvard University Press.

Crapanzano, Vincent

1973   *The Hamadsha. A Study in Moroccan Ethnopsychiatry*. Berkeley: University of California Press.

1985   *Tuhami. Portrait of a Moroccan*. Chicago: [1980] University of Chicago Press.

Culler, Jonathan

1981   *The Pursuit of Signs: Semiotics, Literature, Deconstruction*. Ithaca, NY: Cornell University Press.

Dakhlia, Jocelyne
   1967   "Le sens des origines: comment on raconte l'histoire dans une
           société maghrébine." *Revue historique* 2: 401–427.
Daniel, E. Valentine
   1984   *Fluid Signs: Being a Person the Tamil Way*. Berkeley: University
           of California Press.
Darmon, Raoul
   1930   *La Situation des cultes en Tunisie*. Paris: Rousseau.
Davis, John H. R.
   1977   "Anthropologists and History in the Mediterranean." In *People
           of the Mediterranean: An Essay in Comparative Social Anthropol-
           ogy*. Idem. London: Routledge and Kegan Paul.
de Certeau, Michel
   1984   *The Practice of Everyday Life*. Translated by Stephen Rendall.
           Berkeley: University of California Press.
Dégh, Linda
   1988   "Introduction." In *How About Demons? Possession and Exorcism
           in the Modern World* by Felicitous Goodman. Bloomington: In-
           diana University Press.
Dégh, Linda, editor
   1978   *Studies in East European Folk Narrative*. A.F.S. Bibliographical
           and Special Series 30. Indiana University Folklore Monographs
           Series 25. Bloomington, IN: Folklore Institute.
Dégh, Linda and Andrew Vazsonyi
   1976   "Legend and Belief." In *Folklore Genres*. Edited by Dan Ben-
           Amos. Austin: University of Texas Press.
deMan, Paul
   1971   *Blindness and Insight: Essays in the Rhetoric of Contemporary Crit-
           icism*. New York: Oxford University Press.
Demeerseman, André
   1964   "Le Culte des walis en Kroumirie." *Revue de l'Institut des Belles
           Lettres Arabes* 27 (106–107): 119–163.
Depont, Octave and X. Cuppolani
   1897   *Les Confréries religieuses musulmanes*. Algiers: A. Jourdan.
Dermenghem, Emile
   1954   *Le Culte des saints dans l'Islam maghrébin*. Paris: Librairie Gilli-
           mard.

Desparmet, Joseph

1932   Le Mal magique: Ethnographie traditionnelle de la Mettidja. Paris: Paul Geuthner. Algiers: Jules Carbonel.

Despois, Jean

1961   La Tunisie, ses régions. Paris: Librairie Armand Colin.

Dobos, Ilona

1978   "True Stories (1964)." In Dégh 1978.

Dorson, Richard M.

1952   Bloodstoppers and Bearwalkers: Folk Traditions of the Upper Peninsula. Cambridge, MA: Harvard University Press.

Dossier des affaires indigènes

1885   Zone Septentrionale, centré sur Kélibia. La Dakhla des Maouine. October 30. 158 pages.

Drague, Georges [Georges Spillmann]

1952   Esquisse d'histoire religieuse du Maroc: confréries et zaouias. Cahiers de l'Afrique et l'Asie. Volume 2. Paris: Peyronnet.

Dubouloz-Laffin, Madeleine

1934   "Quelques croyances relatives aux maladies dûes aux Jnoun." Revue tunisienne 18(2):227–266.

Dundes, Alan

1961   "Brown County Superstitions." Midwest Folklore 11:25–56.

1964   "Texture, Text, and Context." Southern Folklore Quarterly 28:251–265.

1965   The Study of Folklore. Englewood Cliffs, NJ: Prentice-Hall.

1966   "The American Concept of Folklore." Journal of the Folklore Institute 3:226–249.

1969   "The Devolutionary Premise in Folklore Theory." Journal of the Folklore Insitute 6:5–19.

1971   "Folk Ideas as Units of Worldview." Journal of American Folklore 84: 93–103.

Duvignaud, Jean

1970   Change at Shebika: Report from a North African Village. Translated by Frances Frenaye. Austin: University of Texas Press.

Dwyer, Daisy Hilse

1978   Images and Self-Images: Male and Female in Morocco. New York: Columbia University Press.

Dwyer, Kevin
  1982   *Moroccan Dialogues: Anthropology in Question.* Baltimore: Johns Hopkins University Press.
Early, Evelyn
  1985   "Catharsis and Creation: The Everyday Narratives of Baladi Women of Cairo." *Anthropology Quarterly* 58 (4):172–181.
Eickelman, Dale F.
  1976   *Moroccan Islam. Tradition and Society in a Pilgrimage Center.* Austin: University of Texas Press.
  1977   "Form and Composition in Islamic Myths: Four Texts from Western Morocco." *Anthropos* 72:447–464.
  1979   "The Political Economy of Meaning." *American Ethnologist* 6:386–393.
  1984   "New Directions in Interpreting North African Society." In *Connaissances du Maghreb: Sciences sociales et colonisation.* Paris: CRESM.
  1985   "Introduction: Self and Community in Middle Eastern Societies." *Anthropological Quarterly* 58: 135–140.
  1989   *The Middle East: An Anthropological Approach.* Second edi-
  [1981] tion. Englewood Cliffs, NJ: Prentice-Hall.
Eickelman, Dale F. and Bouzekri Draioui
  1973   "Islamic Myths from Western Morocco: Three Texts." *Hespéris-Tamuda* 14:195–225.
El-Shamy, Hasan M., editor and translator
  1980   *Folktales of Egypt.* Chicago: University of Chicago Press.
Encyclopédie de l'Islam.
  1924–1934 "Wakf." 4: 1154–1162. Paris: Auguste Picard.
Errington, S.
  1979   "Some Comments on Style in the Meanings of the Past." *Journal of Asian Studies* 38: 231–244.
Evans-Pritchard, E. E.
  1949   *The Sanusi of Cyrenaica.* Oxford: Clarendon Press.
  1962   "Anthropology and History: A Lecture." In *Essays in Social Anthropology.* London: Faber and Faber.
Fantar, Mohamed
  1972   "Madinat Qalibiyya." *al-Fikr* 17(5):12–20

Fares, Nabile

1976   "Propositions introductives à des études d'expression populaire et particulier à propos du conte populaire d'expression orale." *Revue de l'Occident Musulman et de la Méditerranée* 22:11–15.

Ferchiou, Sophie

1972   "Survivances mystiques et culte de possession dans le maraboutisme tunisien." *L'homme* 12:47–69.

Ferenczi, Imre

1978   "History, Folk Legend, and Oral Tradition." In Dégh 1978.

Ferguson, Charles A.

1959   "Diglossia." *Word* 15:325–340.

Fernandez, James W.

1971   "Persuasions and Performances: Of the Beast in Everybody and the Metaphors of Every Man." In *Myth, Symbol and Culture.* Edited by Clifford Geertz. New York: W. W. Norton.

Fernea, Elizabeth Warnock

1965   *Guests of the Sheik.* New York: Doubleday.

1970   *A View of the Nile.* New York: Doubleday.

1975   *A Street in Marrakech.* New York: Doubleday.

1979   *Saints and Spirits: Religious Expression in Morocco, Guide to the Film.* Austin: University of Texas Press.

Fernea, Robert A. and Elizabeth W. Fernea

1972   "Variation in Religious Observance Among Islamic Women." In *Women in the Muslim World.* Edited by L. Beck & N. Keddie. Cambridge, MA: Harvard University Press.

1985   *The Arab World: Personal Encounters.* New York: Doubleday.

Fernea, Robert A. and James M. Malarkey

1975   "Anthropology of the Middle East and North Africa: A Critical Assessment." In *Annual Review of Anthropology.* Volume 4. Edited by Bernard J. Siegel. Palo Alto, CA: Annual Reviews.

Findley, Carter V. and John Alexander Murray Rothney

1986   *Twentieth-Century World.* Boston: Houghton Mifflin

Finnegan, Ruth and Robin Horton, editors

1973   *Modes of Thought: Essays on Thinking in Western and non-Western Societies.* London: Faber and Faber.

Fish, Stanley E.

1980   *Is There a Text in This Class?: The Authority of Interpretive Communities.* Cambridge, MA: Harvard University Press.

Foucault, Michel

1972 *The Archaeology of Knowledge and The Discourse on Language.*
[1969; Translated by A. M. Scheridan Smith. New York: Harper and
1971] Row.

Fowler, Roger

1981 *Literature as Social Discourse: The Practice of Linguistic Criticism.*
London: Batsford.

Fox, Richard

1985 *Lions of the Punjab: Culture in the Making.* Berkeley: University
of California Press.

Fyzee, Asaf A. A.

1964 *Outlines of Muhammadan Law.* London: Oxford University.
[1949]

Gaboriau, Marc

1970 "Structural Anthropology and History." In *Introduction to
Structuralism.* Edited by Michael Lane. New York: Basic Books.

Gallagher, Nancy Elizabeth

1983 *Medicine and Power in Tunisia, 1780–1900.* Cambridge: Cambridge University Press.

Gans, Eric

1985 *The End of Culture: Toward a Generative Anthropology.* Berkeley:
University of California Press.

Geertz, Clifford

1968 *Islam Observed.* New Haven, CT: Yale University Press.

1972 "Deep Play: Notes on the Balinese Cockfight." *Daedalus* 101:
1–37.

1983 *Local Knowledge: Further Essays in Interpretive Anthropology.*
[1976] New York: Basic Books.

Gellner, Ernest

1969 *Saints of the Atlas.* Chicago: University of Chicago Press.

1970 "Saints of the Atlas." In *Peoples and Cultures of the Middle East:
An Anthropological Reader.* Volume 1. Edited by Louise E.
Sweet. New York: The Natural History Press.

1981 *Muslim Society.* Cambridge: Cambridge University Press.

Gellner, Ernest, editor

1985 *Islamic Dilemmas: Reformers Nationalists, Industrialization: The
Southern Shore of the Mediterranean.* Berlin and New York:
Mouton.

Georges, Robert A.

1969　"Toward an Understanding of Storytelling Events." *Journal of American Folklore* 82:313-328.

Gerhardt, Mia

1963　*The Art of Storytelling: A Literary Study of the Thousand and One Nights*. Leiden: E. J. Brill.

Gibb, H. A. R. and J. H. Kramers, editors

1974　*Shorter Encyclopedia of Islam*. Ithaca, NY: Cornell University
[1953]　Press.

Givōn, T., editor

1979　*Discourse and Syntax: Syntax and Semantics*. Volume 12. London: Academic Press.

Glassie, Henry

1977　"Meaningful Things and Appropriate Myths: The Artifact's Place in American Studies." *Prospects* 3:1–49.

1982　*Passing the Time in Ballymenone: Culture and History of an Ulster Community*. Philadelphia: University of Pennsylvania Press.

Goffman, Erving

1963　*Behavior in Public Places: Notes on the Social Organization of Gatherings*. New York: Free Press.

1974　*Frame Analysis: An Essay on the Organization of Experience*. Cambridge, MA: Harvard University Press.

Goldziher, I.

1971　*Muslim Studies*. Volume 2: *Hadith: The 'Traditions' Ascribed to Muhammed*. Albany: State University of New York Press.

Goody, Jack

1977　*The Domestication of the Savage Mind*. Cambridge: Cambridge University Press.

1986　*The Logic of Writing and the Organization of Society*. Cambridge: Cambridge University Press.

Green, Archie

1980　"Threads and Tasks in American Folklore." Paper read at Georgetown University, Washington, DC. November 1. [Copy in my files.]

Gumperz, John J.

1975　"Foreword." In *Sociocultural Dimensions of Language Use*. Edited by Mary Sanchez and Ben G. Blount. London: Academic Press.

Gumperz, John J. and Dell Hymes

1972   *Directions in Sociolinguistics: The Ethnography of Communication.*
        New York: Holt, Rinehart and Winston.

Hand, Wayland Debs

1971   *American Folk Legend: A Symposium.* Los Angeles: University of
        California Press.

Hannerz, Ulf

1969   *Soulside: Inquiries into Ghetto Culture and Community.* New
        York: Columbia University Press.

Hawkes, Terence

1977   *Structuralism and Semiotics.* London: Methuen.

Hegel, Georg Wilhelm Friedrich

1900   *The Philosophy of History.* Translated by J. Sibree. New York: The
        Colonial Press.

Herzfeld, Michael

1985   *Poetics of Manhood: Contest and Identity in a Cretan Mountain
        Village.* Princeton, NJ: Princeton University Press.

1987   *Anthropology Through the Looking Glass: Critical Ethnography in
        the Margins of Europe.* Cambridge: Cambridge University Press.

Hess, Andrew C.

1978   *The Forgotten Frontier: A History of the Sixteenth-Century Ibero-
        African Frontier.* Chicago: University of Chicago Press.

Hobsbawm, Eric and Terence Ranger, editors

1983   *The Invention of Tradition.* London: Cambridge University
        Press.

Hodge, Herbert A.

1952   *The Philosophy of Wilhelm Dilthey.* London: Routledge and Ke-
        gan Paul.

Hodgson, Marshall G. S.

1974   *The Venture of Islam: Conscience and History in World Civiliza-
        tion.* 3 volumes. Chicago: University of Chicago Press.

Hollinger, David A.

1980   "T. S. Kuhn's Theory of Science and Its Implications for His-
        tory." In *Paradigms and Revolutions: Appraisals and Applications
        of Thomas Kuhn's Philosophy of Science.* Edited by Gary Gutting.
        Notre Dame: University of Notre Dame Press.

Hymes, Dell

1974a   *Foundations in Sociolinguistic: An Ethnographic Approach*. Philadelphia: University of Pennsylvania Press.

1974b   "Introduction." In *Reinventing Anthropology*. Edited by Dell
[1969]   Hymes. New York: Vintage Books.

1975   "Breakthrough into Performance." In *Folklore: Communication and Performance*. Edited by Dan Ben-Amos and Kenneth S. Goldstein. The Hague: Mouton.

Jakobson, Roman

1960   "Concluding Statement: Linguistics and Poetics." In *Style in Language*. Edited by Thomas Sebeok. Cambridge, MA: MIT Press.

Jameson, Fredric

1981   *The Political Unconscious. Narrative as a Socially Symbolic Act*. Ithaca, NY: Cornell University Press.

Jason, Heda

1972   "Concerning the 'Historical' and the 'Local' Legends and Their Relatives." In *Toward New Perspectives in Folklore*. Edited by Américo Paredes and Richard Bauman. Austin: University of Texas Press.

Jung, C. G.

1965   *Memories, Dreams, Reflections*. Translated by Richard and Clara Winston. New York: Vintage Books.

Karamustafa, Ahmet

n.d.   "The Antinomian Dervish." Work in Progress.

Katriel, Tamar

1986   *Talking Straight: Dugri Speech in Israeli Sabra Culture*. Cambridge: Cambridge University Press.

Keesing, Roger M.

1974   "Theories of Culture." In *Annual Review of Anthropology*. Volume 3. Edited by Bernard J. Siegel, A. Beals, and S. Tyler. Palo Alto, CA: Annual Reviews.

King, M. D.

1980   "Reason, Tradition, Progressiveness of Science." In *Paradigms and Revolutions: Appraisals and Applications of Thomas Kuhn's Philosophy of Science*. Edited by Gary Gutting. Notre Dame: University of Notre Dame Press.

Kirshenblatt-Gimblett, Barbara
1975   A Parable in Context: A Social Interactional Analysis of a Storytelling Performance. In *Folklore: Performance and Communication*. Edited by Dan Ben-Amos and Kenneth S. Goldstein. The Hague: Mouton.

Kodish, Debora
1987   "Absent Gender, Silent Encounter." *Journal of American Folklore* 100: 573–578.

Kuczynski, Liliane
1989   "Figures de l'Islam." *Archives de science social des religions* 68: 39–50.

Labov, William
1972   *Language in the Inner City: Studies in the Black English Vernacular*. Philadelphia: University of Pennsylvania Press.

Labov, William and Joshua Waletzky
1967   "Narrative Analysis." In *American Ethnological Society Essays on the Verbal and Visual Arts*. Edited by June Helm. Seattle: University of Washington Press.

Lacoste-Dujardin, Camille
1970   *Le Conte kabyle: Etude ethnologique*. Paris: François Maspero.
1985   *Des mères contre les femmes: maternité et patriarcat au Maghreb*. Paris: Editions la Découverte.

Laline d'Epinay, Christian, et al.
1982   "Persistance de la culture populaire dans les sociétés industrielles avancées." *Revue française de sociologie* 23(1):87–109.

Laoust, E.
1919   *Mots et choses berbères: Notes de linguistique et d'ethnographie— dialects du Maroc*. Paris: Augustin Challamel.

Laroui, Abdallah
1975   *L'histoire du Maghreb: Un essai de synthèses*. 2 volumes. Paris: François Maspero.
1976   *The Crisis of the Arab Intellectual: Traditionalism or Historicism?*
[1974] Berkeley: University of California Press.

Leach, Edmund
1964   "Anthropological Aspects of Language: Animal Categories and Verbal Abuse." In *New Directions in the Study of Language*. Edited by Eric H. Lenneberg. Cambridge, MA: MIT Press.

Le Goff, Jacques
1967   "Culture cléricale et traditions folkloriques dans la civilisation mérovingienne." *Annales* 4:780–791.

Le Guin, Ursula K.
1980   "It Was a Dark and Stormy Night: or, Why Are We Huddling About the Campfire?" *Critical Inquiry* 7(1):191–199.

Levi-Provençal, Evariste
1919–20 "Notes d'hagiographie marocaine." *Archives Berbères* 4(1–2): 67–87.

Lévi-Strauss, Claude
1950   "Introduction to M. Mauss." In *Sociologie et anthropologie*. Paris: Presses Universitaires de France.
1966   *The Savage Mind*. Chicago: University of Chicago Press.
[1962]

Limón, José
1983   "Western Marxism and Folklore: A Critical Introduction." *Journal of American Folklore* 96: 34–52.

Limón, José and Jane Young
1986   "Frontiers, Settlements, and Development in Folklore Studies, 1972–1985." In *Annual Review of Anthropology*. Volume 15. Edited by Bernard J. Siegel. Palo Alto, CA: Annual Reviews.

Lings, M.
1961   *A Moslem Saint of the Twentieth Century*. London: Allen Unwin.

Loubignac, Victorien
1944   "Un saint Berbère." *Hespéris* 31: 15–34.

Louis, André
1964a   "Villes et villages de Tunisie: Kelibia I (XXI)." Radio-diffusion Télévision Tunisienne, Service International, Programme de Langue Française. July 24. Tunis: L'Institut des Belles Lettres Arabes.
1964b   "Villes et villages de Tunisie: Kelibia II (XXII)." Radio-diffusion Télévision Tunisienne, Service International, Programme de Langue Française. July 31. Tunis: L'Institut des Belles Lettres Arabes.
1977   *Bibliographie ethno-sociologique de la Tunisie*. Tunis: L'Institut des Belles Lettres Arabes.

Lucas, Philippe et Jean-Claude Vatin
1975   *L'Algérie des anthropologues*. Paris: François Maspero.

Lüthi, Max
  1967   "Parallel Themes in Folk Narrative and in Art Literature." *Journal of the Folklore Institute* 4:3–16.
  1976   *Once Upon a Time: On the Nature of Fairy Tales*. Bloomington: Indiana University Press.
Lutz, Catherine and Geoffrey M. White
  1986   "The Anthropology of Emotions." *Annual Review of Anthropology* 15:405–436.
Mammeri, Mouloud and Pierre Bourdieu
  1978   "Dialogue sur la poésie orale en Kabylie." *Actes de la recherche en sciences sociales* 23:51–66.
Marçais, William and Abderrahmân Guîga
  1925   *Textes arabes de Takrouna: transcription, traduction, traduction annotée, glossaire*. Paris: Imprimérie Nationale.
Marcus, George E.
  1986   "Contemporary Problems of Ethnography in the Modern World System." In Clifford and Marcus 1986.
Marcus, George E. and Michael M. J. Fischer, editors
  1986   *Anthropology as Cultural Critique: An Experimental Moment in the Human Sciences*. Chicago: University of Chicago Press.
Marcus, Michael A.
  1985   "History on the Moroccan Periphery: Moral Imagination, Poetry and Islam." *Anthropological Quarterly* 58(4): 152–160.
Meeker, Michael E.
  1979   *Literature and Violence in North Arabia*. Cambridge: Cambridge University Press.
Mehan, Hugh and Houston Wood
  1975   *The Reality of Ethnomethodology*. New York: John Wiley and Sons.
Memmi, Albert
  1965   *The Colonizer and the Colonized*. Boston: Beacon Press.
Michaux-Bellaire, E.
  1921   *Essai sur l'histoire des confréries marocaines*. Paris: Hespéris.
Montell, William Lynwood
  1970   *The Saga of Coe Ridge: A Study in Oral History*. Knoxville: University of Tennessee Press.
Moudoud, Ezzidine
  1989   *Modernization, the State, and Regional Disparity in Developing*

Countries: Tunisia in Historical Perspective. 1881-1982. Boulder, CO: Westview Press.

Mouliéras, Auguste Jean

1965   *Légendes et contes merveilleux de la Grande Kabylie.* 2 volumes. Translated by Camille Lacoste. Paris: Paul Geuthner.

Muhawi, Ibrahim and Sharif Kanaana

1988   *Speak, Bird, Speak Again: Palestinian Arab Folktales.* Berkeley: University of California Press.

Mukařovský, Jan

1964   "Standard Language and Poetic Language." In *A Prague School Reader on Esthetics: Literary* Structure and Style. Edited by Paul L. Garvin. Washington, DC: Georgetown University Press.

1977   *The Word and Verbal Art: Selected Essays by Jan Mukařovský.* New Haven, CT: Yale University Press.

Mullen, Patrick B.

1978   *I heard the Old Fisherman Say: Folklore of the Texas Gulf Coast.* Logan, UT: Utah State UniversityPress.

Munson, Henry, Jr.

1984   *The House of Si Abd Allah.* New Haven, CT: Yale University Press.

Nader, Laura

1974   "Up the Anthropologist: Perspectives Gained from Studying Up." In Hymes 1974b.

Nicholson, R. A.

1975   *The Mystics of Islam.* London: Routledge and Kegan Paul.
[1914]

Ong , Aihwa

1987   *Spirits of Resistance and Capitalist Discipline: Factory Women in Malaysia.* Albany: State University of New York Press.

Paollilo, Guy

1972   Place des activités non agricoles dans la vie des populations de l'agglomération de Kélibia (Cap Bon, Tunisie). Mémoire de géographie urbaine Université de Paris—Sorbonne U.E.R. de Géographie.

Paredes, Américo

1961   "Folklore and History." In *Singers and Storytellers.* Edited by Mody C. Boatright. Dallas: Southern Methodist University Press.

1969   "Concepts About Folklore in Latin America and the United States." *Journal of the Folklore Institute*, 6:20–38.

Peacock, James

1969   "Society as Narrative." In *Forms of Symbolic Action*. Edited by Robert Spencer. Seattle: University of Washington Press.

Peyssonnel, Jean André (1694–1759)

1857   *Voyages dans les régences de Tunis et d'Alger*. Paris: Librairie
[1838]   de Gide.

Pirsig, Robert M.

1974   *Zen and the Art of Motorcycle Maintenance*. New York: Bantam Books.

Pitt-Rivers, J., editor

1963   *Mediterranean Countrymen: Essays in the Social Anthropology of the Mediterranean*. Paris: Mouton.

Polanyi, Livia

1982   "Literary Complexity in Everyday Storytelling." In *Spoken and Written Language: Exploring Orality and Literacy*. Edited by Deborah Tannen. Norwood, NJ: Ablex.

Pratt, Mary Louise

1977   *Toward a Speech Act Theory of Literary Discourse*. Bloomington: Indiana University Press.

1986   "Fieldwork in Common Places." In Clifford and Marcus 1986.

Rabinow, Paul

1975   *Symbolic Domination: Cultural Form and Historical Change in Morocco*. Chicago: University of Chicago Press.

1977   *Reflections on Fieldwork in Morocco*. Berkeley: University of California Press.

Ranger, Terence

1983   "The Invention of Tradition in Colonial Africa." In Hobsbawm and Ranger 1983.

Reesink, Pieter

1977   *Contes et récits maghrébins*. Québec, Can.: Editions Naaman de Sherbrooke.

Renwick, Roger de V.

1980   *English Folk Poetry: Structure and Meaning*. Philadelphia: University of Pennsylvania Press.

Reswick, Irmtraud
1985   *Traditional Textiles of Tunisia and Related North African Weavings*. Los Angeles: Craft and Folk Art Museum.

Ricoeur, Paul
1988   *Time and Narrative*. Volume 3. Translated by Kathleen Blamey and David Pellauer. Chicago: Chicago University Press.

Rinn, Louis
1884   *Marabouts et Khouan: Etude sur l'Islam en Algérie*. Algiers: Adolphe Jourdan.

Romanska, Tsvetena
1978   "Djado Lako: A Representative Bulgarian Narrator (1962)." In Dégh 1978.

Rosaldo, Renato
1980   *Ilongot Headhunting, 1883–1974: A Study in Society and History*. Stanford, CA: Stanford University Press.
1983   "Grief and a Headhunter's Rage: On the Cultural Force of Emotions."

Ruby, Jay, editor
1981   *A Crack in the Mirror: Reflexive Perspectives in Anthropology*. Philadelphia: University of Pennsylvania Press.

Said, Edward
1978   *Orientalism*. New York: Pantheon.

Scelles-Millie, Jeanne
1970   *Contes arabes du Maghreb*. Paris: G.-P. Maisonneuve et Larose.
1972   *Contes mystérieux d'Afrique du Nord*. Paris: G.-P. Maisonneuve et Larose.

Schegloff, Emanuel A. and Harvey Sacks
1973   "Opening Up Closings." *Semiotica* 8:289–327.

Scheibe, Karl E.
1986   "Self Narrative and Adventure." In *Narrative Psychology, The Storied Nature of Human Conduct*. Edited by Theodore R. Sarbin. New York: Frederick A. Praeger.

Schieffelin, Edward
1976   *The Sorrow of the Lonely and the Burning of the Dancers*. New York: St. Martin's Press.

Scholes, Robert and Robert Kellogg
1966   *The Nature of Narrative*. New York: Oxford University Press.

Scholte, Bob
  1966   "Epistemic Paradigms: Some Problems in Cross-Cultural Re-
          search on Social Anthropological History and Theory." *Ameri-
          can Anthropologist*. 68:1192–1201.
Scott, James C.
  1976   *The Moral Economy of the Peasant: Rebellion and Subsistence in
          Southeast Asia*. New Haven, CT: Yale University Press.
Sethom, Hafedh
  1976   "Liquidation des habous et évolution des campagnes dans la
          presqu'île du Cap Bon." *Les Cahiers de Tunisie* 24(95–96):227–
          242.
  1977   "Les Fellahs de la presqu'île du Cap Bon (Tunisie)." Etude de
          Géographie Sociale Régionale. Publications de l'Université de
          Tunis. Faculté des Lettres et sciences humaines de Tunis Deux-
          ième Série: Géographie, Vol IV.
Sherzer, Joel
  1979   "Strategies in Text and Context: *Cuna Kaa Kwento*." *Journal of
          American Folklore* 92:145–163.
Shuman, Amy
  1986   *Storytelling Rights: The Uses of Oral and Written Texts by Urban
          Adolescents*. Cambridge: Cambridge University Press.
Smith, Barbara Herrnstein
  1980   "Narrative Versions, Narrative Theories." *Critical Inquiry* 7(1):
          213–236.
Smith, Robert J.
  1975   *The Art of Festival: As Exemplified by the Fiesta to the Patroness of
          Otuzco, la Virgen de la Puerta*. University of Kansas
          Publications in Anthropology, No. 6. Lawrence: University of
          Kansas Press.
Sowayan, Saad Abdullah
  1985   *Nabati Poetry: The Oral Poetry of Arabia*. Berkeley: University
          of California Press.
Speck, Ernest, editor
  1973   *Mody Boatright, Folklorist: A Collection of Essays*. Austin: Univer-
          sity of Texas Press.
Spradley, James P. and David W. McCurdy, editors
  1978   *Conformity and Conflict: Readings in Cultural Anthropology*. Bos-
          ton: Little, Brown.

Stahl, Sandra K. D.
  1977   "The Personal Narrative as Folklore." *Journal of the Folklore Institute* 14(1–2):9–30.

Stewart, Susan
  1982   "The Epistemology of the Horror Story." *Journal of American Folklore* 95(375):33–50.

Stock, Brian
  1983   *The Implications of Literacy: Written Language and Models of Interpretation in the 11th and 12th Centuries.* Princeton, NJ: Princeton University Press.

Stoller, Paul
  1984   "Eye, Mind and Word in Anthropology." *L'Homme; Revue française d'anthropologie* 3–4: 91–114.
  1986   "The Reconstruction of Ethnography." In Chock and Wyman 1986.
  1989a   *Fusion of the Worlds: An Ethnography of Possession Among the Songhay of Niger.* Chicago: University of Chicago Press.
  1989b   *The Taste of Ethnographic Things: The Senses in Anthropology.* Philadelphia: University of Pennsylvania Press.

Stoller, Paul and Cheryl Olkes
  1987   *In Sorcery's Shadow: A Memoir of Apprenticeship Among the Songhay of Niger.* Chicago: The University of Chicago Press.

Street, Brian V.
  1984   *Literacy in Theory and Practice.* Cambridge: Cambridge University Press.

Tallman, Richard
  1975   "Where Stories Are Told: A Nova Scotia Storyteller's Milieu." *American Review of Canadian Studies* 5:17–41.

Tannen, Deborah, editor
  1984   *Coherence in Spoken and Written Discourse.* Norwood, NJ: Ablex.

Taussig, Michael
  1987   *Shamanism, Colonialism, and the Wild Man: A Study in Terror and Healing.* Chicago: University of Chicago Press.

Tedlock, Dennis
  1983   *The Spoken Word and the Work of Interpretation.* Philadelphia: University of Pennsylvania Press.

Thompson, Stith
1955–58   *Motif-Index of Folk Literature*. 6 volumes. Bloomington: Indiana
          University Press.
Titon, Jeff Todd
1980   "The Life Story." *Journal of American Folklore* 93: 276–292.
Todorov, Tzvetan
1968   *Qu'est-ce que le structuralisme?* Paris: Editions du Seuil.
1977   *The Poetics of Prose*. Translated by Richard Howard, with a new
          foreword by Jonathan Culler. Oxford: Basil Blackwell.
1984   "A Dialogic Criticism?" In *Critique de la Critique*. Paris: Édi-
          tions du Seuil.
Tuan, Yi-fu
1977   *Space and Place: The Perspective of Experience*. Minneapolis: Uni-
          versity of Minnesota Press.
Turner, Bryan
1974   *Weber and Islam: A Critical Study*. Boston: Routledge and Ke-
          gan Paul.
Turner, Victor W.
1974   "Hidalgo: History as Social Drama." In *Dramas, Fields, and
          Metaphors*. Ithaca, NY: Cornell University Press.
1978   "Comments and Conclusions." In Babcock 1978.
1981   "Social Dramas and Stories about Them." In *On Narrative*. Ed-
          ited by W. J. T. Mitchell. Chicago: University of Chicago Press.
Turner, Victor W. and Edward M. Bruner, editors
1986   *The Anthropology of Experience*. Urbana: University of Illinois
          Press.
Tyler, Stephen A.
1986   "Post-Modern Ethnography: From Document of the Occult to
          Occult Document." In Clifford and Marcus 1986.
Van Binsbergen, W. M. J.
1985   "The Cult of Saints in North-Western Tunisia: An Analysis of
          Contemporary Pilgramage [sic] Structures." In *Islamic Dilem-
          mas*. Edited by Ernest Gellner. Amsterdam: Mouton.
Vatin, Jean-Claude
1976   "Défense (et illustration) de l'anthropologie: 1. A propos de: *Le
          mal de voir*." *Annuaire de l'Afrique du Nord*. 15:965–989.
Wachtel, Nathan
1967   "La vision des vaincus: la conquête espagnole dans le folklore
          indigène." *Annales ESC* 3:554–585.

Wagner, Roy
  1978 *Lethal Speech: Daribi Myth as Symbolic Obviation*. Ithaca, NY: Cornell University Press.
  1981 *The Invention of Culture*. Chicago: The University of Chicago Press.

Webber, Sabra Jean
  1969 *Lis-sigharina (For Our Children)*. Tunis, Tunisia.
  1980 "A Review of Pierre Bourdieu's *Outline of a Theory of Practice*." *Middle East Research in Anthropology* 4(3):12–14. Issue edited by L. O. Michalak.
  1981a "Comment by Pierre Bourdieu on Review of *Outline of a Theory of Practice* and Reply by Sabra Webber." *Middle East Research in Anthropology* 5(3): 6–7. Issue edited by L. O. Michalak.
  1981b "Local History Legends in a Tunisian, Mediterranean Town." Ph.D. dissertation. University of Texas, Austin.
  1984 "Between Two Folklores." In *Connaissances du Maghreb: Sciences sociales et colonisation*. Paris: CRESM.
  1985 "Women's Folk Narratives and Social Change." In *Women and the Family in the Middle East*. Edited by Elizabeth Fernea. Austin: University of Texas Press.
  1986 "Diglossia and Children's Literature." Paper presented to International Conference on "Children's Literature: Past, Present and Future." Cairo.
  1987 "The Social Significance of the Cairene Nukta: Some Preliminary Observations." *American Research Center in Egypt Newsletter* 138: 1–9.
  1990 "Les fonctions communicatives des devinettes de Kelibia." *IBLA (Revue de l'Institut des Belles Lettres Arabes)* 53(166): 275–295.
  n.d.a "An Outline of French Folklore Scholarship in the Maghrib from 1830–1978." Manuscript. 32 pages. On file in the Division of Comparative Studies in the Humanities, The Ohio State University.
  n.d.b "Canonicity and Middle Eastern Folk Narrative." In *Edebiyyat: Journal of Middle Eastern Literatures*. Forthcoming.

Weimann, Robert
  1984 *Structure and Society in Literary History: Studies in the History and*

Theory of Historical Criticism. Baltimore: Johns Hopkins University Press.

Westermarck, Edward
1926 *Ritual and Belief in Morocco*. 2 volumes. London: MacMillan.

Weyland, Joseph
1926 *Le Cap-Bon: Essai historique et économique*. Tunis: Société Anonyme de l'Imprimerie Rapide.

White, Hayden
1973 *Metahistory: The Historical Imagination in Nineteenth-Century Europe*. Baltimore: The Johns Hopkins University Press.
1978 *Tropics of Discourse: Essays in Cultural Criticism*. Baltimore: Johns Hopkins University Press.
1980 "The Value of Narrativity in the Representation of Reality." *Critical Inquiry* 7(1): 5–27.

Willeford, William
1969 *The Fool and His Scepter: A Study in Clowns and Jesters and Their Audience*. Evanston, IL: Northwestern University Press.

Williams, Raymond
1977 *Marxism and Literature*. Oxford: Oxford University Press.

Wolf, Eric R.
1982 *Europe and the People Without History*. Berkeley: University of California Press.

Wolf, Eric R., editor
1984 *Religion, Power, and Protest in Local Communities: The Northern Shore of the Mediterranean*. Berlin and New York: Mouton.

el-Zein, Abdul Hamid M.
1974 *The Sacred Meadows: A Structural Analysis of Religious Symbolism in an East African Town*. Evanston, IL: Northwestern University Press.

Zwettler, Michael
1976 "Classical Arabic Poetry between Folk and Oral Tradition," *Journal of the American Oriental Society* 92: 198–212.

Author Index

Boldface numbers in parentheses refer to individual hikayat. Tellers' names also appear in the Subject Index.

Subject Index

Boldface numbers in parentheses refer to individual hikayat in the text. The label "n" refers to notes; "m" refers to maps.

This book has been set in Linotron Galliard. Galliard was designed for Mergenthaler in 1978 by Matthew Carter. Galliard retains many of the features of a sixteenth century typeface cut by Robert Granjon but has some modifications that give it a more contemporary look.

Printed on acid-free paper.